Driving in the Dark

Driving in the Dark

A CHILDHOOD MEMOIR

Zoe Niklas with Janice Harper

ISBN: 1507589077
ISBN 13: 9781507589076
Library of Congress Control Number: 2015900860
CreateSpace Independent Publishing Platform
North Charleston, South Carolina

Table of Contents

Part One

Prologue

SHE WAS SUCH A TERRIFYING woman, even as she lay motionless in that bed, swaddled in white sheets. Her body was so withered and curled. She looked as if she'd lived a century at least, although she was half that age.

I stared at Zodie's tiny, wrinkled hands clutching the covers in her sleep. The red-lacquer polish was long gone, revealing the nicotine-stained nails that had turned brittle and cracked with age. Her bleached-blond hair had grown into a matted mess; the dark roots were nearly three inches long. Her hazel eyes, the eyes we shared, were closed.

"She looks great, doesn't she?" Gale said aloud, and I turned to my sister, wondering what in the world she was thinking. I thought our mother looked like hell.

"I mean, since George brought her in," she added. "She looks so much better."

George was our stepfather, the seventh of Zodie's many husbands. Each time my mother married a new man, my name was changed to his, and I learned to call him daddy.

But unlike the others, Daddy George had stayed. He stayed through Zodie's rages and breakdowns, he stayed through the fires and filth, and he stayed through all the affairs. And Zodie had stayed through all his beatings. Theirs was an unbreakable, primitive bond—two broken souls brought together in some semblance of a fractured whole.

Zodie moaned and tossed her head from side to side, and I turned back to her hospital bed, alert to any sudden movement. It was a hot day for Seattle, and sweat trickled down my back. I readjusted myself in the uncomfortable folding metal chair, as if I might have to leap from it at any moment. It had become reflex to ready myself for any change in Zodie's moods or movements, and now, though I was grown and free of her and she lay dying, I instinctively readied for flight or fight.

Her eyes flickered open, wandered about the room, and then landed on Gale and lit up. Her drawn face perked up at the sight of her favorite daughter, and her mouth blossomed into a smile.

"Hi, Mom," I ventured from the other side of her bed.

Turning in my direction, her face seemed to slam shut. "Well, God damn. Look what the cat dragged in," she said.

Inwardly, I groaned. This wasn't going well.

Gale began the cheerful chatter about how good Mom looked, how nice the facility was, and wasn't it nice that we could be together because of the break in my college schedule?

Zodie showed no interest. "Okay, so what do I attribute this visit to?" she asked, gazing in my direction, as if annoyed by the intrusion. Turning to Gale, she asked, "Did you bring me my cigarettes?"

"No, Mama," Gale responded. "You know you aren't supposed to smoke."

"The hell with that! If I want a smoke, I'll have a smoke!" Frantically, her thin hands searched the blankets as if she had just left them sitting there.

"Mama, the doctor said no!"

"God damn doctor, what does he know?" Then she softened. "I'll get George to bring me some." Chuckling, she mumbled, "He'll get me anything I want. He always has."

She drifted off, a smile settling on her face, comforted by her memories. I smiled, too, remembering the last time she was in hospital care. She'd been placed in a nursing home, but like every other one she'd been admitted to, she'd been thrown out. This time, the eviction came after she'd left for a recreational visit with George, only to return near midnight dressed in a black cocktail dress, stumbling, and carrying a pair of gold stilettos in her hands, her feet bare.

Fiddling with my engagement ring, I turned it so that she could see the pretty diamond and forced a bright smile. "Mom, I'm engaged to be married," I said, holding out my hand and shattering her daydreams.

She looked at me through tired eyes, eyes which suddenly looked sad, and then she looked away. Her tiny hand lay on the white coverlet. I got up from my chair, reached across the bed, and cradled her hand in both of mine. "He's a really good man, Mom. We met in college, and we'll get married when I graduate."

There was only silence.

After what seemed a very long time, Zodie sighed and faced me. But instead of the anger that I feared or the joy that I longed for, I saw in her face something I had never seen on her face before. It was sorrow.

"I hope you have better luck with men than I did," she said, her voice barely audible. "I never could find one worth a damn." Then her face grew stern once again and settled into its familiar, angry scowl.

I took a few deep breaths, as I weighed whether I should say what I'd promised myself I would say, the words I needed my mother to hear before she died. I knew it was futile, I knew she'd only explode, but I also knew I needed to say them. I needed to ask them. I needed to tell her what she had done to me and ask her why she had done it.

"What?" she said, seeing my torment etched on my face. "What is it this time?"

"Nothing, Mom, really. I was just thinking."

"Didn't I always say you thought too much? And you had to come here to my deathbed to do it?" Her annoyance was palpable. "What's the awful secret you can't tell me?"

"It isn't a secret, Mama; it's something else."

She glared at me. "Are you pregnant?"

"Oh, Mom, no, of course not. I just have something I've wanted to say to you for a really long time, and maybe now isn't the time to tell you."

"Tell me what?" I knew she was curious, but she wasn't about to admit it.

The room grew loud with our silence. Finally, I blurted it out.

"I just don't understand, Mom. I don't understand why you made us live like that, all those years."

"Oh no! Not that old bullshit! You can't pull that old chestnut on me. It was crap then, and it's crap now. You think it was easy for me? Let me tell you—" She began coughing, her lungs so damaged I feared she'd cough them right out of her throat. But the glare from her eyes told me that her anger meant more to her than her suffering. "You don't know the half of it!" she said the moment she could squeeze out some words. "I treated you better than I was ever treated, and God damn it, you, came out okay!"

I took a deep breath before replying, but before I could utter a word, my mother added, "I taught you to be tough."

I took a deeper breath. "No, Mom, we *didn't* have it easy. You have no idea what you put us through, and—" But Gale cut me off.

"Zoe, this isn't the time," she said. "Mama needs to rest." She cast me a stern look, clearly meant to stop me from going any further.

"No, I want to hear it!" my mother snapped. "If she thinks she's gotta tell me off before I die, then God damn it, let's hear it." She fiddled around, searching for the control to the hospital bed. When she found it, she switched it on, and the bed raised her to a sitting position. She seemed to be suddenly growing bigger while I felt as if I were growing smaller. She snatched up a Styrofoam cup filled with melting ice water, and sucking on the straw as if it were her treasured cigarette, she said, "Oh for Christ's sake! Go ahead and tell your damned story."

ZODIE CIRCA 1950

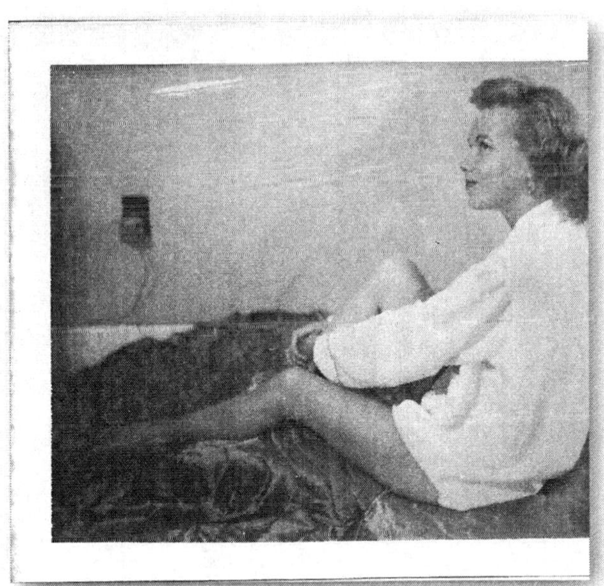

ZODIE CIRCA 1950

Zodie and Mary Gale circa 1950

CHAPTER 1

A Toddler's Tale

MAMA AND I WERE LIVING in a trailer park in California in 1956. I was four years old and standing outside. All was quiet except for the trucks that rumbled past on the highway. I could feel the world vibrate under my feet when the big ones passed by.

It was fiery hot. The sun beat down on my head with such force that I could feel my short ash-blond hair practically cooking on top of my head. But the heat on my head was nothing compared to the blinding-white heat of the gravel that burned through the soles of my thin tennis shoes. Sweat trickled down my face.

Mama was in the trailer. She told me I could play outside but not to go near the busy street. stood alone in front of the trailer, surrounded by the hot rocks, looking through the wire fence that bordered our lot where I could see the other trailers. I looked past them to the trees just beyond my reach and stared in fascination at their leaves, so still and silent in the shimmering heat. No breath of air stirred them into life; they hung, almost limply, as if they'd given up.

A shout of pleasure and a splash of water caught my attention, and I turned my head to the noise. More shouts and voices and laughter changed my silence to joy. I ran right up to the cyclone fence and put my face to the cage-like wire grid, peering through to the other side. Through a wall of bushes, I could see a wonderland of green—cool green grass, green bushes, and bright, colorful flowers. In the center of the emerald coolness was a blue wading pool with some children splashing in it, laughing and squealing and howling with happiness. A mother stood by the pool with a hose, laughing along with the children as she sprayed them with the cool water.

I wanted that coolness. I wanted to be where it was green and a mother would play. My mama never played.

Looking up at the fence, I realized it was too tall for me to climb over. To get to the green yard, I had to move along the fence to the front gate. But that would bring me close to the road and Mama had told me not to go near the road. One thing I knew was I couldn't disobey Mama.

I stood stock-still, biting my lip as the gravel warmed the soles of my feet. Suddenly, I knew what I could do. I could hold onto the fence and follow it to the gate, and then I'd get to play in the green coolness. I would stay next to the fence and not even get close to the road. The road was bad, Mama had said. So I'd stay away from it.

My mind made up, I began to walk along the fence, watching the children play and running my hand across the wire mesh as I walked, feeling the way the bumpy fencing strummed across my fingers, turning them numb. The roar of the highway was getting louder and louder, but I kept my hand on the fence, so I wouldn't break any rules. I knew to follow the rules. I was nearing the gate, and with every step, I became more excited as I got closer to the happy children.

Suddenly, the whole world turned upside down, and Mama grabbed me around the waist, hung me upside down, and started spanking me and yelling. She yelled and yelled and yelled and shook me harder and harder. Then she yanked me back to the trailer and pushed me through the door into the baking-hot trailer, spanking me even more while she kept screaming at me. When she finished spanking me, she sent me to bed without any dinner.

I cried into my pillow until my throat was raw. It was so unfair. I wouldn't have stepped into the road. I just wanted to play with the children in the green yard. I wanted that green yard.

Someday, I promised myself, I'd be big and I would have my own green yard and swimming pool. I knew it.

Mama was so mean.

I didn't always live with Mama. Lots of times, she sent me away to whoever would have me. When she did that, Sissy and I got split up. Sissy was nine years older than me and I thought she was the best big sister in the whole world. She loved and hugged me fiercely, and whenever we were together, she would take care of me, because Mama usually couldn't. She'd kiss me good night every night and tuck me into bed. When I got older, she'd shake me awake to get ready for school and she'd have breakfast ready and my clothes all pressed and ready to wear.

When Mama said we had to go away, Sissy would go to one house and I'd go to another and then Mama would just be gone. Lots of times, that meant she'd come back with a new husband and he'd become our new daddy.

I didn't even really know what a daddy was, other than Mama's new husband. Daddies kissed Mama and put their hands up her dresses and slept in Mama's bed. Sometimes they'd touch me in ways that I didn't like at all.

Each daddy had a different set of rules, and it was hard figuring them out without getting in trouble. Some were really, really mean, and some just ignored me, but once in a while, Mama came home with a nice one.

I never knew the first one, but somehow, he always seemed to be in our lives. His name was David Grossman, and he was Sissy's father.

"Your daddy was the love of my life," Mama would say to Sissy whenever his name came up or whenever she was getting rid of one of her husbands. "Not a damn one of them could ever hold a candle to him, not a damn one!" Then she'd pour another drink.

"We loved each other," she'd mumble, mostly into her ice cubes. Her words got blurry and stumbled into each other like they didn't know their own sounds. "If David was alive today, we wouldn't be living like this," she'd rant, getting madder and madder. "If he hadn't been killed, my life wouldn't be crap and I wouldn't have to put up with all this *shit*!" When Mama got like that, I got scared.

David Grossman was killed in a car accident in 1946. Mama had insisted that they take a vacation to Northern California, but he didn't want to go. His International Harvester truck was acting up, but Mama had insisted. So, to make her happy, he finally agreed. They got as far as Weed when the truck broke down. David Grossman got out of the truck and tried to fix the vapor lock in the engine when a logging truck made a wide turn and plowed right into them, knocking them both over an embankment.

While they waited for the ambulance, Mama cradled David Grossman's head in her lap and watched his life flow away.

Mama was severely injured and had to have plastic surgery on her mouth and never looked the same after that. It turned her mouth into a barely perceptible pucker, like she was trying to say something in French or had a mouthful of water she could spit out at any moment.

Sissy told me that Mama changed after David Grossman died, that she was never the same loving woman. That's when she became haunted. And that's when she began drinking and taking pills to cope, and that's when the string of husbands began, or at least that's the way Sissy told it.

Not long after David Grossman died, Mama got a new husband and had a baby boy, my brother, Larry Lee, but I never even knew him. His daddy took him away from Mama, but she didn't seem to mind and she never saw him again until he was all grown up. Larry Lee's daddy said he'd take Sissy too, but Mama said no, he couldn't do that, even though Mama said he'd adopted her.

"If you take Gale, who'll look after me?" she said she told him, so Sissy had to stay to look after Mama.

Then Mama married an Irish singer named Johnny Carmichael, who was a rogue and a drunk, at least that's what she told me. Johnny Carmichael was my father, but I hardly knew him because she divorced him when I was just a newborn. After Johnny Carmichael, she married Bill Ashton, but he hanged himself in the shed, and that's where Mama found him. She ran crying and screaming from the shed and grabbed a butcher knife and said she was going to kill herself, but our neighbor Mrs. Schneller stopped her.

Then she married Bill Wallace, who tried to push Mama's head through the windshield of a car, and he ended up in Sing-Sing, though I can't remember why.

When she'd send us off to other people's houses, it would get awfully boring. In order to make the time bearable, I watched a lot of movies on TV and pretended my mama was Doris Day and just busy with her career. I learned to appreciate the families I stayed with, and I quickly learned how to make friends. I was always polite and well mannered, as I found that got me along with strangers better. I trained myself to remember the good survivor qualities of each household. I watched how the mothers cleaned and cooked, so that I could use those skills as well. I learned how to break eggs into a dish at one home and was amazed to learn that the egg was really a yellow chick that didn't develop. I realized if I didn't develop properly myself, I might end up cracked up just like a chicken's egg, so I learned as fast as I could. I knew instinctively that I had to work hard to survive, so I studied the people I stayed with. I learned to recognize strengths in each one, and I purposefully focused on acquiring those strengths for myself.

At one home where Mama left me, there was a large pool in the grassy backyard. I stood on the grass in the hot sun and watched the other children play in the water, just like the time when I was four. But I wasn't allowed to go in the water. I was too little, their mother had said. "When you're bigger, Mary Zoe, then you'll be able to join in. Right now, you're too short!"

I really wanted to play with the other children. Stepping closer to the side of the pool, I could see the outline of the water on the plastic walls. My chin was level with it. The pool was on the grass, and I was standing on the grass, too. Thinking hard, I walked around the whole pool. The outline of the water never got higher than my chin. I knew I could stand in it and hold onto the side.

I took my discovery to the mother of the house and explained that the water was not over my head. She followed me as I walked all around the pool, showing her that I was always taller than the water. She smiled at me and said, "You're right, honey. You *are* big enough. But I don't have a bathing suit for you; you'll have to go in with your undies."

And so I did. I held onto the side while cool water lapped at my overheated face and arms. It felt wonderful to me. It was thrilling to be with the other kids, and I felt a glow of pride that I had managed to prove I was finally big enough!

Another time, I stayed with my aunt Lulu. Auntie Lulu was shorter than she was wide. She had gray, curly hair, laughing eyes, and a mouth like a Valentine's card. She told me she was my daddy Johnny's sister. I was supposed to stay with her until Mama came back for me.

Auntie Lulu lived in a white stucco house on a very steep hill in Oakland. She had a tiny staircase that curved from the driveway up to the kitchen, and she told me it was the servants' entrance, but I never saw any servants. Her house smelled of furniture polish and soap. In her living room, there was the biggest ruby-red rug I had ever seen. Auntie Lulu told me it was an Oriental rug. I loved to lie on my belly and stroke that rug, because it had such a soft feel to it. In one direction, it felt like silk, and in the other direction, it felt like rubbing cats' fur the wrong way. I spent many hours sitting on that rug watching *The Mickey Mouse Club*, waiting for Mama to come get me. The days went by, and still Mama didn't come, but I kept waiting.

Auntie Lulu served breakfast on a lace-covered table, and she ate a soft-boiled egg each morning out of something she said was an eggcup. I was fascinated to watch her tap the egg, remove the top, and dip inside, eating the white and runny yellow in its shell. I tried to do it, but I never could.

Unlike Mama, Auntie Lulu kept a clean house. She was always dusting and cleaning and vacuuming the rug. I hated her vacuum. It looked like a red-eyed demon that roared. I tried to stay away from the vacuum when Auntie Lulu worked, but it seemed to follow me wherever I moved. I ran from it into the living room, calling to Auntie Lulu to stop the red-eyed monster. Finally, tear-stained and trembling, I climbed on top of the sofa back and stared round-eyed at my roaring nemesis. I knew it couldn't climb. Suddenly, it stopped roaring. Laughter filled the room, and Auntie Lulu dropped into a chair, wiping her eyes. "That had to be the funniest thing I've ever seen!" she howled. "Mary Zoe, it's just a vacuum. Don't be daft!"

Climbing off the sofa, I didn't think it was funny at all. I hated that machine. I knew it was evil. I had to get away from it.

The next thing I knew, I was lugging a brown paper bag down the hill. Inside it were all my toys. I was going to leave Auntie Lulu. I was going to find Mama. I walked and walked. But the bag was big. I hadn't realized I had so many stuffed animals, but I had to bring all of them with me; I couldn't leave any of them behind. I dragged the bag along the sidewalk since it was too big for me to carry, and that made it rip. The more I tugged the bag, the larger the rip became until my toys started to fall out, spilling all over the concrete.

Finally, I sat down. It was no good. I didn't know where to find Mama, and my toys would never make the trip. I had a decision to make. I could go back and face Auntie Lulu and the demon vacuum, or I could leave my toys behind. I couldn't leave my stuffed animals, I thought as I wiped my nose on my sleeve, because I was their mama. How would they feel if I left them like Mama left me?

I couldn't do it. Scooping up the ragged ends of the bag, I dragged my toys back up the hill to Auntie Lulu's house.

One time, I was sent to stay with Auntie Jane. Auntie Jane was Mama's friend. She and Mama would go out drinking together, but I didn't really know her until I started staying with her. Auntie Jane was a bony little woman, hardly bigger than me, with walnut-colored eyes that were soft and kind. She always had a cigarette either in her hand or in her mouth. When she smoked, she would pop the smoke out of the corner of her mouth, and then the smoke would stream from her wrinkled lips like a genie coming out of the bottle. It was fascinating to watch her.

Auntie Jane lived in a little house a couple of blocks from my school with her husband, who did a lot of drinking. One time, I had to go to the bathroom really bad, and when I went into the bathroom, I saw Auntie Jane's husband asleep in the bathtub. He was completely naked. That startled me something awful, and I ran out of there and hollered for Auntie Jane. I almost wet my pants before she got him out of there and sent him off to bed.

I liked staying with Auntie Jane. She taught me to play some card games, introduced me to Chinese checkers, and taught me how to cook some things. She even showed me how to save money, by using a bar of Ivory soap to make the suds for the dishes. I liked washing dishes for Auntie Jane. She really appreciated my help, and she taught me how to run a clean house. In the evenings, we'd watch *Gunsmoke*, *Death Valley Day*, and *The Lawrence Welk Show* together. I thought the shows were pretty boring, but since she seemed to enjoy them, I found parts of them I could enjoy. I liked watching TV with Auntie Jane.

In the daytime, we'd talk for hours. She'd tell me about how wonderful it was to be loved by a good man. When her husband wasn't around, she'd tell me stories of her life with her first husband, "Dr. Brady." Dr. Brady had died twenty years before, but still, Auntie Jane mourned him, I could tell. Auntie Jane agreed with Mama that some men were "no damn good," but all you had to do was keep your eyes open, she said, and you could find the good ones.

"You'll find your good man one day, Mary Zoe," Auntie Jane promised me. "He's out there. You're just going to have to deal with a few no damn good ones first." And then she laughed, a warm and gentle laugh, and made up the sofa for me to go to sleep.

Auntie Jane made my bed on the sofa every night. She would place a sheet on the cushions and then an apricot quilt over it. Then she'd put a chair at the edge of the sofa, so I wouldn't fall out. I never did, but I thought it was sweet that she worried about such a thing. I had so much more to worry about. I lay in the dark of the living room, grateful beyond words that I was safe in her house.

Then one day, Mama came to get me, and I had to go home.

Sometimes, Mama would send me to the neighbor across the road. Mrs. Church was a heavyset, short woman whose wide mouth made her look like a good-natured frog. She loved flowers and grew roses, cosmos, daisies, and geraniums in her yard. There was always something blooming at Mrs. Church's. In the evenings, I would stand in her yard and talk about her garden, and she would show me how to water the plants with a hose. Standing on the green lawn with Mrs. Church encouraging me, I learned to water the flowers properly, giving them enough water to soak through the mulch and into the soil, but not so much I'd drown them. They smelled sweet and earthy, and the gentle twilight of summer would gild the leaves. It was peaceful at her house.

Mrs. Church's husband was blind, so to help her out, I'd take him on walks and describe what the houses looked like and if there was a curb or a street to cross. He would tell me stories of his life as a barber in West Seattle, not far from where they lived. I kept imagining him poking people in the head with his scissors, even though he explained that was before he got sick and lost his sight. But since I didn't know him then, all I could do was imagine a blind barber, and I thought that was pretty funny. Mr. Church and I got along very well. He laughed at my jokes, and I learned to put his food in precise places on his dinner plate—meat at six o'clock, potatoes at twelve, and vegetables at nine. Mrs. Church said I was a great help to her. She kept a tidy house, because Mr. Church had to have furniture in certain positions, so he wouldn't fall. I liked how tidy she kept it. There was an order to her home that gave me comfort. I wanted that order in my home.

There were beautiful things in Mrs. Church's house. In the kitchen, she had a black Kit-Kat clock that had green rhinestone eyes and a red rhinestone tie. I would watch that clock swish its tail with every tick and every tock, as Mrs. Church cooked dinner.

The prettiest thing she had was a red lacquer Chinese bowl in her living room, which was filled with peppermints. I would sit in the armchair by that bowl of peppermints and listen to Mrs. Church tell me what it was like growing up in the "old west." She had wonderful stories. I especially liked the one she told of facing a mountain lion. She said it took all her self-control not to run, to stand absolutely still. The mountain lion looked at her but then just casually walked away. I thought Mrs. Church was very brave. I always looked forward to being with her. Whenever I stayed at her home, I slept well. I didn't have to worry about anything. I was safe.

Sometimes, I got to visit my grandma. Nana was Mama's mama. She was tall and slim like Mama, with curly blond hair that was practically lemon yellow. She had Gloria Swanson eyebrows, arched and thin, and she always wore scarlet lipstick that clashed with her pale face and yellow hair and made her look menacing. She wasn't very warm and cuddly, that's true, at least not to me, but she *loved* her son Tucker, who was as good as Mama was bad, which was pretty much how Nana explained it.

"Your mama never has been of any help to me at all," Nana would tell me. "Thank goodness I have my boy, Tucker. Tucker is such a gentleman; he takes me anywhere I need to go and never complains. Why, if it weren't for Tucker..."

Tucker this, Tucker that, was about all that ever came out of Nana's mouth, which was all the more fun because as everyone knew, Tucker had killed a boy in a fight and spent years in reform school and still didn't seem quite reformed. Aside from killing someone, I didn't have anything against my uncle Tucker, and it was true Mama was less than perfect, but I still didn't like to always be told that. It made me feel bad for Mama. Mama always said that Nana loved Tucker more than her, and she certainly was right about that. I could tell that Mama wanted Nana to love her, but I knew Nana probably never would as long as she had Tucker.

Nana lived in a very nice house, but Mama said that before she moved there, she was so poor that Tucker had to sleep in the same bed with her until he was sixteen. I don't know if it was true or not, but that's what Mama said. I was just glad I got my own bed when I stayed with Nana.

Nana always seemed to be sniffing with displeasure whenever I was around, but later, I found out it was allergies, at least that's what she explained. There was something about her that frightened me, just a little bit, but she was also kind of amazing. Before Mama was born, Nana had been an opera singer and had sung in Carnegie Hall. I didn't know what Carnegie Hall was and couldn't quite understand why singing in a hallway was something very special, but I did figure out that it meant that Nana was someone really special. I also kind of got the feeling that she wished she still sang in Carnegie Hall and maybe that's why she was so mad at Mama, for being born and all.

Sometimes, when she was happy, Nana would sit down to her piano and play and sing so loudly and beautifully that I thought the roof might come right off of her house. I loved hearing Nana sing and play her piano.

Every Sunday, we would get dressed up and Nana would take me to church. I got to sing when I went there, but I was afraid I didn't sing well enough for Nana, much less well enough for God. But she told me that we are all children of God. "And God doesn't give a crap if you can sing or not," Nana explained, which helped me to feel a lot better.

After church, we'd go to Nana's open houses. Nana sold houses to people. I would carefully watch her as she moved from room to room, explaining the features of each room in each house. If a house had lots of windows, she made sure people knew that, even if they could see the windows for themselves. If it didn't have many windows, she told them how private and cozy the house was. No matter what it was, she made it sound like it was just what everybody wanted.

If a lot of people came to an open house, I would get to lead groups around the houses. Just like Nana, I explained all the details I could remember, like how many square feet each room had or whether or not it had enough windows or privacy. After one particularly busy afternoon, Nana smiled at me as we drove away. "You did great!" she told me. "The clients thought you made one good little salesgirl. And so do I!" Sniffing, she added, "There is hope for you after all."

Whenever Mama did come for me, I'd be really happy. Each time, I'd imagine that she'd take me to a new, beautiful, clean home and we would play happily ever after. But then we'd get back home, and every time, things still weren't like the images I saw on TV or the movie screen or even like the homes that I'd been staying in. Whether it was the same home I left or a different home, the dishes would be piled up in the sink, and the trash would be spilling over. Empty cans of food would be strewn across the counter, and Mama would sleep most of the day. When she finally got up, she'd turn the TV on real loud and clean up a little bit and sometimes fix me dinner. If we had some money, it might be something like porcupine meatballs. I thought the name was funny, but they were good. They weren't made out of porcupines, which would be really yucky; they were made out of hamburger and rice instead. The rice was like the prickers on a porcupine, but they didn't prick at all. Mama made them in a pressure cooker, though, and that really scared me, because sometimes she didn't pay attention and then we had a real mess.

But I paid attention. I learned to pay really close attention to Mama so nothing bad would happen—like watching Mama's toes. Mama liked to wear her slip around the house, so lots of the time, she'd be barefoot in her slip with a cigarette in one hand and a drink in another. When I saw her like that, I paid real close attention to her feet, because when her toes would start to curl like she was gripping the floor, I knew she was afraid of losing her balance. That meant she'd been drinking too much and I'd better be extra careful.

Sometimes, Mama made macaroni and cheese from scratch, and I liked those dinners. But when we ran out of money and didn't have much cheese to go with the macaroni, she'd add ketchup to it.

"This'll make it stretch," Mama said, "and taste better."

But I didn't think it tasted better at all; I thought it tasted disgusting.

Also, we had a lot of animals. We had birds and cats and dogs, and sometimes there were more than I could count and their fur was all over everything. Sometimes, it smelled really bad, but other times, I didn't really notice.

I tried to be extra good and make Mama happy, but my best efforts were not always good enough. Once, when I was about four years old, I tried to sing so she would love me.

I sat on my bed wearing my best dress, the pink gingham skirt all puffed up by the petticoats that were scratching my thighs. My hair was cut in a pageboy and held back with a pretty barrette. I looked down at my white socks and black patent-leather shoes. They were so shiny that I hoped I wouldn't scuff them. That would make Mama real mad.

Mama had told me to wait until I was called, so I waited. She had a visitor, and I was to come out and sing when she told me to. Until then, I was not to get dirty. So I sat with my hands gripped together. My shoulders ached, I was so nervous.

"When will you call me?" I asked her. "I'm scared to sing."

"Children do as they're told," she responded as she lit her cigarette and tossed her head upward to exhale. "Besides, children are to be seen and not heard, unless called upon. So you can wait, Mary Zoe."

I waited.

After a while, I was so tired and my shoulders hurt from keeping still so long. But I was too scared to move. So I kept waiting.

Then, after a really long time, I heard Mama's voice through the closed bedroom door.

"Mary Zoe, come here!" Her voice was all singsong, like she wasn't really talking to me but to her guest. At least she wasn't mad at me. Still, I was really scared I might disappoint her or do something wrong.

I walked to the living room, keeping my eyes on the floor, careful not to do anything wrong.

"Sing your song," Mama said, and then she turned to her guest. "She does it very well for being so little."

I began. "Jesus Loves Me, This I Know." It was the only song I knew. I didn't dare look at the guest or at Mama. I just watched her red fingernails as she smoked. I sang as well as I could, praying I wouldn't make a mistake. When I finished, Mama said I could go.

As I began to dash from the room, I saw her hands tighten on the cigarette. I had forgotten something very important. Turning around, I faced Mama's guest and curtsied. Then Mama smiled.

To this day, I don't know who taught me that song, since we didn't really go to church.

I just know that somehow it helped me to get through what was up ahead. And what was up ahead was a lot scarier than singing for Mama's company.

MARY ZOE AND DADDY JOHNNY 1952

CHAPTER 2

Zodie's Men

ONE OF MY FAVORITE TIMES Mama sent me away was when I was six years old and got to go visit Daddy Johnny, my real daddy.

She put me on a plane all by myself, and the stewardess gave me a pair of wings to pin to my dress. Mama had given me a pair of white gloves and a little purse that snapped closed with a pearl on the top. It was so beautiful that I held it in my lap and played with the clasp all the way there. I loved the airplane because it was just like a little playhouse, and when I looked out the window and saw clouds, I pretended they were mashed potatoes. I imagined giving a gift to God, since we were so close to heaven, and if the gift fell when I reached up to offer it, that would be okay because it would just fall on the mashed potatoes, where God could pick it up.

I spent the whole summer with Daddy Johnny. He could sing and dance and play all kinds of instruments. In my little girl's mind, I got him confused with the actor Van Johnson, who could also sing and dance and play music, because I saw Van Johnson in the movies more than I saw my father. So that summer, it was like going to see a movie star, and I was really, really happy. I thought my daddy must be a sailor or a soldier or some kind of hero because that's the kind of man that Van Johnson was in the movies.

Daddy Johnny was so tall that when I looked up at him, the California sunshine shone full in my little eyes, momentarily blinding me. He laughed a lot, and he called me his "Princess," especially when he brought me to those dark bars. They were strange and kind of scary, but Daddy Johnny made me feel safe there.

"Give my princess a Shirley Temple!" he'd shout to the bartender, and I felt really special. I loved watching Shirley Temple. She was always having adventures, but no matter what happened to her, she always got the good family in the end. And she did it by being a good little girl, so that's what I tried to do. She won her enemies over by turning their hearts and getting them to love her, so I stored that little bit of information away because I figured it might help me. Mama always said, "You get more flies with honey than you do with vinegar," so I knew there was some truth to it.

I was dazzled by the sparkling bubbles in my Shirley Temple drink, and I especially loved the red cherry. I'd save the cherry for last because we stayed for some time in those dark places and I'd get really hungry. Daddy Johnny let me play on the shiny bar with a leather cup filled with dice, but eventually, I shook it too hard and the little cubes spilled onto the floor. That's when he made me sit in the booths.

I didn't like the booths because the upholstery scratched my legs. I always wore my prettiest dress and my patent-leather Mary Janes when I was out with Daddy Johnny, but my starched dress and petticoats were no protection against those prickly seats in the booths.

I remember Daddy Johnny eating some pink meat from a big jar, laughing and telling me, "Pickled pig's feet are great! Wait'll yer older; you'll love 'em." I didn't think I'd ever want to eat a pig's foot, even if it did taste like a pickle.

One time, after a particularly long time in the dark booth and several Shirley Temples, the front door of the bar opened and a white-haired lady stormed in. She had hair like Jayne Mansfield, so blond it looked almost like Christmas snow, the kind made out of spun glass that we used to lay across our mantle and set the manger on. She grabbed my arm and began pulling me out of the dark bar. It was so bright outside I was blinded. I heard her yell at Daddy Johnny about taking a child "in such a place." But I thought the place was nice, except for the prickly booth seats.

Later, I learned her name was Bernice and she was married to Daddy Johnny. Bernice was always good to me. But she'd get mad at my daddy and yell at him sometimes.

Daddy Johnny laughed a lot around me. He gave me hugs, and he sang. He had a warm, booming voice, and it made me happy just to hear it. He'd sing, "Off we go into the wild blue yonder..." And he loved airplanes. We'd climb into his station wagon, the kind with wood paneling on the sides, and we'd go to the airport and watch the jets and blimps. Sometimes, we'd even get to walk into their "mouths." I thought the front of the plane looked like Mickey Mouse's nose. Daddy Johnny made everything fun for me. I loved Daddy Johnny, at least as much as I had a chance to love him.

One time, I skinned my knee and he told me he was going to put iodine on it. I knew that was going to hurt. But he said, "Princess, I won't let it hurt you. See, I'll put it on my tongue and if it doesn't hurt me, it can't hurt you."

I was amazed. There he was, a big man with a red slash of iodine on his tongue, just for me. I skinned myself a lot that summer, but still, I fell for it every time. Of course, when he applied the medicine, it stung, but he would blow on it and give me a little pat.

"You're such a brave little princess," he'd say, and I'd give him a great big hug.

After I got home and she saw how much fun I'd had, Zodie wasn't happy. She told me that Daddy Johnny had a temper. She said that when she was seven months pregnant with me, Daddy Johnny pulled her off the couch in a rage and she hit the floor hard. I was born just after that, two months premature. She said I spent the first two months of my life in an incubator because of Daddy Johnny. I weighed two pounds and eleven ounces, wore a lady's handkerchief for a diaper, and was so small I could fit inside a shoebox. It was a miracle I survived, Mama said, or that I wasn't blind, since in 1952, medical care for premature babies was pretty bad. She told me that sometimes they burned out the retinas of the babies by mistakenly using too much oxygen in the incubators.

"So you're lucky I divorced him," Mama reminded me. "You could have been blinded or killed because of that SOB." Then she took a long drag on her cigarette, blew the smoke up into the air, and poured another drink.

After that, I started kindergarten. And that's when I met Daddy David.

One day while I was playing on the playground, I saw Mama and Sissy. Sissy was really pretty and had a big smile and pretty blond hair. She was already in junior high and almost ready for high school. We rarely got to see each other, since we lived with different people most of the time.

I ran from the playground straight to Sissy and gave her a monstrous hug. Mama thanked the principal, and we got into a car driven by a black-haired man. He was introduced as Mama's new husband, David Walz. David Walz was going to be my new daddy, and we were all going up north to a city called Seattle, which would be our new home.

But before we left California, she said we had to visit Grandma Kizer. Grandma Kizer was a tiny old woman in a big hospital bed. She was Nana's mother, Mama's grandmother. Her name was Haddie Maude Kizer, but everybody called her Rattlesnake Haddie, since she used to kill rattlesnakes with a bullwhip. Sissy had lived with her most of the time. I didn't know Grandma Kizer, but I had heard of her from Sissy whenever we were together.

"She's real nice sometimes, but she runs a tight ship," Sissy explained. I had to have her explain what she meant by running a tight ship, because at first, I thought it meant she lived on a boat, but Sissy said it meant that there were a lot of rules to learn, but once you learned them, everything was smooth sailing.

That was another expression, Sissy explained, and I just nodded like I knew that.

Visiting Grandma Kizer was a new experience for me, and I was kind of scared, since she killed rattlesnakes and all. When I got close to her bed, I wrinkled my nose because she smelled like Noxzema. But when she smiled at me, her eyes twinkled. She handed me a pink crocheted hat for my doll. The hat was lovely. It had ruffles all around the edge and tiny roses along the top. I immediately put it on my doll and was delighted. I never saw Grandma Kizer again.

Mama's new husband, David Walz, was a lot shorter than Daddy Johnny. But he was stocky and very strong and seemed to vibrate with a secret energy that only he could feel. He had searing eyes like the movie star Yul Brynner, but he looked more like a mean Chihuahua than a handsome movie star. He watched me with a reptilian intensity that I didn't quite understand. I just knew he made me feel really nervous. But so did lots of things at home, so I just decided to be careful around him and see how long he stayed with Mama.

We moved to a house on Genesee Hill. A half-porch sported a window, which Mama always kept covered, like a blind eye. As with everywhere we lived, the porch was never used and collected debris and leaves blown in by the wind, giving it the appearance of being abandoned.

In some ways, that's just what it was, although four of us lived inside it.

The house was all brown, inside and out. The outside was the color of dung, and the inside was dark as mud. Even my room was brown, but it had a white leafy vine with a birdcage painted on the wall. Mama painted it for me free hand, so that I could look for birds when I lay down for my nap. I loved looking for birds, and I loved even more knowing that Mama had done that for me.

The living room had a large front window, facing the road, but Mama also kept that covered with heavy curtains, so even when it was light outside, it was like nighttime inside. The walls were covered in thick, dark wallpaper that had big flowers on it. I remember that because when I had to stand in the corner (which was often), I punched holes in the space between the two walls, leaving little half-moon tears in the wallpaper about two feet up, which was how high my punches landed at the time. That was the home where I had a play kitchen. Daddy David built a wooden stove with an oven door that opened and knobs I could turn. He and Mama even bought a pretend fridge and plastic food so that I could "cook" like Mama, which I thought was funny since it was Sissy who did most of the cooking.

David Walz was the only husband Zodie ever had who seemed to have any money. He was in the Coast Guard, so he was gone a lot, and when he wasn't in the Coast Guard, he was in real estate, like Nana, which meant he was always walking out the door or walking right back in it. I didn't help David Walz sell his houses, though, like I did for Nana, because he made me so nervous.

Mama was happy for a while with David Walz because she liked being able to buy things. She bought herself beautiful clothes and shoes and furniture, including a brand-new maple coffee table in the Early American style that was popular back then; she thought it made our home look elegant, but I thought it was just plain ugly.

Mama was happy when she polished that table, as if owning such a polished piece of furniture was her greatest source of pride. It meant she'd made it; she was a proper lady. Her jewelry was like that, too.

"The more jewelry you can get from a man, the better off you'll be, Mary Zoe; you remember that!" I watched with fascination as she'd clip big, glittery earrings onto her earlobes and then drape a string of sparkly gems around her long, thin neck. Turning her back toward me, she would stoop down and lift her wavy blond hair with one hand, while clutching the clasp with the other, which I fastened for her. When she stood up and twirled around in her high heels, there it would be, a string of beautiful, sparkly gems glittering like diamonds, rubies, and emeralds around Mama's neck, proof that she was worth something.

David Walz gave her lots of pretty jewelry. But they fought a lot, and when that happened, usually something got broken. Mama would throw a lamp at David Walz, and David Walz would slam the door and drive off, making a terrible racket. Sometimes, she'd throw our best dishes or beautiful statues, and lots of times, they both threw their whiskey glasses at each other. One time, liquor was splattered all over the floors and walls when my babysitter Dolores came over. She did her best to clean it up, but she couldn't clean up the wallpaper. That was permanent, she explained.

Sometimes, David Walz would beat Mama up, and she'd be all black and blue the next day. Then he'd buy her something really special, and they'd make up. Once he got her a beautiful gold lighter that sat on top of the coffee table, and every time she lit a cigarette, she lifted it up like a magnificent piece of art, holding it in her hands with her red-lacquered nails, which looked like Chinese porcelain against the sparkly gold. Then she would almost close her eyes, but not quite, and the flame would flicker with a big *poof* as Mama ignited her Camel.

Another time after he beat her up, he got her a beautiful matching ashtray.

Mama smoked three packs of Camels every day, so there was always a cloud of smoke swirling around her that made her look mysterious and almost spooky. She never seemed to completely open her eyes, maybe on account of the smoke, so she sort of squinted at the world like she didn't quite trust it and had its number.

Mama was always saying she had someone's number and no one could fool her because she'd seen so much of the world, but she seemed to get a lot of numbers wrong whenever she got married.

At first, it was okay with Daddy David, because Sissy got to live with us after Grandma Kizer got sick. I loved having Sissy home with us; she took good care of me and taught me lots of things about survival, like how to fold my sweaters so they didn't get ruined. We didn't have many clothes, and if something happened to them, Mama wouldn't replace them, so we learned to take real good care of whatever we had.

"If you're real careful and fold the arms like this and then fold it over like this," she explained, "your sweaters won't stretch out or get wrinkled and they'll last longer." I learned quickly that being poor meant it was a good idea to take care of your clothes, so I always folded my sweaters and hung my dresses just like Gale did so that they would stay pretty. Sissy taught me lots of other things as well, like how to iron, how to fix grilled cheese sandwiches, and how to dance.

Sissy loved to dance, and her dream was to be a ballerina. One time, she took me to the opera house and we watched the ballet. It was so beautiful. We were enthralled, especially Sissy. She had a pair of pink ballet slippers that she kept hung in her bedroom, just like a real ballerina. Sissy wanted to take ballet lessons, but Mama said no and gave her roller skates instead.

"Ballet takes years to learn, and I need you here at home," Mama said, "to keep an eye on Mary Zoe. Besides, you won't stick with it and I don't have money for that sort of thing." Mama always seemed to have money to go out drinking, but there was no use in pointing that out. We knew that Mama needed Sissy to watch after me and fix us dinners and do the dishes because if Sissy didn't do it, it probably wouldn't get done. I guess that was what she meant when she said that Sissy couldn't go away with Larry Lee.

But it was good for Mama to have Sissy home because she made everything so much more fun. Mama would spend more time going out or sleeping late, but she also spent more time with us sometimes. When that happened, we'd sit at the table and make arts and crafts together, if money allowed. She'd hide her money in the *Encyclopedia Britannica* because she said that was the safest place in the house.

"David wouldn't open a book if his life depended on it," she said, "So this is where I keep our money."

Daddy David thought things like arts and crafts were a waste of money, so Mama would tell him the art supplies came from Auntie Lulu or someone like that, and he wouldn't ask any more questions.

I especially liked paint-by-numbers and mosaics. I loved the crushed-rock mosaics the best. The tiny pieces of glass looked like jewels. Or Mama would help me make paper dolls, which I really loved. She would draw them free hand, and I would color them. Mama was really good at arts and crafts. One time, she painted a Santa Claus on a plaque and hung it on our front door at Christmastime, and I thought it was the most magical Santa I'd ever seen. The colors were so bright and the curls in Santa's beard so real that I thought if I touched it, I could make Santa smile.

When we did things like that together, Mama was always happy and laughed right along with us.

I loved making Mama laugh. One time, I finished reading my Dick and Jane book and I tossed it on the coffee table just like Mama did with her books, and I announced, "Well, I'm glad *that's* done!" Mama laughed so hard I thought copying her was a good idea. So next time I dressed up in plastic high heels with my candy cigarette in my hand and went outside strutting on the sidewalk swearing a blue streak. Mama burst out the front door, swept me up, and pushed me back inside, just like that time at the trailer but without the spankings. It was a perfect performance, Mama admitted, but I made sure I never did it again because I could tell it made her mad that I did it outside where the neighbors could see it.

"At least you got my look down," Mama said with pride.

Sometimes, when Daddy David was gone away with the Coast Guard, other men would come over. When that happened, I would have to wait outside until they left. I never liked those men and didn't understand why they were inside our house with Mama.

One time, I came home from school sick, and a whole bunch of men were in the house with Mama. The couch, rug, and table were covered with booze that had spilled all over. Dolores, our neighbor, came over. She took one look at the room and asked those men what they were doing there, and they all ran off. But as soon as Dolores left, Mama made a phone call and pretty soon, they all came back.

I was so sick that afternoon I just wished they'd stay away.

Then there was my grandpa. Grandfather Jerre was Mama's daddy. He had snow-white hair and a very red face. There was no kindness in his eyes or in his smiles. He looked like the devil would look, if the devil was a grandpa.

My grandpa had a tiny little shoe shop in the Big Junction at the top of the hill, up the street from Kress department store. The walls were covered in shoe boxes, and it smelled of leather. The floor was made of tiny white tiles with a black outline around the edges of the shop. Mama would visit Grandpa regularly and sometimes when she visited him, she brought me. Sometimes, I was fitted for school shoes, and other times, I just sat, waiting for Mama and Grandpa to finish up. Those times, they would leave me in the front of the store while they went into Grandpa's inner office. I would ride the horsy ride or sit in front of Grandpa's roll top desk and play with his adding machine. Pushing in different colored ivory buttons, I could hear the clunk inside, and then I'd crank the arm. I was so small that I had to stand on something to work the crank with both hands.

Although I couldn't see or hear anything, I knew for sure something was going on in that office that I wasn't supposed to know about, in that way that children have a sixth sense for something really creepy. I spent a lot of time looking at that black-and-white floor waiting for them.

Then Grandpa lost his shoe shop, and when that happened, he started coming to the house during the day whenever Daddy David was away at work. That's when Grandpa brought Mama her "presents," which weren't presents at all but pills in a bottle. He gave Mama lots of attention, and in return, she was really friendly to him, in the same way she was friendly to her husbands. But it felt dark and nasty. Mama never wore any underpants ("It ruins the lines of the clothing," she said to me), and Grandpa took advantage of that fact. Lots of times, I watched him reach up her legs when she was driving and push up her skirt. He would cuddle close to her and whisper, "Do you like this? How about this now?"

Mama would moan and say, "Not now, the baby is in the car!"

I never liked that, not at all.

Grandpa was always touching Mama, cupping her behind with his hands in a way that just felt wrong for grandpas to do. One day, our neighbor Dolores came over to ask Mama something, but I told her she was in the room with Grandpa and we weren't supposed to disturb them. It wasn't bedtime yet, because I still hadn't had any dinner, but I had a cold so I was in my jammies watching TV. Sissy wasn't home, so I was really hungry.

"Grandpa's been in there with Mommy an awful long time," I told Dolores. "I don't understand what's going on. When I went to the bathroom, I could see them through the door and they were doing things that weren't nice."

Dolores had a real surprised look on her face, and then she said, "I'm sure you misunderstood it, Mary Zoe. Your grandpa and mommy were probably just discussing something serious."

Then Grandpa came out of the bedroom with his pants undone and saw us sitting there. He just walked right past us and got his belt, which he'd left on Daddy David's roll top desk. Then he put it on, giving Dolores a creepy smile like he was going to eat her right up.

Daddy David came home right after that, and there was a really huge fight, right in front of Dolores. She went home looking like she'd seen a zombie, and I couldn't blame her.

I felt like that every time that Grandpa came around.

We hadn't lived together in Seattle very long before Mama told me that Grandma Kizer had died. She said that she and Sissy had to leave to go to Grandma's funeral. I was to stay with Daddy David for a few days until they returned. By that time, we lived in a brown house on Walnut Street across from West Seattle High School. I usually ran around the grounds of the high school or in Hiawatha Playfield, which was right next door to the high school.

One afternoon when I was playing outside, Daddy David called me inside. He had insisted that I wear a dress that day. It was hard to play in a dress in the playfield, so I played in the backyard. When I went into the living room, Daddy David was sitting in an armchair in his wool plaid robe, holding a windup clock. He said he was going to teach me how to tell time.

"Come on, Mary Zoe, climb up on Daddy's lap and I'll show you what time it is," he said. His eyes were looking at me in that reptilian stare, but he was chuckling like he was happy.

I obediently climbed onto his lap, but the wool from his robe was scratchy on my legs, and I tried to shift my position, pulling my skirt down more around my legs to stop the scratching.

"Stop fussing," he ordered, no longer chuckling. "Don't worry about your dress, just hold the clock." He seemed really irritated, like he was almost mad at me, so I did what I was told so I wouldn't make him angry.

As he showed me the hands on the clock, he spread his legs, which made me slide down between them, exposing more of my bottom and legs. He pointed out the big hand and the little hands on the dial, and I tried to pay attention, but one of his hands began rubbing along my leg. I didn't care for it at all and tried to pull away.

"Stay," he ordered. "Good little girls obey their fathers, and smart little girls learn to tell time." So the lesson progressed, as did his hand on my leg. Then he moved his position, and suddenly out from beneath his robe, I saw a pink thing that looked like some kind of animal's head. Startled, I looked into his eyes. They were very black.

"What's that?" I asked him, feeling scared for some reason, though I wasn't sure why.

"A mouse," he responded. "Now just get on with your lesson."

But it was hard to concentrate. I kept seeing the mouse. Pink. Hidden. Pink. It felt wrong, sitting on his lap, him being in his robe in the middle of the day, his hand on my leg and that mouse peeking out from the robe. Pink. I averted my eyes from the mouse, his hand on my leg and the clock. It was odd, I thought, that that mouse didn't have any ears. Finally, I said, "Daddy, I'd rather go outside and play."

I looked up at his face, and his eyes glittered.

"Good little girls keep secrets, and this one is ours," he told me firmly. He pushed me off his lap and said, "Lesson over. Go play."

I ran.

We didn't talk about the mouse or the windup clock after that, but after dinner, I went to my room and played by myself until bedtime. After I went to sleep, though, I felt a hand reach out of the darkness and grab my left arm, waking me up in terror. It was Daddy David.

"Shh...Keep your eyes closed," he instructed me.

I wanted to pull my hand back, but he held my wrist firmly.

"Open your hand," I heard through the darkness. "I want you to hold something."

I was scared. I wanted my mama. He forced my fist open and filled it with something, something similar to a finger, only bigger. Tears welled in my eyes and spilled down my cheeks as the something began to move. It was loose skin, I could tell, and it was getting bigger and moving faster.

"Don't look at me," he said again, his voice sounding funny, like he was running out of breath. "Good little girls do as they're told, and you're a good little girl, aren't you?" The dark room was filled with his heavy breathing and the fast movement of the thing in my hand. Suddenly, the movement stopped and I could feel a pulsing. I felt sick. I knew then. It was naughty. I had done a bad thing. He released his hold on my arm.

"Good girl, my good little girl. Now you know this is our secret. Good girls don't tell." Then he left. And I cried alone in the dark, wishing Mama would come home. By the next morning, everything seemed normal and I wondered if I'd made it all up in my imagination.

The next night, I had a terrible nightmare and I was so scared something would get me. I was afraid of being alone. I had to go to Daddy, since he was the only other one in the house. I thought maybe he'd play his big music box for me so I could go back to sleep.

"Daddy?" I said, shaking him awake. "Daddy, I had a bad dream. I'm scared."

I remember him pulling me into his bed with the music box playing. All I could see was his face like a big yellow moon hanging over me. I don't remember anything else.

When Mama came back from Grandma Kizer's funeral, I buried my doll and Grandma's crocheted hat in the backyard. It was all Grandma's fault. She died, and I was left behind. I never wanted to play with the doll or the hat again because I didn't want to remember my time alone with Daddy David.

I told Mama what had happened to me when she came back. There was all kinds of yelling soon after that, and she made me stand in the living room and tell that Daddy David had touched me. I cried, doubled over with stomach pain, and ran from the room. Later, Mama made me lie on the bed so she could check me for "virginity," even though I didn't know what that meant. She made me take off my panties, and she spread my legs and looked at me, while *King Kong* played on the TV in the background.

To this day, I can't stand the thought of King Kong.

Mama divorced him soon after that, which I thought meant Daddy David was gone.

But he wasn't.

CHAPTER 3
Sissy

"I'M GOING OUT, AND I won't be back until late," Mama instructed Sissy, "unless I come back in the morning." She smiled into the mirror as she applied her mascara, saving the fiery-orange lipstick for last, which she blotted on a Kleenex before giving herself one final, approving inspection. We knew where our mama was going—off to the bars to persuade some man to give her money, gifts, or a wedding ring. That was how she survived. "Financial contributions," she called them.

"You be sure Mary Zoe has a bath before bedtime, Gale. And get that laundry done!" Then she was out the door, and it was just me and Sissy.

Sissy had started running the household ever since she came back from Grandma Kizer's. She did the laundry, the housekeeping, the cooking, and the shopping, even though she was still in high school. And she took care of me.

One day, Sissy was cooking something that smelled wonderful. "Please give me a big portion," I pleaded. I was so hungry.

Sissy smiled. "Sure, Mary Zoe," she said and filled my plate with the beef and onions she was cooking.

I took a bite of the onions and smiled. They were so good; my Sissy sure knew how to cook. Then I took a big bite into the delicious-looking meat and felt as if my tongue had been slapped! The meat was awful! It felt greasy on my tongue, not like meat at all. I smiled at Sissy.

"Thank you," was all that I said. She didn't need to know that I thought the food she'd made was terrible.

"You liked that?" she asked me.

"Sure, Sissy," I lied. "What's it called?"

"Liver and onions," she said.

When she wasn't looking, I spat out the chewed meat and stuffed it into the cushions of the sofa, telling myself that whatever "liver and onions" were, I never wanted to eat them again.

After that, she made it often.

And each time, I'd stuff it into the cushions. By the time it was found, it looked like something the dogs had thrown up and no one ever knew.

When we ate together without Mama, Sissy would read from the Bible first. I didn't know much about the Bible, because Mama never took me to church, but Sissy had made friends at the church and she would go all by herself. I wasn't sure why, but it seemed to make her happy, so I figured it had to be something good.

"The Lord is my shepherd; I shall not want," she intoned, her face bowed humbly into her opened book of onion-skin pages, her soft blond curls falling around her face, giving her the look of a gentle angel. "He makes me to lie down in green pastures; He leads me beside the still waters. He restores my soul; He leads me in the paths of righteousness for His name's sake. Yea, though I walk through the valley of the shadow of death, I will fear no evil; For You are with me; Your rod and Your staff, they comfort me."

She'd go on and on with talk that made no sense to me at all, as I would watch the food get cold and my stomach would growl. But I never complained. I was grateful to Sissy for feeding us. If she wasn't home, sometimes I had nothing to eat at all. A little Bible reading was a small price to pay for having something to eat for supper.

Sissy was also the one who bought and cleaned my clothes. She was the one who met me at school and walked me home, the one who sang hymns with me as she cleaned the house, the one who read me even more Bible stories, made my meals, put me to bed at night, and got me up for school in the morning. I wanted to please Sissy as much as I wanted to please Mama, but for different reasons. I wanted to please Mama so she'd love me and not be so mean, and I wanted to please Sissy because it made her so happy and me so proud.

Sissy was the only constant in my life, and I couldn't afford to lose her love—if that ever happened, it would have been like having the wobbly earth drop from beneath my feet and I'd be left all alone in the cold, dark universe. Even though Sissy was always sweet to me, I was so afraid of making her mad. If she got mad at me, she might not just spank me—she might even leave! Mama left all the time, but if Sissy left, I'd be alone with Mama—and the thought frightened me to the marrow.

Although Sissy had all the responsibilities for the household, if Zodie thought that she had overstepped her authority, the punishment was swift and painful.

One time, Mama overheard me mention that I was afraid of getting a spanking from Sissy. She never asked what I meant; she just grabbed Sissy's head and beat her into the wall.

"You lay one damn hand on my baby girl and you'll wish a beating is all you got!" Mama screamed at her. "Now knock off your crying act and get dinner on!" I was so sorry I'd ever said anything, and I hoped Sissy wouldn't be mad at me. Thank goodness she wasn't.

Sissy just gave me a great big hug and whispered, "Don't worry, Mary Zoe; I'll never hurt you."

"I know you won't, Sissy," I blubbered, afraid that Mama would hear. "Please forgive me!"

"I can't forgive you because you didn't do anything wrong. It's Mama who's wrong, Mary Zoe, and don't you ever forget that—you're perfect just the way you are!"

Mama just wasn't there when I needed her the most, but Sissy always was—at least, she was when she lived with us. When I was seven years old, I had pneumonia. It was Sissy who took care of me when she got home from school, stripping the sweat-soaked pajamas off of me and sponging me down as I trembled with fever. I don't remember Mama even being there at all. It was Sissy who made Mama leave me alone at night so I could sleep. Mama wanted me to stay up to keep her company or bring her whatever she wanted. But instead, Sissy stayed up to take care of Mama. Sissy didn't like having to wake up, but Mama made her.

If Mama couldn't find something in the night, she'd wake Sissy up. If Sissy hid Mama's pills or alcohol, Mama woke her up. Sometimes she just had a question, and she'd wake Sissy up for the answer or sometimes she'd wake her up just to argue.

"You don't love me, do you?" she'd demand to know.

"Who should I marry?"

"Get up! I need you to dial this number for me and I'm too sick to see the numbers."

Lots of times, Sissy was up all night with Mama and still went to school in the morning.

She did it all. Sissy was the only good in my whole world, the bright star across the dark sky. The greatest role she ever played was protector. She protected those she loved, even if it hurt. And when she couldn't protect them, it utterly broke her heart.

I missed so much school on account of getting pneumonia that I got real behind on my schoolwork. But every time I tried to practice my reading, if I stumbled over a word, Mama would slap me hard, right in front of Sissy.

When I did my times tables, I always screwed up, and Mama would really get mad.

"How can you be so stupid?" she'd yell, and I cried because I was so stupid. I really wanted to make Mama happy, and I knew she was frustrated that I was so foolish, but the more I thought about that, the harder it all became and the more I messed up.

I knew Sissy wanted to help me, but she was too afraid of Mama. Even our neighbor Dolores saw Mama slap me over my homework; she was afraid too, and she was a grown-up. So I knew there were some things that no one could protect me from, not even Sissy.

"You're not stupid," she'd remind me. "And don't you ever believe it for a minute!" Then she'd kiss me on the forehead and help me with my homework when Mama wasn't looking.

Sissy's first boyfriend was a nice dark-haired boy with a ready smile. His name was Jerry Flagg. Jerry always wore crisp, button-down shirts and nice slacks. Underneath his slacks were metal braces that were clamped onto his legs, which made him walk funny. But Jerry was such a sweet guy that nobody ever noticed how he walked, and he didn't even seem to notice them himself. He was the nicest guy either of us had ever met, and he always made Sissy laugh, revealing her adorable dimples. Sissy was such a pretty girl, with wavy blond hair and a figure like Brigitte Bardot's, so naturally, lots of boys liked her. But Sissy was only interested in Jerry Flagg because he made her so happy. And since seeing Sissy happy made me happy, I hung around them a lot whenever Jerry came around.

"Hey, Mary Zoe," Jerry would say. "How are your stuffed animals doing?"

Jerry didn't just think of other people's feelings; he even considered the feelings of stuffed animals; he was that kind of guy. So I'd climb on his lap and tell him just how they were doing, and if any weren't feeling well, Jerry would take a look at them and tickle their fur or whisper something into their ears, and wouldn't you know, it worked every time. He could make even a teddy bear smile.

He never complained when I would climb onto the sofa and sit down between him and Sissy to show him whatever new thing I had to show off, even if it was just a schoolbook I was learning to read. I'd just wave my little reader and jump up and down with excitement, and he welcomed me every time.

"Come on up, little one!" he'd declare. "Show me what you got!"

And in no time at all, Sissy would be sighing heavily and shooing me off to go play while Jerry would just wink at her and let me steal the show.

But everything changed in an afternoon, and Sissy's world came crashing down with a terrible banging on the door. I went to answer it. It was our neighbor, Mrs. Snyder.

"I need to speak to Gale!" she said, in a frantic sort of way. Whatever it was, I could tell it was something really important, and I was afraid that Sissy might be in big trouble. I didn't want to turn her over to Mrs. Snyder if she was going to get in trouble.

"Gale?" I said, stalling for time.

"Yes, Mary Zoe, something terrible has happened! Something's happened to Jerry!" Before I could say anything more, Sissy came to the doorway.

"What is it?" she asked. "What's happened to Jerry?"

And that was when we learned that the TV news had just reported that Jerry had drowned in Puget Sound. He and some friends had gone out in a small boat without lifejackets or adults. Their boat capsized, and they hung onto the boat while one swam to shore. But Jerry couldn't keep his head above the cold water, since the metal braces were so heavy and his legs were too weak to kick. Though his friend tried to help him stay afloat, Jerry eventually slipped from his grip and died.

Even Mama was torn up to hear the news. She took Sissy in her arms, and everyone cried. We cried for days.

I don't really remember much about the funeral, except that I was scared by the pastor in his long black robe. He stood talking to Mama and Sissy, while I hid behind Mama and peeked around her legs to look up to him. He was so tall and thin that I figured he must have been ten feet tall. He had gold-rimmed glasses that framed his sky-blue eyes, but they didn't look scary at all. They looked very kind. He noticed me peeking up at him, and he smiled a gentle, warm smile. I blushed and ducked back behind Mama's legs once more.

That's all I remember—that and how terribly sad everyone was, especially Sissy.

Just like when David Grossman died and Mama started drinking, Sissy seemed haunted after that. She didn't start drinking, of course, but she didn't smile as much and slowly turned sadder and sadder.

Aunt Licha, Nana, and Uncle Tucker wedding circa 1950

It was shortly after Jerry Flagg's funeral that Nana showed up for Tucker's wedding to a sweet but shy woman named Licha. Before that, Tucker had found a girlfriend he really loved, but Nana didn't like her.

"She had him wrapped around her finger, and he was so lovestruck he just couldn't see it," Nana told Zodie. "I had to step in for his own good."

"That's damn white of you," Mama said, stamping out her cigarette with a mean half-smile on her face.

Nana gave her a mean look back, but she wasn't smiling. She was mad.

"And just what is that supposed to mean?" she asked.

"Oh, come on, Mom, you know as well as I do that you just can't stand the thought of Tucker marrying anyone. No one will ever be good enough for your little Tucker, as far as you're concerned." She lit another cigarette and reached for her drink.

"I beg your pardon? Do you think I would come all the way here for my son's wedding if I didn't approve of the woman he's marrying?" After Nana had made Tucker break up with the woman he loved, Nana said he could marry Licha, who was sweeter than pecan pie and just as silent.

"If you ask me," Mama went on, "the only finger Tucker's wrapped around is your middle one, and now that he's found some compliant little mouse to marry, you're going to put on an act and play the role to the hilt just as long as it takes to get through the wedding. And then you're going to have your nose so deep in their marriage that Tucker won't know which woman he's married to."

Then they started screaming at each other, and I went to my room until it was over.

When it came time for the wedding and Nana arrived for the ceremony, everyone gasped but Mama. Nana walked through the doors of the church dressed in the exact same white dress the bride was wearing, but Nana got to be seen in it first.

Mama just smiled and shook her head, like she wasn't sure which one of them had won that battle.

"Here comes the bride," was all Mama said.

CHAPTER 4

The Sound

AFTER JERRY FLAGG DIED, YOU'D think that I'd have sense enough to avoid Puget Sound. But I didn't. Why I ended up on the beach that August day in 1960 remains unclear to me, but what happened that day is forever etched in my memory. I was new to the neighborhood; we'd moved from the top of the hill by the high school to the bottom of the hill by the beach. School was out, so I was running around on the rocky beach looking for some kids to play with, any kids. I didn't find anyone my age or any girls for that matter, but I did find two older boys who were real old, like twelve or something.

They were building a raft and excitedly describing the foes they would slay once they got it finished. It was a really hot day, and I so wanted to play in the water with them, but I knew I'd get into big trouble if I did. Mama forbade me from going into the water.

"That's the Puget Sound, and it's as deep as the ocean," she said, "Remember what happened to Jerry Flagg! And it's full of jellyfish and river otters that could kill you!" I used to see the jellyfish washed up on the rocks at low tide, and the river otters would roll around in the water and play like water clowns, so I knew she was right about them being in there. But they didn't look like they would kill me, and besides, lots of kids would play in the water whenever the weather was warm. So I didn't understand why Mama was so afraid of me playing with them. Besides, I would never go out in a boat without a life jacket or grown-up like Jerry Flagg had done.

The boys noticed me climbing around on the rocky shore behind them, trying to keep my balance on the slippery black seaweed-covered rocks that covered the beach for as far as I could see.

"You know there's a sandy beach just on the other side of the point!" one of them hollered to me.

"I know, but it's too far," I answered. "My mama won't let me go that far."

"It's not that far—it's just past the lighthouse. That's where we're going. Why don't you follow us?"

I knew I shouldn't follow them, and I knew better than to go past the lighthouse, but it was so hot and I really wanted someone to play with. Besides, Mama wasn't home and she'd never know just as long as I wasn't gone too long.

They hoisted the raft over their heads and headed north, toward the lighthouse, and I followed them from a safe distance. I was too shy to get any closer, and they didn't seem to notice me once they set out. Once in a while, one or the other would glance back at me, jerk their head for me to keep following, and then they'd seem to forget me, lost in their banter.

When we got to the enormous rocks that were piled high beneath the lighthouse, we rounded Alki Point, and there it was—a long sandy beach as far as I could see. We walked a bit further, and they set the raft into the sand and finished tying the ropes that held it together.

I watched as the boys waded into the water, getting soaked up to their knees. They climbed onto the raft, each shouting ideas to the other about the games they could play, but it wasn't moving much, since it was still set in the sand. I stood on the beach and watched as they pretended they were pirates and started shouting orders around, swinging sticks in the air.

"Ahoy, Matey!" one cried.

"Aaaarrrrggggghhh! Batten down ye hatches, a storm's a brewin'!"

"Aye, aye, Cap'n!"

In the midst of their madcap play, they noticed me still lurking around, watching them with joy and fascination. One of the boys, the blond one, stopped swinging his stick and called out to me

"Ahoy, lassie! Wanna help us?" he called. He gestured for me to give them a push into the water.

I shoved the raft as hard as I could, but only got my sneakers filled with wet sand. Then the blonde boy jumped off the raft and we pushed it together. With one hard push, the raft floated free of the bottom! I could see its shadow on the sand and stared at it in awe. The boy climbed back on board, shouting at me the whole time to get on the raft. "Come on!" he called, with a big smile on his face.

"Yeah, come aboard!" the other said, gesturing for me to join them. He was darker and heavier than the blond boy but seemed to be as friendly.

I was wet only to my mid-thighs, so I thought it was okay where I was standing; it couldn't be very deep. So I got on. Once I climbed on the raft, the heavier boy said, "Let's row out away from the shore!"

"No!" I screamed. "Stay shallow!" Dread filled my stomach. The heavy boy only laughed and continued pushing with his pole. I couldn't go into deep water because that was forbidden. I had to make him understand. "I knew a boy who *died* in Puget Sound," I explained. "I'm not supposed to be in it!"

"Really?" he said. "Then you better hurry!" He yelled out and pushed harder on his pole.

I looked down. I could still see the shadow on the sand, so I figured we were at the same spot. I jumped off the raft expecting to be wet to my knees, but I dropped much deeper and the water shot up past my knees, rushed up my legs, swirled at my waist, and gripped my chest, squeezing the breath out of me. Seawater splashed my face, and I tasted the briny salt as it shot down my throat. Fear made me gasp, and I sucked in more water. Seawater stinging my eyes, I coughed and panted as I stood teetering on the tips of my toes with my arms stretched out to keep my balance.

The water was up to my armpits. I had to get to shore without falling into deeper water. I could feel the cold grip of the current just wanting to swallow me up and kill me too. I struggled to walk through the heavy water toward the shore. It seemed to take me a very long time, as I walked on tiptoe against the current. I was at the mercy of the water, as the waves pushed me this way and that. It was so slow I thought I'd never get there, but I was determined not to die.

After making it to shore, I rested with my hands on my knees and bent forward to catch my breath. That was when I caught sight of the raft. It was farther out than I remembered, and the boys looked much smaller to me. The blond boy waved. I didn't wave back, because I didn't need friends that much. I was sure that if I had stayed on the raft, one of two things would have happened: I would have drowned, or Mama would have killed me. Fatalistically, I went home.

We faced each other that afternoon, looking much alike, Sissy with her hands on her hips and her hazel eyes flashing in anger, me with my hands at my sides and my hazel eyes focused on the kitchen floor and the spreading puddle of water pooling around my feet. Under Sissy's gaze, I hung my head and shifted my weight from foot to foot, making squishing sounds in my Keds. I had upset my sister. It was the water. I had been in Puget Sound, and that was forbidden. People drowned in Puget Sound. Her boyfriend did.

"You could have drowned, just like Jerry!" she shouted, before bursting in tears. "Promise me, Mary Zoe, that you will never, ever go in the Puget Sound again!"

I promised. Then I started crying, too.

"Mary Zoe, what were you thinking?" Sissy scolded again, after she had calmed down. She was still upset. "You know how dangerous Puget Sound is! I'd hate to have anything happen to you, too." Sissy knelt on the floor, her knees in the puddle pooling beneath my feet, and she hugged me tight. She released me, and her dimples flashed with her warm smile. Then she held my hand and led me to the bathroom to wipe off the water still dripping off me.

"You know you'll have to stay wet, so that when Mama comes home, you'll be punished." I watched her in growing anxiety as she wiped up the floor where I had tracked muddy water. "You know you are not to go near the water! You can't swim!"

"But, Sissy, I got off as soon as I knew the boys were pushing away from the sand! Please don't let Mama punish me," I pleaded. "I'm sorry! Please don't tell Mama!"

Getting up from the floor, Sissy put both hands on my damp cheeks, "Sweetie, don't you know how precious you are to me? I don't want anything bad to happen to you. I can't protect you from everything, so you'll have to obey the rules in order to be safe. You broke the rules, and now you have to face your consequences." As she towel-dried my back, she smiled. "But I'll fix you a nice dinner before Mama comes home."

And she did. Fixing a dinner meant more than food to me; my hunger was more than physical. I felt protected by her love as my stomach filled.

Suddenly, the kitchen door slammed and high heels clicked a rapid beat across the linoleum. Mama was home. Sissy put her arm around me, and we turned as a unit to face the thin, agitated woman with the red fingernails who was furiously smoking a cigarette.

"Okay, what happened?" Mama snapped, looking down at us through her squinting eyes as the smoke billowed around her head.

Sissy stood by me with her hand on my thin shoulder and repeated the whole beach incident. I sneaked a quick peek at Mama but dropped my eyes right away. She was mad.

Silence ballooned. Mama continued to scowl as she smoked.

"All right, Mary Zoe, you were a good girl to get off the raft when you did, but you shouldn't have gotten on the raft in the first place." She exhaled a cloud of smoke. "Go outside and pick a branch. You're going to get a beating, but I'll let you pick out the shillelagh."

With stooped shoulders, I went into the yard to pick out the stick. I understood. Sissy was powerless against Mama. I had to be punished because if Mama ever found out that Sissy had kept the water incident a secret, it would be very bad for my sister. It was better this way, and both Sissy and I knew it.

Mama favored thin sticks because they made vicious welts on the thighs, so I picked out the thickest one I could find that would still satisfy Mama's determination to teach me a lesson.

As I lay across the bed with my wet pants and panties down, she slashed away at my wet, upper legs with the branch I'd brought her. She punished me that way because no one could see the welts except me. Afterward, it was Sissy who helped me into my pajamas, heard my prayers, and kissed me good night.

"I don't kiss bad girls," Mama said from the doorway. Then she turned and walked away.

But Sissy kissed me anyway and whispered, "Sometimes, you have to hurt those you want to protect." She stroked my hair. "Now, you'll remember to stay out of the sound."

I never went into the sound after that.

Sissy continued to do her best to create a normal household, but the more work she did, the more responsibilities Mama heaped on her. And as I was soon to learn, even Sissy's formidable strength had its limits.

CHAPTER 5

Martha

AFTER ZODIE DIVORCED DAVID WALZ, she got a job working nights as a dispatcher for Grey Top Taxis. She worked from midnight until six or seven in the morning, and it terrified me to have her leave us home alone. What if something bad happened?

I also worried about what could happen to Mama when she went off to work at night. A lot of times, she was already having trouble walking straight by the time she had to go to work, and when she'd come home in the morning, she was often in even worse shape. Sometimes, she brought some of the cab drivers home with her. When that happened, Sissy and I had to stay in our room or Mama would lock us outside, unless it was a school day and we could just go to school. Other times, she'd bring just one cab driver home, like Frank Mahoney, one of Mama's boyfriends. If she did that, he'd wait for Mama to change her clothes and then they'd leave and Sissy or a neighbor would usually take care of me.

If it was Mama's night off, instead of staying home with us, she usually just took off and didn't come home at all in the morning. "I don't want you kids to see me drinking," she explained, as if she was just looking out for us.

Pretty soon, Mama started inviting David Walz over and they'd get drunk and throw things at each other. I hated having David Walz come over, so whenever he did, I stayed in my room with the door closed.

It was one of those nights when I fell asleep to the sounds of crashing and cussing and really loud, ugly laughs that I woke up just before dawn. I had to go to the bathroom and heard a man snoring real loud. When I was heading back to my room, I peeked into the living room and saw two big men sleeping on the floor, with empty glasses and bottles strewn all over the place. I couldn't tell who they were at first, but

I could tell that neither was David Walz, because they were so big, so I crept into the living room to have a better look.

And that was when I saw my Daddy Johnny.

He was sprawled out on the floor with his mouth hanging open and snoring as loud as a truck. Another dark-haired man I'd never seen before was sleeping a few feet away from him. Mama was alone in her bed, snoring loudly.

I stood over Daddy Johnny, hoping he'd wake up, but he kept on snoring. Inside, my heart started beating like a happy little bird, and I hurried back to my bedroom so happy that my daddy had come back! When I woke up later in the morning, I felt like it was Christmas and hurried straight to the living room to make sure it was real.

But only the dark-haired man was sleeping on the floor.

There was no more Daddy Johnny.

"Oh, your father was here, all right," Mama said later when she woke up. By then, it was almost time for supper and I'd spent the whole day staring at the strange man on the floor and wondering if Daddy Johnny had really been there or if it was all just a dream.

"Is he coming back?" I asked, almost begging.

"I doubt it," Mama answered. "He said he came by to see you, but all he wanted was money."

"Then he *will* be back!" I insisted. I knew my Daddy Johnny wanted to see me and Mama was just being mean and making it up about the money.

"Don't hold your breath. He went to your room and gave you a kiss, but who's he kidding? He wasn't here five minutes before he had his hand out."

"You're just being mean!" I told her. "You chased him away! You didn't *want* him to see me!"

She stared at me for a good long moment and then burst out laughing. "You keep telling yourself that, sweetie pie, if that's what you want to believe."

"I believe it because it's *true*! You *hate* him because he loves me!"

Mama took a long draw on her cigarette, tipped her head to the ceiling, and slowly blew out the smoke. Then she turned her head toward me and said, "I wouldn't give him a dime."

That was the last time I ever saw Daddy Johnny. He never did come back.

With Mama working nights and partying with so many men, when I went to bed at night, I never knew what might happen before morning. I felt safest when Sissy was with me, but she was almost all grown up and sometimes she would do something with one of her friends. She took really good care of me, but I understood. Sometimes, she just had to go out.

"If you need anything, you call Dolores, you promise?"

I would always promise, but I was pretty good at taking care of myself most of the time so I usually didn't need to call anyone, as long as Sissy fixed me my supper and gave me my bath before she left.

It was one of those nights when Sissy was gone that I woke up all alone and I was so scared I started to panic. I walked to the manager's apartment in my nightie and knocked on their door, even though I knew it was so late that they'd be sleeping. But when the manager lady saw me crying, she wasn't mad I woke her up. Instead, she took me back to our apartment and stayed with me until Sissy came home. She left a note on the front door for Mama, but as soon as she left, I took it down because I knew I'd get in trouble for going to the manager.

The big change in our lives came in June of 1960 when I was eight years old and Mama married the cab driver I'd seen sleeping next to Daddy Johnny. He was a French-Canadian man named George Victor. George Victor was a handsome man of about forty, and he was powerfully strong. He was much taller than Zodie, and he had huge biceps that he liked to show off by rolling up his shirtsleeves. He also had a well-developed hairy chest that he liked to show off just as much, by unbuttoning his shirt. His hair was thick and black with white wings at the temple, and he pushed it back from his face so often that it made a big black wave at the top of his forehead, like an exotic bird. His dark eyes sparkled with humor, though sometimes they flashed with rage.

Right before they got married, Mama told me we had to move again, so there would be room for our new step-daddy. So once again, we put everything into boxes and moved to a new house. It wasn't too far away, but it was too far to see my old neighborhood friends, so once again, I'd have to make some new ones. But before I could do that, we had to have Mama's wedding. It seemed that Mama had more weddings than I'd had Christmases, so it was sort of like a tradition.

Sissy and George's sister, Charlotte, drove Mama and George to the town of Everett for their wedding. All the way there, Mama and George insisted that

Charlotte stop at all the taverns, until finally they were both too drunk to go any further. Sissy thought they should just cancel the wedding altogether, but they found a justice of the peace somewhere near the highway and Mama and George Victor got married. They were too wobbly to even stand up straight, but at least they made it legal.

The next day, Mama was so sick that she couldn't even see Sissy standing there right in front of her, bringing her some aspirin. She stayed in bed all day, and George Victor went back to work.

A week later, Mama and George went out to a bar and had a really big fight. Mama came home, locked the door, and said, "Don't let that SOB in no matter what he does. I never should have married him! Why didn't you stop me?"

The next day, Daddy George showed up at the house really early in the morning to get his clothes. Mama let him in and then there was a lot of screaming and banging. Finally, he left, still angry. As soon as he was gone Mama went to visit Grandpa to get some pills to calm down.

Sissy and I finally went out to get some groceries so Sissy could fix us something to eat. Mama still wasn't home when we got back, but while we were putting the groceries away, the phone rang. It was Mama. She was at David Walz's and not talking very clearly. She said she had come home while we were gone but had forgotten her keys so she was locked out. She wanted Sissy to come get her.

"I'll be right back, Mary Zoe," Sissy said and kissed me on the forehead. "Just watch some TV, and when I get home, I'll fix you some supper!"

But Sissy didn't come home that night because Mama wouldn't let her. When Sissy got to David Walz's house, Mama was so mad she'd been locked out that she pulled Sissy's hair and told her to never, ever come home again. She kicked her out and told her to go live with the Flaggs.

So that was what Sissy had to do; she went to say with Jerry Flagg's family. Mama sure hated that, even though she'd made her do it, and the next day, she called Sissy and told her she had to come home.

"Not unless you quit drinking and stop taking your pills," Sissy later told me she told her. I was standing right there by the phone, so I heard Mama's answer.

"What do you want? A Puritan mother?"

I didn't know what a "pure-tan mother" was, but I thought that might be better.

Sissy was gone a week, and I had to fix my own dinner and put myself to sleep. Mama slept all day, and when she woke up, she took her pills and started drinking. She wasn't working anymore on account of marrying George Victor, but after she kicked him out, she spent her nights with David Walz or Grandpa. After a week of that, Sissy called and said she'd come home, but by then, Mama said she didn't need to.

"You'd might as well stay another week," she said. "Because George and I have reconciled and we're going to Vancouver for our honeymoon. I'm sending Mary Zoe to Aunt Charlotte's."

Aunt Charlotte lived in a trailer. It was really small and dark, and I hated every minute of it, but after a couple of days, Aunt Charlotte said she was going camping and took me to the Flaggs' house. The Flaggs said I was filthy, and Sissy gave me a bath and washed all my clothes. Then she spent hours combing the mats out of my hair, but finally, I looked and felt so much better. Sissy took me home and said she'd watch me while Mama finished having her honeymoon.

While they were gone, I made up my mind to get to know as many kids in the neighborhood as possible. The best place to do that, I quickly discovered, was at the McWains'. The McWains had four kids and a big house just down the street, so there was always someone to play with if I went to their house. That was where I met Martha. She lived next door to the McWain's.

Martha had curly dark hair, black-rimmed glasses, and a blinding white smile. When I first met her, she was organizing a fort-building project with the neighborhood kids. I got to know her really well and to appreciate the way that she'd take charge. When she was intent in her directions, she'd push her glasses up her nose or she'd wrinkle her nose to reposition the glasses. Either way, it gave her an air of serious intellect that no one dared question.

"Mary Zoe, you stand there and hold this end," she instructed, like we'd known each other forever. "And, Julie, you take that other end." Martha put us all to work building the fort, and we all happily fell into line.

Martha could build the best forts and tents. Not only did they remain standing; she even made tunnels in them. And she would think up such wonderful games for us to play. As far as I could tell, Martha could do anything.

Martha and I hit it off right away, and on the first day we met, she took me to her house to meet her family. "I have two brothers, but they won't bother us, and my mom and dad are real nice. Come on," she said. "We can play in my room. I have lots of art supplies!"

So I went to Martha's house. She lived in a big white house with red door and a bluish-gray porch. The bright colors looked and felt so clean, nothing like the dingy brown house that I lived in. On one side of the house was a carefully tended rose garden, full of fat yellow roses. It smelled heavenly. The dining room window had something Martha called a storm window; I had never seen one of those before. Martha said it was to keep the bad weather out and keep the glass from "sweating." I didn't know that windows "sweated." Her windows were clean, whereas our windows were dirty and had black mold on the wooden frame, so I wished we had storm windows, too.

"It's a parsonage," Martha explained as she showed me around her house. I didn't know what that meant, but it sounded very impressive, so I decided then and there that one day when I grew up, I would live in a parsonage just like Martha.

The house also had a great big yard where her brothers, Jon and Larry, were busy playing and laughing and challenging each other. I suddenly wanted brothers, too, and stood in the yard watching them for a minute, just to enjoy their happiness.

"Come on, Mary Zoe!" Martha said, tugging at my arm. "Let's go inside so I can show you my room!"

We went inside. Martha's mom was in the kitchen cooking something, and she greeted us pleasantly. She had hair as dark as Martha's, and she was thin, but not skinny like my mama. Her eyes sparkled, and she had such a nice smile. Her kitchen smelled of good things to eat. She was just the kind of mom they had on the TV shows, the kind I dreamed about.

"I'm Mrs. Dimock," she said in the kindest voice. "What's your name?"

"My name is Mary Zoe Victor," I replied as grown up as I could sound, and she smiled as if I'd made a joke.

"It's nice to meet you, Mary Zoe," Mrs. Dimock answered. "How old are you?"

"I'm eight and a half years old," I said, hoping I didn't sound too young to play with Martha, who was nine.

"Eight and a half? Well, that's a fine age! And you're just in time, Mary Zoe, because I've made some cookies. Would you like some with a nice tall glass of milk?"

I readily agreed, and we sat down. Mrs. Dimock brought out a whole plate of homemade cookies and two glasses of ice-cold milk, and we sat at the kitchen table eating the cookies and drinking the milk like two ladies at a tea party. Homemade cookies! On little tiny flowered plates! I never knew cookies could taste so good. We just had cookies from the store. I knew then that Martha was the luckiest kid in the world!

Then, just as we were finishing the last of the cookies, a really tall man with wire-rimmed glasses came into the kitchen and smiled. Snatching a cookie from us with a wink, he said, "Hello! I'm Martha's daddy. What's your name?"

I stared at him, confused. I'd seen him before, but I couldn't quite place him. Then it struck me—he was the man from the church! He was the minister from Jerry Flagg's funeral, the one I'd hidden from behind Mama's wool skirt.

He was so tall standing in front of Martha's mama that I had to look straight up to see him.

"Hello," I answered. "My name is Mary Zoe Victor." Then I blurted out, "You're the man with the funny glasses!" Feeling my face flush and trying to cover my blunder, I added, "I saw you in church."

Martha tugged at my arm. "Come on! You can talk to Dad later." So before he could even answer, we dashed away to play.

Martha had everything: a warm family, food, and safety. I basked in her warm friendship.

We played the whole day and into the evening, a day that became a blur of games and dancing in the living room and delicious homemade food served on flowered plates. She shared all of what she had with me that day, until it began to grow dark and Martha's mom called her and Larry and Jon to dinner.

"Mary Zoe," Mrs. Dimock said in a friendly tone, "you'd better go home now; your dinner will be ready."

I wished that that was true, but the truth was I knew it wasn't. "I don't think my mama is home yet," I said, knowing Mama and George were still on their honeymoon, but I was too embarrassed to say that. "Can I call to see if she's home?"

Sissy had gone to play tennis, and I knew she wasn't going to be home until late, but I didn't want to get Sissy in trouble, especially after Mama had just thrown her out.

"Of course," Mrs. Dimock said, and I went to the phone and called home, but the phone just rang and rang. I hung it up and said, "There's no answer. Can I just wait in the front room while you eat? I'm sure she'll be home soon."

"Of course you can," Mrs. Dimock said, and she took me into the front room and gave me some coloring books to play with.

The dinner smelled so delicious, and I was so hungry. I wished I could sit with them at the table and be a part of their TV-perfect family, but I knew I couldn't do that so I just colored and imagined I was Martha's little sister and I just wasn't hungry. But my growling tummy told me otherwise, so I had to just pretend.

After they finished eating and Martha and her brothers cleared the table, Mrs. Dimock suggested I try to call Mama again. So I called home again, but still there was no answer.

"My goodness," Mrs. Dimock said, "I hope nothing has happened. Where did your mother say she was going?"

I felt my face turn red, and I said, "My sister Gale went out with some friends, but I'm sure she'll be home soon. She's a really good sister; she'll come get me."

Mrs. Dimock looked down at me, and I could see her face deciding what to do. Then she said, "I'm sure she will, too, but it's getting late and you need some supper. Let me get you something." Then she went into the kitchen, came back with a whole plate of yummy-looking food, and set it before me at the table. Martha sat with me while I ate it, and every bite was warm and delicious. I could hear Mr. and Mrs. Dimock talking very seriously in the background, and then Mrs. Dimock made some phone calls. She was trying to find my mama, but I could tell from the little bits I heard coming from the phone conversation that what she was finding was the story of Mama.

After I finished eating, I played with Martha some more, and then the phone rang. It was Sissy. She felt really bad about being out so late but told me that Mrs. Dimock said I could spend the night with them. I was thrilled!

That night, Mrs. Dimock made up the extra bed in Martha's room for me to sleep in and told us it was bedtime just when it got dark. It was summertime, so it got dark late. Still, that seemed awfully early to me since I usually stayed up way past midnight, but I didn't want to make any trouble so I eagerly put on one of Martha's nighties and got ready for bed.

"I hope I'm not being too much trouble for you," I said to Mrs. Dimock, accustomed to having strangers put me to bed and well aware that for many of them, it wasn't what they wanted to do.

"You are no trouble at all, Mary Zoe," Mrs. Dimock said. "We are delighted to have you stay, and I know Martha is delighted to have you as her new friend."

Mrs. Dimock was so warm and kind that I mustered up my courage and asked, "Mrs. Dimock, could you please tuck me in so it would seem more like home?"

She smiled again and didn't hesitate. "Of course, Mary Zoe," and she tucked the sheets in all around me and pulled the blanket up to my chin. "How's this?"

It was like heaven, but I asked for one thing more. "Will you listen to my prayers, like my Sissy does?" I asked her.

"I'd love to," she said, and I could tell she really was happy to hear my prayers. So I folded my hands together and said, "Now I lay me down to sleep..." as Mrs. Dimock listened and stroked my head. I fell asleep that night the happiest I'd ever been in my life.

If only I could have stayed forever and not returned to the nightmare up ahead.

Zodie and George circa 1960

CHAPTER 6

Charleston Street

SINCE MAMA QUIT HER JOB after she and George got married, she stayed home all day and George was always gone. Mama drank, and George worked. That was all she'd do, and that was all he'd do. He would either be working for the gas company during the day or the taxi company during the night. Either way, he was gone all the time, and when he wasn't gone, he was sleeping. And what that meant for me and Sissy was that when Mama was messed up, Sissy and I had to take care of not just the house but Mama, too. When she wasn't messed up, which wasn't very often, it was even worse. Then Sissy and I had to be obedient daughters—but no matter how good we were, we could never be obedient enough to please Mama.

Just one look from her half-closed eyes glaring down on us was enough to get us to stop whatever we were doing, or start whatever she wanted us to be doing. We learned not to wait for the explosion, because if it came, it would be brutal. But when George was around, she wasn't as mean to us. As long as he was home, she saved her meanness for him and was a little bit nicer to us.

Of all of Mama's husbands, George was turning out to be the best. He wasn't around much, and when he was around, he and Mama fought an awful lot or danced and laughed and kissed an awful lot. He didn't get mad at me and Sissy the way some of Mama's other husbands used to do, and he was nothing at all like David Walz, which was a huge relief to me. I liked George because he kept an eye out for us, at least the best he could. When he was heading off to his car to drive to work sometimes, if Mama was in a bad state, I'd beg for him to stay. "Why can't you stay?" I'd plead with him. "Why do you have to work all the time?"

Half in and half out of his car, he would pause and answer the same thing every time: "Because your mother is expensive." He would sigh and shrug his shoulders, and then he'd be off. But always, just before pulling away, he'd roll down his window and add, "If you need me, just call the taxi company and ask for cab seven-O." That always reassured me, though I never did call because I didn't know how to do it unless I called the operator and if Mama found out I'd done that, her punishments would be too much to bear. So I took the pragmatic approach and did everything I could to make her comfortable. We all did.

With Daddy George in the house, life remained chaotic, but at least there was steady money coming in and another adult in the house who understood that Mama wasn't normal. But he wasn't entirely normal himself and came with a menagerie of pets that seemed to get bigger and bigger. We had birds, cats, and lots of dogs, and once in a while a gerbil or two. The animals brought with them added noise, stink, fur, and filth and pretty much came down to a whole lot more work for Sissy. But seeing Daddy George love those animals so much was somewhat comforting. If he could love a stray dog, he could love Mama, and that was what she needed the most.

When he wasn't working, he loved to watch wrestling and cartoons. I didn't care so much for the wrestling, but I did like watching cartoons. Our favorite was *The Flintstones*, and when we watched that, we laughed and laughed, maybe because Daddy George looked so much like Fred Flintstone. Daddy George had a high-pitched chuckle that was so odd coming from such a big man that it always made me smile.

I watched a lot of TV and movies because I liked to imagine I lived in a home with a happy family, just like on *Father Knows Best*. That's who the Dimocks reminded me of, so I knew those TV families could be real.

I also really loved the movies. If she was in a good mood, Mama and I would get dressed up in our prettiest dresses and go to the Admiral Theater in West Seattle to watch a Sunday matinee. Mama would buy us the biggest popcorn and soda they had and a giant box of candy or a great big candy bar the size of a license plate, and we'd eat it all in the balcony watching the latest movies.

We were watching *Irma la Douce*, with Shirley MacLaine, when Mama leaned over and whispered loudly into my ear, "She gets money from men."

I thought it was Mama who got money from men, but I knew not to say it. Instead, in an effort to impress Mama, I chirped up with, "Oh, a woman parasite!"

Mama laughed so loud the people around us shushed us, but she just told them to shush themselves. Then she whispered, "Not quite."

I loved those Sunday matinees. But they became fewer and fewer, until after a while, we never saw any more matinees together. After that, she would send me alone.

When I was watching movies or TV, I could be anyone I wanted to be and imagine that my life was completely perfect. Other times, it was like getting an education. Like the time Mama and I were watching the Pink Panther movie, *A Shot in the Dark*. I had no idea what was going on and kept wondering when the pink cartoon panther would come back on, when George came into the room, stopped, and looked at the TV. Nodding toward the screen, where Peter Sellers and Elke Sommer were jumping into bed to make love, he said, "Isn't this a little raw for Mary Zoe?"

"Hell no!" Mama shot back. "She can handle it—can't you, Mary Zoe?" Not to let her down, I nodded, though I had no idea what they were talking about. "My little girl isn't scared of this. Are you?"

I shook my head rapidly, and after that, I sat wide-eyed, fascinated by the action on the screen and forgot all about the pink cartoon cat. Whatever it was I was watching, I knew it was something I could handle. I just couldn't figure out why Mama thought I ought to.

Other times, when I was sitting in front of the TV, Mama and George would start fighting, and when that happened, nothing could drown out the screaming and slamming and Mama's crying and cursing.

Daddy George wasn't a mean man, but he did have a wicked temper, and he beat Mama really bad sometimes. I really hated it when he did that. Sometimes I thought he might outright kill her. But most of the time, he took care of her, and most of the time, she seemed to really like him. He tried to be a good stepfather to me, and he never once did anything naughty like David Walz, but he wasn't always nice to Mama and she wasn't always nice to him. I learned about grindstones in third grade, and that's when I figured out that life with Mama and George was a perpetual grinding of incompatible personalities, and Sissy and I were caught right in the center of their grindstone.

Running out the kitchen door, I was greeted by the early summer morning, and it smelled so sweet. It was a Saturday, and nobody was up yet, but I'd already finished my breakfast and was ready to start playing! It felt good to get out of our musty house. I had the whole day of freedom ahead of me before I had to return home. I was happy.

I ran down the Charleston hill, across the street, and a few blocks to Martha's house to spend the day. I crossed the large covered porch and rapped on the big front door. And waited. Nothing. No answer. I rapped again, even louder. I could hear someone walking to the door. Finally, the door swung wide and Martha's mom stood there wearing a pink robe, fuzzy slippers, and a stern look.

"Can Martha play?" I asked hopefully.

"Mary Zoe, I'm sorry. Martha is still asleep. You should go home and come back later when she is awake, about nine."

Fear rose from my stomach, up to my throat. I couldn't go back home. I couldn't tell time very well, and Mama wouldn't help me. When she was sleeping, she only wanted to be awakened because of an emergency. I knew asking the time was not an emergency. But it was to me. I didn't want to go home and sit in my room, not making any noise all day long until Mama woke up. It was so beautiful here, and it was so dark and cold and unfriendly in my room. I couldn't play with my toys because it could wake Mama. Besides, the house smelled. We'd gotten a new dog, which made everything even messier, and they had both messed again, since Mama wouldn't let them go outside.

"Please don't make me go home, Mrs. Dimock," I pleaded. "I'm sorry it's so early. Is it okay if I wait?" I dreaded going home. There was no telling what would happen once I passed inside those doors.

Martha's mom looked down at me, her face a strange mixture of irritation, curiosity, and kindness.

"Could I do some chores for you?" I asked in a small voice. "I promise to be a good girl. Please let me wait."

Martha's mother was quiet for a moment, just standing in the doorway looking at me. Suddenly, she pushed her glasses up on her nose, just like Martha did, stood straighter, and smiled. "Sure, you can stay, Mary Zoe. I do need some extra help. You can help me by sweeping the porch."

Joy spread over me like warm butterscotch. I didn't have to go home! I could stay! I'd make sure I did a good job on the porch. I was glad to help. At least it meant for the moment that I didn't have to go home.

I began to sweep the huge gray porch, and as I did so, I gazed in wonder through the dining room window. Although I'd been inside many times already, standing outside looking in gave it a completely different appearance, as if it had suddenly become magical. In the center of the room was a large brown table covered in a lace tablecloth with yellow roses in a green vase in the center. A sideboard sporting a China tea set sat in the middle of the far wall. Gazing past the dining room, I could see the large sweeping staircase that led to the upstairs and Martha's room.

I knew that Martha's room was large and filled with sunlight. Her bed was covered with a white ruffled bedspread sprinkled with red roses. She had a glass case filled with dolls.

But the best part of the house was the secret staircase. The back staircase was dark and small, and it snaked from the upstairs to the kitchen, like a secret passage. It wasn't really a secret, though, since all the kids used that back staircase, especially Jon and Larry. When they came down those stairs, they'd jump down the steps four at a time, hitting the top of the kitchen doorjamb with their hands as they flew through the air and landed at the foot of the stairway like some kind of superheroes.

Everyone was happy there, and it was a beautiful house, filled with beautiful things. I sighed happily as I resumed sweeping; at least for the moment, I could pretend that Martha's house was mine.

As the school year approached, I was very excited. Since Mama had married Daddy George, she said I could get new school clothes that year! I was thrilled—it wasn't every year that I got new school clothes. For days, I daydreamed about the pretty dresses I'd wear, the shiny new shoes I would get, the new socks without any holes. But when it came time to go shopping for them, she didn't want to take me.

"Sissy can take you," she said, polishing her coffee table before company arrived. "I have enough to do already." My heart sank, like someone had filled it with stones. I bit my lip to keep from crying because I knew if Mama saw me cry over that, it would probably only get worse.

The coffee table polished, Mama smiled and then reached down, picked up the gold-filigreed lighter, and lit a cigarette. Then she got one of her dirty books, sat down, and started reading.

I went to my room to cry.

But shortly after, Sissy came home and took me to buy shoes and dresses and a new red jacket with furry white lining, and I felt like a movie star with all my new clothes. When we came home and I tried to show them off to Mama, her only comment was, "You'll never get a boyfriend wearing square-toed shoes like that. Next time, get pointed toes. You'll thank me later."

A few days before school started, there was a knock at the front door and I went to answer it. I figured it would be someone for Sissy, but I was thrilled to see that it was Martha and Mrs. Dimock.

"We were just going up to the junction to run some errands, and we wondered if you wanted to join us, Mary Zoe," Mrs. Dimock explained. "I thought we'd stop at the drugstore for hot dogs—you do like hot dogs, don't you?" There was a twinkle in her eye, and I knew she knew that of course I loved hot dogs!

"Yes, I'd love to!" I said, jumping up and down and hugging Martha.

"But first we have to ask your mama," Mrs. Dimock said, "to be sure it's all right with her." She looked around the house, which Sissy had just finished cleaning, and I could tell she approved of how clean and shiny the house was. There was even a pot of stew simmering on the back burner, so the whole house smelled delicious. I couldn't have asked for a better time for her to drop by—most any other time, I would have been mortified for her to see how I really lived. But thankfully, when she had the time, Sissy did a good job of cleaning up after Mama, George, and the animals.

"It looks like your mama has been working hard," Mrs. Dimock said. "But we'll get you home by dinnertime."

"Oh, Mama's not home," I told her. "But my Sissy is. She's taking a bath. I'll just tell her I'm going."

"I have to be sure it's okay with her," Mrs. Dimock said. "How about I just call through the door to be sure?"

Mrs. Dimock called through the bathroom door asking for permission. Sissy hollered back through the bathroom door that it was okay to go, so I grabbed my new red coat off the hook and we were off.

It was one of the best days of my life, and a hot dog never tasted so good! I wanted to go everywhere with the Dimocks from then on.

After school started, I stopped at the Dimock's house every day to walk to school with Martha. But it seemed no matter how much I tried to be on time, I always came too early. I would explain to Mrs. Dimock that I didn't know what time it was and I was afraid to wake Mama up and ask her because she'd be mad. So after a while

Mrs. Dimock just set up a card table in the living room and gave me coloring books and things to play with while they ate breakfast. Sometimes she'd ask what I had for breakfast, and since I didn't want to tell her that we didn't always have breakfast at our house, I'd just say I was afraid I'd be late so I came straight away.

Mrs. Dimock would look at me and say, "You're so thin I think you could use a little something extra to keep you warm," and she'd give me a bowl of cereal or some toast and juice. I loved it when she did that.

Martha became my first true friend. Like Sissy, she found me loveable and fun. We made houses out of nothing but junk and then judged which one designed the best house. We staged puppet shows for kids in the neighborhood and even made puppet and built a stage for our performances. We built forts in the woods behind Martha's house. And we built elaborate tents in Martha's living room, using blankets, clothespins, card tables, and other furniture. If I'd ever done anything like that at home, Mama would have hit the roof. But Martha's parents didn't mind at all and sometimes they even helped us. Martha's world was exactly what I desperately wanted for my own life, and the more time I spent with her and her family, the more my own life and family seemed so terribly wrong and unendurable.

One night after playing all day with Martha at her house, I stayed for dinner, and as it got dark, Mama still wasn't home. Mrs. Dimock wrote a note, took it down to our house, and left it on the door for Mama, explaining that she was going to put me to bed and she'd send me home in the morning. I loved spending the night at Martha's. We laughed together in the dark of her room when we were supposed to be asleep. I was so happy when I cuddled down in my new friend's spare bed. I couldn't remember when I'd been as warm and content. Mrs. Dimock even tucked me in and listened to my prayers, just like the first night I'd spent there.

But just after I had fallen fast to sleep, the hall light cut across the dark warmth of Martha's room and I woke up in fear—cold, numbing fear. I could hear Mama and Daddy George in the next room—they had shown up in the middle of the night and wanted me home. I couldn't make out everything they said, but I knew I couldn't continue to sleep over at Martha's house. And sure enough, Mrs. Dimock came and got me out of bed, telling me in a hushed voice that I had to go home with my mama. I got out of bed and went downstairs, feeling like I'd just been punished for something I hadn't done.

Cold nibbled at my toes while I watched the grownups talk by the big front door. All I wanted to do was sleep, where I was safe and quiet. Silently, I pleaded with them to let me stay. I'd be a good girl. I wouldn't giggle anymore. I'd be real quiet. But nothing could stop the cold; it seeped inside my coat as I left Martha's house and settled in my stomach as I traveled home with my angry mother and stepfather.

Mama didn't say much. She just yanked me by the hand into the house and ordered me to go straight to bed. I placed my stuffed animals around the entire edge of the bed and crawled into the shelter they provided. It was all I had. The icy sheets were unfriendly and uncomfortable; they hadn't been washed for as long as I could remember and smelled sour and stinky—nothing like the flowery smell of Martha's sheets. I burrowed deep into the blankets, trying to shut out Mama's sharp staccato coming from the other room. I didn't want to hear how mad she was at me for going to my friend's instead of staying home to keep her company.

I wished I had a mama like Martha's mama.

CHAPTER 7

Home for the Holidays

WE WERE ALL LOOKING FORWARD to having a halfway normal Thanksgiving that first year with George, one with a proper turkey and stuffing, mashed potatoes and gravy, and pumpkin pie. Mama had bought all the groceries, including the cranberry sauce that came out of the can like a wobbly cylinder of Jell-O, and she promised to bake pumpkin pies. I was so excited! After watching the Macy's Day Parade on TV, I ran to the kitchen to see how Mama was coming with dinner and see if I could sneak a bite—I was starving, and we hadn't had any breakfast—but when I got to the kitchen, I saw that nothing had been done to start the dinner, nothing at all. Soon, I found out why.

It seems the bourbon got poured before the pies got made, and by midafternoon, Mama and George were too busy fighting to bother with any cooking. There'd be no turkey dinner after all, and I couldn't have been more disappointed.

"Don't worry, Mary Zoe," Sissy told me, as the screaming in the next room made the whole house shake. "I'll fix the turkey."

I couldn't imagine how Sissy could cook a whole turkey; that was something only a grown-up could do, I was certain. But she pulled out the giblets, patted the turkey dry, stuffed it with some stuffing she'd mixed up, plopped it in a big roasting pan, and sprinkled it with salt and pepper. Then she put it in the oven, and sure enough, after a while the whole house started to smell wonderful as the smell of the turkey grew stronger and stronger. I stood in the kitchen transfixed as Sissy basted the bird until it turned a deep golden brown. We hadn't eaten all day on account of the fighting, and we would have gone to bed without anything at all except maybe a bowl of cereal if Sissy hadn't taken charge.

"You overcooked the breast," Mama said, her mouth fixed in a pucker of displeasure. "That turkey cost us good money, and now you've ruined it."

"Tastes great to me!" George said, giving Sissy a wink and an understanding smile.

Mama just glared at him and left the room. Then she started screaming at George from the other room. After a while, he put his fork down and went into the living room to fight some more.

Sissy and I finished Thanksgiving dinner all alone.

The big trouble came with the New Year in 1961. When Mama and Daddy George tucked me into bed that New Year's Eve, everything was fine. I didn't often get tucked in by Mama, and Daddy George was usually sleeping to get ready to work the night shift. But this night, Sissy had gone out to a dance, and Mama and George were laughing and having a good time; they had been drinking to celebrate the New Year, and both were very happy. They came into my room together, listened to my prayers, and kissed me good night. I went to sleep happy and hopeful for the New Year.

I don't know how long I'd been sleeping when the angry voices woke me. They got really loud and mean and awful. I peeked out of my blankets and through the light from the hallway, I saw Mama weaving toward my room. When she passed under the hall light, I saw she was splattered with blood. When I saw that, I started to cry.

Mama came into my room and knelt by my bed, but she smelled funny and her words were sloppy. I pulled away from her, cringing. As she reached out to grab my hands, that was when I saw the cuts. Her wrists were slashed open, and in the dim light, I could see the red meat inside.

I screamed at the top of my lungs.

Daddy George rushed into the room and threw on the light. There was bright-red blood all over Mama and all over my bed and the floor. It was everywhere. Daddy George pulled Mama away from me and took her out of the room. Mama stumbled into the dining room, talking rapidly to Daddy George, but I couldn't understand what she was saying because someone was screaming and crying too loud. I didn't realize that that someone was me. I just heard the screaming and crying and saw all the blood and felt terrified.

I watched Daddy George chasing Mama around the dining table. One of the dogs was so frightened by the fighting that he messed on the dining room floor, but Daddy

George was so angry with Mama that he didn't even notice and stepped right in it. He just kept after Mama, tracking the smelly mess all over.

Suddenly, just as he cornered her, Mama made a break for the living room door, but Daddy George blocked her escape. Screaming at him, she grabbed a porcelain statue and raised it over her head. It was a statue of a Chinese man that Mama had painted herself. The colors were so beautiful they seemed to glow. He was such a delicate little man, and I liked to spend time running my fingers over his smooth robes and playing with his tiny hands. As she held it high to threaten George, I saw once again the gaping wounds from her arms and the blood pouring from them.

Daddy lunged at Mama, grabbed the Chinese man, and smashed him on the table. The little man exploded, sending splinters of porcelain through the air. Then Daddy dragged Mama into the living room. I could see through the doorway and watched horrified as he seemed to be pounding a rag doll's head into the floor. But the rag doll was my mama.

Then the kitchen door opened, and there was Sissy standing in the doorway in her pink party dress, with a look of horror on her face. She dashed to the kitchen phone, and I watched her desperately saying something to someone on the other end. Hanging up, she took a long look at me, nodded once, and then she ran outside. Daddy kept fighting with Mama but suddenly stopped when Sissy came back in with the police. I watched as the policemen strode through the kitchen doorway and disappeared into the small living room. I strained to see what was happening, but all I could see was a small amount of red-splattered floor. I heard shouts and then banging and meaty thuds. Daddy George was fighting with the police. Suddenly, everything became very quiet, and I ran back to my room to hide.

Footsteps echoed through the house as a big policeman came into my room. I peeked at him from the safety of my blankets. He towered over me. He seemed to take up all the space in the room. I knew enough about the police from the movies, so I watched his gun carefully, fully expecting him to draw the weapon and aim it right at me. It gleamed like a snake, and it was so black, it looked blue.

But the policeman didn't draw his weapon. He smiled at me instead. That's when I began to breathe again. He picked up one of my stuffed animals that had fallen on the floor. Passing it to my outstretched hands, he smiled and told me he had a little girl about my age. He squatted by my bed and asked, "Do you need some help with your stuffed animals?" Again, he smiled.

"Yes," I answered shyly. "I always put my babies around me. They protect me."

"You're a brave little girl," he said as he helped me rearrange my stuffed animals. "The worst is over now. Your sister did the right thing. She called the police, and now she's home and you don't have to be scared anymore."

But I wasn't so sure. When he left, Mama would really be mad. And then I remembered the blood.

"Don't worry," he said, noticing my unmistakable fear. "We stopped the fight, and we'll take care of your parents. Your Mama will be okay."

I learned later that Gale was busy putting tourniquets on Mama's wrists, so she was unable to assist me when the fighting stopped.

After the policeman left me, Daddy George came in my room to tell me that he and the officers were going away for a little while and that they were going to take Mama to the hospital to fix her slashed wrists. As Daddy spoke, his words slurred and I saw that he had bloody bruises and purple lips so swollen he could barely speak. The blood on his face looked wrong. He shouldn't have hit that policeman. He was lucky he hadn't got shot. I knew. I saw the gun.

"Try and sleep, Mary Zoe," Daddy George said through his swollen lips. "Everything'll be fine and your mama and I'll be back real soon." He patted my blankets and added, "I won't be in jail for long."

Then he left. I lay in the dark with the room dimly lit from the hall and stared at the ceiling as my ears rang. The quiet was deafening.

In total quiet, I watched Sissy come into the room, switch on the small lamp on the nightstand between our beds, and hang up her dance dress. There was a wet spot on her skirt where she had tried to wash off Mama's blood. Sissy stood in front of her dress and touched the wet spot, which we knew would never wash out. Then she sighed and climbed wearily into her bed. Watching her blond curls settle onto the pillow, I knew I was safe and could finally fall back to sleep.

I awoke to a cold morning. I dressed for church, being careful not to wake Sissy. She was very tired. Mama and Daddy were both back home, sleeping together in their bed off the living room and snoring loudly, as if everything was normal. Sidestepping the dog mess and smashed breakables, I entered the kitchen and fixed myself a bowl of cereal. The dogs had broken into the sugar bag again and had eaten some of it. I carefully took some sugar from the untouched edges and sprinkled it on my cereal and then poured cold milk over it. After I finished it, I placed my bowl in the sink, and that was when I saw Mama's gold watch. It was covered with brown dried stuff. It was her blood. I picked it up, and the blood flaked off when I scraped it, so I took a scrubbing pad and scraped until the gold gleamed. Then I placed the watch on the TV set where Mama would be sure to find it when she got up.

That fight had been the last straw for Sissy. She had made up her mind. After years of watching Mama's husbands come and go, being shunted from place to place, placating Mama and protecting me, she had had enough.

The next day, it was time to go back to school, and instead letting me go to the Dimocks' that morning, Sissy walked me to the corner where she would go off in one direction to her high school, and I would go off in another direction to my elementary school. When we reached the corner, Sissy suddenly grabbed me by the shoulders and turned my face toward hers.

"You know I love you, don't you?" Tears were in her eyes and voice. "Nothing will stop me from loving you, Mary Zoe."

"I love you too, Sissy," I stammered, confused. She squeezed me one more time and then my sister walked away. I knew something was wrong, because I never saw Sissy cry as she walked to school. She liked school, like I did.

"Oh, well," I said, shrugging my shoulders. I figured I'd ask her when she came home, so I turned and walked on.

But Sissy never came home again.

And I was left alone with Mama.

CHAPTER 8

Alone

Mama yelled a lot the night that Sissy left us. Some people from the church had come by and told her that they'd taken her to the youth center. There was a lot of serious talk, and when they left, Mama started pouring drinks and yelling and screaming at everyone and everything in sight. Pretty soon, she couldn't walk straight, and I saw that her toes were curling, so I knew what that meant. She was trying to keep her balance.

"Leave me alone! Can't you see that I'm sick!" Mama yelled. Mama always said she was "sick" when her toes curled or she couldn't walk straight. Sometimes, she'd fall asleep and there was no waking her; she called that "a seizure."

"Bring me my pills!" she screamed, and I had to go into the bathroom to get her tranquilizers. Daddy George tried to keep them away from her, and sometimes, he even flushed them down the toilet, but that only made her angry. So I obediently got her pills and watched her swallow a couple and wash them down with a highball.

"She *had* to go and bring those goddamned church people into our private business!" Mama screamed, her face red with fury. "And now I've got those damned nosy authorities to deal with. As if I needed anymore *crap* in my life! How *dare* she let them take her to the youth center! How could she do this to me? I'm her *mother, goddammit*!"

Then she glared at me, and jabbing her red-polished finger at me, she added, "You ever do anything like that and you'll see just how far it gets you, missy!" I was certain she was going to start beating me at any moment, she was so furious.

"I won't, Mama. I promise," I said, trying to keep from crying.

"You'd damned well better not!" she mumbled, swaying and fumbling to light her Camel with her gold-filigreed lighter, squinting with one eye closed to better focus.

Her cigarette lit. She inhaled long and slow and then blew the smoke up toward the ceiling like it was the most heavenly relief.

"Come here, Mary Zoe," she slurred, falling onto the couch. I didn't want to get near her, but I knew I had to obey. "Come sit with Mama."

I came closer to her, and she reached out and grabbed me, squeezing me tight, her boozy breath strong and foul. "At least I have my baby, and that's all that matters," she said as she fell back into the cushions for her "seizure."

I took the burning cigarette that dangled from between her fingers, stamped it out, and went into the kitchen to fix myself something to eat.

Mama could think what she wanted about how Sissy leaving was so horrible for her, but I knew what really mattered. All that really mattered was that Sissy had gone and I was all alone. The world *had* fallen away from beneath my feet.

Tuesday was garbage day, and that was my favorite day. It meant that the piles of garbage that were strewn all over the kitchen could be hauled out. I loved lugging the big, heavy bags to the curb for the garbage man, because the kitchen looked so much better. I cooked the dinners, washed the dishes, made my bed, and did my best to keep the bathroom clean, just like Sissy had done.

Mama's pill bottles would be scattered all over the bathroom, along with all her makeup and toiletries. Towels were perpetually dropped on the floor, and hair, toothpaste, and soap were on every surface. The living room wasn't much better; dog fur was everywhere, and empty bottles and cigarette packages and dirty ashtrays seemed to cover every inch of the place.

The floor was filthy, and we didn't own a vacuum cleaner and the animals soiled all over the place because they never got let out. The whole place was practically carpeted in pet hair. I'd do my best to sweep it with the broom daily, but nothing I did could make that filthy carpeting look any better.

With Sissy gone, it seemed that not only did the house get much worse, but so did Mama. She still tried to fix her hair and makeup every day, but more times than not, it was more than she could handle and her face would be smudged with mascara and her lipstick looked like she'd scribbled it on her face.

"I look like hell!" she spat out one day, as if fighting with the mirror. "I can't be seen looking like this! That damned SOB George kept me up half the night last night, and now I look like death warmed over." Her cursing and cussing the state of her life began, and I did my best to tune it out and focus on my homework.

How Mama hated my homework. She felt my time could be better spent taking care of her and the house.

"What the hell are you doing? Can't you see that I need some help?" she yelled, snatching my book from my hands. "You can do your damned schoolwork at school! I need you here!"

"But, Mama, I have a homework assignment and—"

"I don't give a damn about your homework. You're in second grade! How hard can it be? I have half a mind to march down to that school of yours right now and have a talk with your teacher about sending you home with all this goddamn work! You have other obligations, and I expect you to be available when I need you! I'm your mother!"

"Yes, Mama," I stammered, starting to cry. I loved school. It was the only escape I had other than watching TV or playing at the Dimocks, and at school, I could learn and be with other people. Nice people.

"I want you to run to the drugstore and pick up my pills for me," she said.

The last time she'd sent me, it had been a nightmare. I had waited so long for her pills that I finally walked up to the tall counter to ask the nice man how much longer it would be. But he was gone! I was completely alone, locked in the pharmacy! I was so frightened that the police would come and find me and say I was a thief that I hid behind the magazine rack on the floor so no one could see me through the glass front door. I didn't know if I'd be there all night or what, so I just lay on the floor and waited.

Sometime later, the pharmacist came back and called out to me, "I'm sorry I had to lock you in, but I had to run an emergency prescription out to someone." I scrambled up from behind the magazines, and brushing off the dirt and dust from the floor, I approached the counter. He smiled at me.

"Besides," he added, "I knew you'd be a good little girl. Here's your mother's medication. Tell her to take it as prescribed." He unlocked the door, and I fled.

Now she wanted me to go back.

"But, M-mama," I stammered, afraid to tell her what I knew I had to tell her. "I just got you a bottle of pills last week, and the pharmacist will remember me. He's going to know you didn't take them as prescribed."

Mama sent me for pills so often that she usually sent me to different pharmacies, but this one was the closest. She wanted me to go there so it would be faster.

"I don't give a damn what that old fart said, just tell him the dog ate my pills."

I knew in my bones that what I had to do to make Mama happy was not right. The TV moms never did the things Mama made me do, but I had no choice. She was my mama.

"And bring me one of my books," she added, handing me an extra two dollars. I went to the drugstore, humiliated to have to pick out a dirty book for my mama and lie to the nice pharmacist.

When I got to the counter, I explained that my mama needed a refill and then told him the lie about the dog.

He stood looking down at me from his tall counter. "And how's your dog now?" he asked.

"Fine," I said, somewhat confused. "Why?' I asked the pharmacist.

"Well, drugs of this strength would have killed him."

"Oh," I said. I could feel my face flush. "Please, mister," I said in a small voice, hanging my head, "give Mama her pills. I'll be in trouble if I come home without them."

He stood there for some time and finally answered, "Okay, but I have to make some calls first."

I went to the book rack and rifled through the dirty books, looking for something that would please Mama. That meant something with a woman's bosom and lots of words about sex. My face always burned red when I had to pay for them. I would always stammer, "It's for my mama; I read comic books," but still the people behind the counter looked at me funny every time.

Searching through the book rack yet again, I looked left and right to be sure no one could see me looking at such awful books. But acting like that made me feel like a thief, which made me feel even worse. Finally, I found one and an Archie comic for me, and then I sat in a cracked green chair, swinging my feet, reading the Archie comic with the dirty book hidden beneath it.

I waited about an hour, finishing the Archie comic book and reading several others, while the sun shone outside the window. I wished I was playing outside, but I had to take care of Mama. Now that Sissy was gone, it was my turn to keep Mama safe.

I had been through this routine so many times before. It always seemed to take forever for the druggists to fill Mama's pills. Finally, the man called me to the counter, and I paid for her pills and dirty book—and a Wonder Woman comic for me.

After he gave me my change, the man looked at me closely and said, "Tell your mama to follow the instructions on the bottle." Then he smiled at me and added, "I hope your dog stays healthy."

"Thank you," I said and left as quickly as I could.

Oh, how I missed my Sissy.

When Sissy was home, I didn't have to make the drugstore trips so much because she had Sissy do it. Sometimes, Mama even made Sissy buy razor blades so she could cut herself. At least that was one thing Mama didn't make me do.

I think that would have killed me.

Every night at 3:00 a.m., George had to be woken up and fed his breakfast before he left for his taxi-driving shift. Mama did this during the weeknights, and I did it on Fridays and Saturdays. Usually, I had already washed and pressed his work shirt and started his breakfast before I went in to wake him. Daddy George slept like a dead man, and getting him up in the middle of the night was never easy. So I came up with two methods to get him out of bed, and each was a little bit manipulative. I'd burst into his room shouting, "Daddy, wake up!" using the urgent tone I saved only for Mama's worst crises. And bless him, no matter how many times I tricked Daddy George that way, he'd jump out of bed every time—because he knew that sometimes it wasn't a trick, and I really did need him on account of whatever Mama was up to. He frowned on this procedure when it was a trick, but I continued doing it because it worked. It got him out the door, so I could go to bed.

The other method I used was my handy sonic torture, while I made his breakfast. I'd iron a clean shirt I had washed, and then I'd start his oatmeal. George always liked his oatmeal. But he hated my whistling! So I'd make sure the door to his and Mama's bedroom was slightly ajar and then I would wet my lips and start on my own weird breathless version of "The Halls of Montezuma" or "As the Caissons Go Rolling Along." Both were military songs, and I would belt them out as sharp and cracking as I could. Whenever I did the whistling trick, George would bound out of bed yelling, "Stop, Mary Zoe! I'm up!" And that was that.

"Mary Zoe, you are a god-awful whistler," he'd groan as he sipped his morning coffee.

"All the better to get you off to work like you wanted me to, right, Daddy?" I'd say playfully.

"Right!" he'd grumble, grabbing his coat. Stopping on his way to the door, he'd usually add, "Remember to call the cab company and ask for me if you need any help."

"Right," I'd answer him, relieved to know he was a phone call away and worried I'd actually have to call him.

Mama never stayed up with me on those weekend nights when it was my turn to get Daddy George up, but on the weeknights, she expected me to stay up with her. Those were school nights, of course, but Mama didn't see it that way. She saw it as mother-daughter bonding time, and if I didn't join her, I wasn't just defying her, I was rejecting her. So I stayed up late on school nights, not until 3:00 a.m., but at least until 1:00 or 2:00, and I'd be up again by six to get ready for school (and try to sneak in some homework while Mama slept off her "sickness" from the night before).

When we stayed up together to awaken George, my favorite times were when we kept busy with arts and crafts. That was how I got pretty good at art. Mama bought me some paints, and one time, I did a painting of Puget Sound and Bainbridge Island. She taught me to keep my hand steady by holding my breath, and she was right, it worked. I kept that painting on my wall for years, until I had to use it to block up a broken window that Mama said she couldn't afford to repair.

But mostly, we watched old movies. We'd sit on the couch and watch the old classic movies from the thirties, forties, and sometimes fifties, but as the night wore on, the movies got stranger and scarier. We'd watch things like *Attack of the Giant Leeches*, where a half-naked woman got kidnapped by atomic leeches, or *The Killer Shrews*, featuring funny dogs wearing little costumes to look like rodents.

"Oh, look!" she'd howl, pointing to the TV. "At that one! And that one! What do you say we dress up these mutts of ours like that, Mary Zoe? Can you imagine Duchess dressed like a rat? Wouldn't that be a hoot?"

Then we'd start cracking up about what our dogs and cats would look like if we dressed them up like killer hamsters.

Mama also liked to point out all the mistakes in the filming, and we'd critique the acting.

"That broad can't act her way out of a paper bag," Mama would say of whatever movie star was being chased by aliens or devoured by flesh-eating bacteria. "I've been more shocked by a run in my stocking than she is by those zombies!"

"And I've been more shocked by running out of hot water!" I'd chime in, thrilled for a moment to bond with Mama.

"And I've been more shocked by running out of my booze!" Mama would say, slapping me on the back and reaching for her near-empty glass.

Then we'd get quiet again and go back to watching the movie.

Those were good times. When we watched *Frankenstein*, Mama explained that the monster was just misunderstood, that he didn't try to be mean.

"It's just who he is," she explained. "He can't help it because it's his nature."

"But why does he want to be so scary?" I asked.

"He doesn't *want* to be scary; he just has to live with the fact that he *is* scary. What he wants is to be understood, but everyone is so scared of him they run away. That's why he's so upset so much. He's lonely."

Mama helped turn the scary monster into someone I could feel empathy for. She made me realize that even bad people have a goodness inside them. They just don't always know how to get it out.

Watching TV with Mama prepared me for the real world in a way. Facing the screen monsters helped me to face the monsters in my own life. It made it easier to fall asleep when the test pattern finally came on telling us the movies were over.

And it made it easier when David Walz came back into our lives.

I came home from school one day, and there he was, his hands all over Mama and his reptilian eyes staring at me with a despicable smile, like he'd somehow conquered me by returning to our home. I ran to my room and closed the door so I wouldn't have to see him, and he left shortly after. Then Mama came into my room.

"Mary Zoe, I know you don't like David, but you're too young to understand these things so I want you to promise me you won't say anything to Daddy about him being here."

"I promise," I told tell her, my disgust unconcealed by my face.

"Besides, he never did any *real* harm to you," she said, straightening her clothes before Daddy George came home from his day job. "It's not like he broke your bones or anything."

I looked at her, astounded, but she just got up and walked out of the room. When the door shut behind her, I buried my head in my pillow and cried. Why couldn't Mama understand? How could she let him back into our lives?

I thought about telling George, but if I did that, he might leave Mama, and then I wouldn't just be alone—Mama would have David Walz move back in. That was unthinkable, so I had to keep the secret from Daddy George.

The visits from David Walz continued, and it wasn't long before he didn't leave when I came home. Sometimes he came by during the day, and sometimes at night, after Daddy George had left for work.

I stayed far away from him and kept their secret.

I watched raindrops sprinkle bright diamonds on the gray living room window. Sitting alone on the sofa, I tucked my legs underneath me to boost me a bit so I could see through the window into the front yard, but even with that, I had to stretch to look out. I was watching for Mama. I wanted to see Mama come home, even though the water cascading from the full gutters on our roof made gazing out pretty blurry. Our driveway glistened, and the puddles shone silver, but black spots of rain marred the smooth surface. The red mud driveway seemed to ooze around the tall grass at the top of the drive, but at the bottom of the hill, the mud turned black where the neighbor's crab apple tree cast a shadow. It was getting dark. I wrapped a thin arm around my chest trying to keep warm in the increasingly cold house. I was hungry and afraid to be alone in the dark. I sighed.

I wish I could go to Martha's house to get something good to eat, I thought. But I couldn't leave. Mama said I was to wait for her. So I waited. My stomach growled.

I licked the peanut butter off my fingers, wishing there was something more to eat than peanut-butter-and-mayonnaise sandwiches. Martha was probably eating roast chicken.

As I bit the crust, some mayonnaise squirted out and a droplet splattered on Mama's hi-fi, settling into the dust. I prodded the milky lump on her prized stereo cabinet and drew circles around it.

Sighing deeply, I remembered Sissy. When she was home, there was no dust. The house smelled of Pine-Sol, there was music on the hi-fi and there was always food to eat.

Finishing the last bite of sandwich, I licked my fingers and peered into the deepening gloom outside the window. My tears had finally stopped, but the strangeness of Sissy's absence hadn't. Luckily, I liked peanut-butter-and-mayonnaise sandwiches since most of the time Mama never felt well enough to cook. *Martha's mom cooks*, I remembered. *Maybe if Mama comes home before dark, I can go to Martha's and get something to eat at her house.* The possibility of a hot, homemade meal made my stomach growl, but it grew darker outside, and still no Mama.

Then, from out of the fuzzy rain, I saw her red Fiat appear around the overgrowth at the mouth of the driveway. It took a jerky turn into the drive and slid wildly side to side, bouncing from one pothole to another. The little red car tried to crawl to the high side of the road where it might get better footing, but it lost ground and glided in slow motion into the neighbor's cedar fence near the crab apple tree. There was an awful sound, and the fence convulsed. The apple tree shuddered. Boards splintered, and the fence sagged with pieces sticking out at weird angles, like broken ribs. Mama was home.

The passenger door opened, and Mama crawled out of the red car. Her face was white. Her eyes looked glazed, and she had that familiar drugged frown I knew so well. She stumbled up the slick driveway to the tall grass at the top of the drive. The yard was flat, but I watched as she deliberately placed her feet before her as if she were climbing up uneven ground. Suddenly, she pitched forward and landed on her knees. Her leather coat and shoes were streaked with brown mud and grass. She struggled to her feet and began her measured pace again. I'd seen this scene a thousand times before. Mama was "sick" again, and there would be no dinner tonight.

I wished Sissy had never left.

CHAPTER 9

The Chicken Lady

I SAT IN THE WAITING room of the juvenile court. Mama had deposited me in a green plastic chair and told me to wait until she came out of the courtroom with Sissy in tow. But that seemed ages ago, and still, I waited. Mama said she wouldn't let the nosy authorities from the youth center keep Sissy. She had come to get Sissy back.

The building was drafty and depressing. The white overhead lights didn't brighten a thing; they just made the furniture appear dull and shabby. I sat quietly, trying to keep my attention on the Golden Books I had brought to read. I was so nervous and kept looking at the door, expecting it to open any minute. But the doors remained stubbornly closed. Bored, I squirmed in the plastic chair and bit a fingernail. Gazing at the holes in the ceiling tiles, I tried to count them. Climbing on the seat of the chair and kneeling on my knees, I lost count and gave up, resting my head on my thin arms on the back of the chair. I had waited alone for a long time.

I was used to waiting for Mama.

What I didn't know at the time was that Sissy had prepared for her escape for a very long time. For months before she left, she had collected interviews and wrote down all of Mama's beatings, all the times that Mama was too "sick" to fix us dinner, all the times that Mama brought another man home to be our daddy, all the times that Mama left us all alone. She had witnesses to Mama's insane behavior, like our neighbor Dolores and Mrs. Flagg, and they told the courts they were willing to support Sissy in court. She even had the support of Mr. and Mrs. Dimock. Sissy had gone to them when she fled to "the church people," since Mr. Dimock was the pastor.

The Dimocks. Martha's parents. I didn't know they even knew Sissy.

How long Sissy had wanted to leave and plan her escape, I had no idea. But I did know that Sissy had stayed with us all those years, taking the abuse, so that she could shield me. I knew that Sissy had stayed until she was seventeen because she loved me. But I also knew that she had to be safe herself. She had to run for help.

Suddenly, the doors burst open and Mama stormed through the waiting room with George striding to keep pace. "Come on, Mary Zoe! We don't have all day!" he said, as he helped me collect my books, which had fallen to the floor when I saw Mama.

"Where's Sissy?" I asked.

"She's not going to live with us anymore. She's going to live with the Dimock family until she graduates," George answered. "They've offered to be her foster family. Let's get in the car."

What? Sissy was going to live with the Dimocks? I couldn't believe my ears. I so badly wanted to go live with the Dimocks myself. And that was where Sissy was going—if only I could join her!

The whole impact of all this information was just overwhelming, and I sat in the backseat trying to make sense of it all. But I didn't dare ask a question or say a word. Mama was quiet in the car, smoking with angry, jerky motions. Daddy George said that we were going to his sister Charlotte's house overnight, because Mama was so upset that she didn't want to go home.

"Okay," I said and looked out the window, thinking about Sissy and the Dimocks.

As for me, that meant spending another night in that dirty trailer with Auntie Charlotte, like it or not.

I don't remember much about that visit, except to see Mama drunk at the kitchen table with her head hanging down. Daddy George sat in stony silence, drinking some amber fluid from a little shot glass.

That night was dark and long for me. I couldn't fall asleep. Sissy wasn't ever coming back. Mama couldn't bring her home. Alarm bells rang in my head. There was never going to be anyone to protect me. I felt lost. I watched the furnace cast firelight shadows on the ceiling for a very long time. But for all its mess, it was so comforting to be warm and momentarily safe in Aunt Charlotte's house. Finally, I slept.

The next morning, it was cold outside, so we bundled up and returned to the shabby little house on Charleston Street. The sky was clear blue and the air sharp with cold. The thin dress I wore was no match for the weather. As we made it up the driveway and onto the high ground of the yard, I noticed that I couldn't see the drapes in the living room window or see through any of the windows—they were shiny obsidian black.

I stood on the ground in front of the living room window and put my face to the black glass. I could see nothing except a reflection of my own thin, pale face; large hazel eyes; and short blond hair. I touched the glass, and my reflection shattered as Mama pierced the quiet morning with a shrill scream.

"Fire!"

I ran from the house, and Mama and I met at the corner. She grabbed me and ran around back to the dog kennel where she sat me on the wet grass and told me not to move.

So I sat.

I watched the firemen run into the house as thick black smoke snaked into the shimmering blue sky.

I watched as Mama stood on the grass and wailed. "My babies!"

I watched as Daddy George ran in and out of the billowing black cloud shouting the names of our dogs. He repeatedly came out from the fire coughing and hacking, bent over with his hands on his knees, but without any of our pets. All of them were dead. The white parakeet Mama called Baby, who used to sit on her shoulder and chirp at the cats sitting quietly in her lap. Duchess the shepherd. Lady the mutt. All were gone.

Eventually, the firemen put the fire out. They said the oil furnace had blown up. "Good thing you were away; that could have killed you," they said.

Oddly, nothing had burned. But the whole house stank. And all our possessions were covered in a layer of black, sticky film and reeked of oil and carbon. The floor had streaks in the ash. At first, I couldn't understand what the streaks were from, but then I realized—it was where George had dragged the bodies of our dogs out of the house.

Later that night, I sat in the backseat of the car. My skin looked blue in the streetlight. I was cold and empty inside. I could feel the load in the back of the car lighten as Daddy removed the black plastic bags that held the bodies of our pets. We had stopped to drop the animals off at the vet's to be cremated. I climbed onto my knees and looked out the back window. Daddy George's face was framed in the window. He was crying. Trails of tears glistened on his cheeks in the streetlight. I quickly sat down. I knew he didn't want me to see him cry.

We drove for a long time in silence, and I fell asleep. I woke up when the car stopped. Daddy George carried me into a large house. It was the landlady's house, he said. She owned the house on Charleston, and we were going to live in her house until our things were clean and we found another place to stay.

The landlady was tall and strong, even though she was old. She had tight, iron-gray curls on her head and a big smile for me. "Put that child on the sofa bed in the living room," she said. "She looks exhausted."

As Mama tucked me in the bed, she seemed so sad. She brushed my blond hair out of my face and kissed me on the cheek.

"Sissy's never coming back," Mama said, her anger still palpable through her sadness. "She's living with that Dimock family now, and you aren't to have anything more to do with them, you hear?"

"But, Mama—" I began, but she cut me off.

"I mean it, Mary Zoe. You stay away from those people. You aren't to go over there, you aren't to play with Martha, and you aren't to call her. And you aren't to call your sister. She's made her bed; let her lie in it."

Then she turned off the light and walked out of the room, and I cried into my pillow. Now I had no Sissy, no home, no animals, no toys, and no friends. I was utterly, totally, completely alone. And there was one unmistakable truth I knew deep in my bones. I had to take care of myself, because I knew Mama wouldn't.

The next morning in the landlady's house, it was gray and cold. I folded up my blankets and managed to push the hide-a-bed back into the sofa. After dressing in the same clothes I wore the night before, I studied the house on my way to find the kitchen. The woodwork was dark, and the ceilings were very tall and slightly curved at the top edge. Lighting fixtures hung from the ceilings in what looked to me to be piles of icing. Waves of swirling plaster adorned the base of every lamp, but they had no shades; the bulbs just hung naked from the decorated ceiling. Somehow, they looked sad.

There was very little furniture in the huge house. It had great open spaces filled with dusty hardwood floors. It was as empty as I felt my soul was with Sissy gone. I found the bathroom, and I finally found the kitchen. There was a round table in the center of the room, and the landlady was at the stove making oatmeal. She invited me to join her at the table. I sat down. I was so hungry.

I never knew the landlady's name. I thought of her as the Chicken Lady, because she drew pictures of chickens and told me stories of life on a farm. We stayed with her for weeks. In that time, I rarely saw Mama and Daddy George. They went to the bars. When I awoke in the night with bad dreams, Mama wasn't there and Sissy wasn't there, so I crawled into bed with the Chicken Lady. She'd fluff a pillow for me and spin stories of her life as a young girl on a farm. I loved her stories. I stayed with the Chicken Lady, and she would feed me mashed potatoes with lots of melted butter.

"Eat up, Mary Zoe. You're much too skinny. This will put some meat on your bones!" she smiled. I liked the Chicken Lady.

I spent days walking around that big house. The only rooms that had furniture in them were the Chicken Lady's bedroom, the living room, the kitchen, and Mama's room. The four bedrooms and hallways upstairs were completely empty with their wires hanging dismally from their icing nests. All the light switches were buttons that went in and out, which I enjoyed pushing, but after a few weeks, the novelty of the house wore off. I set up a little playhouse in an upstairs closet, and I'd sit there for hours looking out the tiny window. I gazed at the empty trees and the gray, colorless sky and felt lost.

I asked the Chicken Lady for some chalk, and I drew a hopscotch grid on the sidewalk and spent a lot of time outside playing alone. I kept watching for other kids, but I never saw them. Finally in frustration, I knocked on each house asking the person in the doorway if they knew where the children were so I could play with them. I never found any kids because they were in school and I was not. Mama didn't want me going.

But before I could search any further, Mama abruptly told me we were leaving.

I never got to say good-bye to the Chicken Lady.

The house we moved into had a knotty pine kitchen, hallway, and bath. The house had very small windows, so it always seemed dark, without a colorful thing in it. All the furniture we salvaged from the house on Charleston was still darkened by the fire, so the house was dismal and lonely. I began going to school again, this time at Gatewood

Elementary. I had to walk a long way to get to school, but it gave me time to daydream what kinds of families lived behind the tidy yards. I wanted a family that was normal. I knew that being kept up in the night by parents fighting was not the way it was supposed to be. When other kids were sleeping, I'd stand crying in my thin pajamas, begging to be allowed to go to sleep. Mama would be yelling to keep me up, and Daddy would be yelling to let me go to bed. I sure missed going to the Dimocks, and I wished more than anything that I could join Sissy there, but I knew there was no room for two of us, and Sissy was sleeping there now.

Without Sissy and without Martha or her family to turn to, life grew lonelier and lonelier. Then, one day in early May, Mama got mad at Daddy George. We had been sitting around the living room. I was on the floor in front of the TV watching Alan Shepard sail into space. Daddy George had asked Mama to get him a beer, and she wouldn't. So Daddy swore at Mama and walked over the top of her freshly waxed coffee table to get a beer. That caused an argument that lasted most of the night. I still don't know why that incident blew up the way it did. I tried to drown out the sound of their bickering by covering my ears. I fell asleep with the pillow over my head. It was the only way I could get to sleep. It still is.

A few days later, Mama got the idea to drive to California, taking me with her. But we never made it.

CHAPTER 10
Road Trip

IT WAS WARM FOR MAY, the day my grandpa came to visit Mama. That meant I had to stay outside even if I was hot or thirsty. I had to stay outside until he was gone; that was the rule. Daddy George was already gone; after his fight with Mama, he took off for who knew where. I knew he'd be back, but I didn't know when. I just wished he were back already.

Whenever my grandpa left, Mama was usually "sick." She didn't cook, clean, or do anything. Mostly, she stumbled and fell. But that May afternoon when I let Grandpa into the living room, something different happened, something that had never happened before. When I turned to call for Mama to tell her Grandpa was here, he reached out and cupped me on my bottom. I didn't like him, and I didn't like his touch. It made me feel dirty. When he touched me, it reminded me of the way that David Walz had touched me, and I knew that it was wrong. It was the way he touched Mama's bottom, and that felt wrong, too. Grandpas weren't supposed to touch like that. And I just knew that if the Dimocks had a grandpa, he wouldn't touch Martha like that. It just wouldn't happen.

So out of his hearing, I told Mama. "What is it?" she asked, irritated that I was trying to get her attention. Then I told her.

"Mama, Grandpa touched me," I said, and I saw from her face that whatever I said, she'd believe me. "In a funny way. On my bottom, like he was holding it. I didn't like it, Mama."

Her face was furious, but for some reason, I knew she wasn't furious with me. I knew she believed me, because I saw how Grandpa was with her. Nasty. Wrong. Not like a daddy at all.

"You run outside," Mama said, her voice serious and determined. "And don't worry. Grandpa will never, ever touch you like that again, I promise." I looked up at her, and I could see that she meant it. Weirdly, it felt like the first time she was really trying to protect me, and I ran outside feeling a strange mixture of relief, joy, shame, anger, and confusion. But Mama was true to her word. Grandpa never touched me again.

When he left that day, coming out of the house as if he was in a hurry to get somewhere, he saw me playing outside. I looked at him, and he turned and scowled at me, paused for a moment, and then he waved his middle finger, got in his car, and drove away. I was paralyzed and ashamed. I knew what the middle finger meant; it meant, "Fuck you." My grandfather had said, "Fuck you," to me! My face burned.

I went into the house, and Mama was furiously grabbing clothes and putting them in pillowcases. "We're leaving," she said. "Get your things."

"Where are we going?" I asked her, even more confused. Had I done something wrong? I thought she was on my side.

"California," was her terse reply. "We're leaving."

I was so scared and confused that I ran through the knotty pine kitchen and bathroom, grabbing items at random, my heart beating fast and my guts churning. Sissy was no longer with me; she had gotten a new life. So I was on my own to deal with Mama.

I had no idea what had ultimately caused Mama to reach the breaking point. Fights with George were common, but a fight with Grandpa was something different. On the other hand, the decision to fight for her child and flee to God knew where with that child was just like Mama. She could throw a screaming child into the deep end of a pool, but she would fight anyone who threatened that child. I knew at the age of eight years old that my only real protection was the very source of my fear—my very own mother.

The little red Fiat was hot when we climbed in with our bundles of clothing in the back. Mama didn't say much. She just said, "Things will be better in California. You'll see."

We drove a long way. Tires over the tar and concrete beat a pounding rhythm in my head. Thumpty-thump, thumpty-thump. I was so tired and hot and hungry.

Around dinnertime, we stopped at a small town, right on the highway. Mama found us a motel with a yard out front that had a swing set. She settled us in for the night and got us pizza, and I played on the swing, running my bare feet on the green grass. It was cool by then and felt good, but I knew that Daddy George was going to be mad when he came home and found us gone.

Mama and I ate our pizza; I washed my face, brushed my teeth, and put on my pajamas. She tucked me in, and I said my prayers, as I did every night: "Now I lay me down to sleep, I pray the Lord my soul to keep; if I should die before I wake, I pray the Lord my soul to take. Bless Mama and Daddy. Bless President Kennedy, Mrs. Kennedy, and all the little Kennedys, and please, Lord, help me to be a good girl." Silently, I prayed for my Sissy. I knew she would never come back.

"Good riddance," Mama had said. But I missed Sissy and always prayed silently for her.

Mama kissed me and whispered, "Tomorrow, we'll be in California, baby, and things will be different. You'll see." Then she patted me on the head and went into the bathroom, leaving me alone in the dark in the great big bed.

Better? I wondered.

All night long, Mama kept getting up and going to the bathroom. It would wake me up, and one time, I saw her taking pills.

"Mama, what's wrong?" I asked her.

"Nothing's wrong, you go to bed," she answered. "I'll come back to bed in a minute." Her words were becoming a little slurred. But she said she was going right to bed, so I rolled over and went to sleep.

Bright light from the bathroom woke me. Mama was a dark silhouette; the light was behind her. She gripped the doorframe to keep from falling. My stomach turned queasy. Mama was "sick" again, and I was all alone in a strange motel in a strange town far away from home.

I watched Mama lurch to the dresser. She shoved it and all of the furniture and even the TV against the door. Then she looked straight at me. "This is to keep your daddy away from us. Go back to sleep."

I knew that if she slept it off, she would be okay again. So I begged her, "Please, Mama, come to bed!"

"Go to sleep!" she ordered and went back to the bathroom. I did fall asleep, but not for long. A loud thud woke me up, and I knew what it was; I'd heard it often enough. Mama had fallen on the floor. I listened closely, but she didn't get up. I waited for her to wake up and get into bed. But she didn't. I was frightened and began to cry. I don't know how long we stayed that way, Mama on the floor and me in bed, crying. I must have dozed off. When I woke up hours later, she was still on the floor. It was still dark, the middle of the night, and I was scared.

But I had to do something, Mama was really sick. Trembling, I lifted the receiver of the motel phone and dialed the operator. I hoped someone would answer, but what if they were sleeping? But they weren't. Somebody answered. A man's voice. "Front desk."

"Please come and help," I pleaded. "My mama is sick." The man asked me some questions and promised to get help. Then I got dressed and went to the door. I had to move all the furniture that Mama had pushed in front of the door. It was so heavy. I broke into a sweat as I struggled with the bureau, the TV, a chair, and a table. I finally got the furniture away and standing on my tiptoes, I released the chain lock and let the adults into the room.

The room filled with light as the manager and the police entered. As I was being taken away by the motel manager, I saw someone throw ice water on her, and then someone who looked like a doctor started treating Mama. She made little moaning sounds, mumbling words that sounded like "bolt hole" and "running." My last view of her was when she tried to slap the doctor.

Although I knew that there would be big trouble because of my call, I was relieved. Mama was alive. I was sitting in the manager's kitchen eating a piece of toast to dull the pain in my stomach when the police came for me.

They asked me many questions about what had happened. Then they started asking about me.

"How old are you, honey? About seven?"

"No. I'm nine," I said, "almost nine and a half in a few months." I hated when people thought I was so little, but I was used to it. Mama said that was because I was scrawny and didn't eat enough, but I knew the truth. I couldn't eat enough, not unless Sissy did the cooking. When she was gone, I was always hungry.

"Is that right? Well, that's a good age! I have a granddaughter just about your age, in fact, but she's a lot bigger."

As if hearing that made me feel better.

Finally, after answering all the policemen's questions, they said that they would have to take Mama to jail "to sleep it off." I'd have to come, too. There was no other place for me. I rode in silence to the jail. They put me in a gray room with a gray scratchy blanket and bars for a door. I climbed into a thin, hard bed, and as a policeman began to close and lock the cage door, a police lady said that wasn't necessary. "Leave the door open a little." Then she turned to me. "You'll be a good little girl and go right to sleep. Okay?"

"Yes," I said, obediently. I always prayed to be good.

Later, she brought me cupcakes. She was real nice to me.

The next day, I got to sit with a nice old lady, the sheriff's grandmother, in her parlor filled with bric-a-brac. We had been watching TV all day. I watched TV with one ear open because I knew Daddy George would come. I knew he'd be mad. And I sure was right. I could hear him yelling all the way down the hall.

Mama refused to come home with Daddy George, so he left Mama in jail and took me back to West Seattle. He didn't say anything to me on the long drive back. His mouth was set in anger, and his knuckles were white on the steering wheel. I was worried about what would happen to Mama, but I found out later that Grandpa got Mama out of jail and they went off together to a hotel for a binge. That was how Mama described it. So Daddy George took me home to the house with the knotty pine kitchen. When we got home, he fixed me a mayonnaise-and-peanut-butter sandwich and made a phone call.

"Yeah, I have a kid here, and her mom's in jail. She's not mine, and I can't take care of her," I heard him say. "No, I've got work to do, I don't want a kid hanging around all the time; she's got to go somewhere."

That was how I got sent the Seattle King County Youth Center.

Again, I entered a room full of bars and long hallways. Daddy George said this was for the best and that I was to be a good girl. I was so frightened. They made me shower and gave me different clothes. I had to sleep on a narrow metal bed in a room filled with other girls. The matron yelled, "Lights out!" and we were all to go to sleep. We had to get up before it was even light out, and every morning was awful—loud clanging and talking and laughing and fighting and screaming and shrill telephones ringing and the matron yelling at us to hurry up. There was nothing but noise, as everyone woke up at once and the room was filled with unhappy girls who'd rather not have to get up.

I tried to behave and be nice to everyone, but I was so alone. There was no Sissy. Mama and Daddy didn't want me. The Dimocks took Sissy instead of me. I wasn't a good girl. If I were a good girl, I wouldn't be alone. Every night at bedtime, I turned my face to the foul-smelling pillow and cried quietly in terror.

Until the night I heard a Voice.

"Don't be afraid. I love you. It will be all right."

I'd never heard such a Voice before, but I suddenly felt calm. I believed the Voice. It would be all right. I rolled over on my cot and slept.

The next day, my caseworker, Mrs. Komoto, asked me to her office. Mrs. Komoto had long blue-black hair sprinkled with white and piled onto her head with decorative combs. I wondered how she kept it so tidy in its gloss rolls, and I would stare at it in fascination when she spoke.

I stood in front of her desk, curious and worried, afraid I might have done something wrong, but wondering if she might have some news about Mama. If so, I hoped that it was good news. Mrs. Komoto smiled officiously, then peered at me through her cat-eye glasses and asked in a friendly voice, "How would you feel about living with Mr. and Mrs. Dimock? I understand you're friends with their daughter, Martha."

How would I feel? I couldn't imagine anything better! I rejoiced at the thought. I hadn't seen the Dimocks since we moved, and I really missed playing with Martha and being tucked in by Mrs. Dimock. And I'd get to see my Sissy!

"I'd love to!" I told her. "But where will I sleep? My sister lives there now, and there's no room for me." I was suddenly afraid that even if they wanted me, the Dimocks had no place to put me. But I'd be thrilled sleeping on the floor, if that was what it took.

"As I understand it, your sister has moved in with another family, the Flaggs, it says here. I don't know anything about that, but the Dimocks are eager to have you."

If Sissy had moved to the Flaggs', it meant there was finally room for me in Martha's family! It was an answer to my deepest prayer.

And just the beginning of heaven and hell.

MARTHA AND MARY ZOE 1962

Part Two

CHAPTER 11

First Morning

IT WAS THE SUNSHINE THAT woke me. In place of the juvenile hall's harsh glare of fluorescent lights, golden sunshine warmed my face, and I heard nothing but birds. I opened my eyes to shining glass windows that framed blue sky and swaying green trees. Everything seemed to shimmer. I rubbed my cheek on the soft white pillowcase and inhaled the smell of soap and fresh air. It was so quiet—no yelling matrons, no grumbling girls, and no shrill telephones, just sunshine, birds, trees, and *me*.

It was my first morning at the Dimocks. Martha and her father had come for me at the youth center the night before. I was surprised that Mama hadn't come.

"Where's my mama?" I asked Mr. Dimock. "Isn't she supposed to be here, too? I need to say good-bye!"

"Your Mama is sick today," Martha's daddy explained, "but you'll see her again soon; don't worry." His smile was so kind and gentle that I knew I didn't need to worry at all; I was thrilled to be going to stay with them. But still I was disappointed that Mama hadn't come to say good-bye. I knew what "sick," meant, even if Mr. Dimock didn't. It meant that Mama had been celebrating the night before and didn't even think about coming to see me.

I didn't ask him about why Daddy George hadn't come. I knew that Daddy George didn't really want me. It hurt me a lot to know that, so I just pushed those thoughts out of my head and went home with the Dimocks, happier than I'd been in years.

Maybe my wish that Mama and Daddy George wanted to see me hadn't been granted, but my wish to live with Martha's family had finally come true, and that was enough for me.

Still under the covers, I listened to the birds singing in the trees. The shining new day was calling to me. I had a new start. Maybe Martha was up and we could play. I crawled out of my bed, and standing in my own pajamas, not the coarse and ill-fitting ones from the youth center, I made my bed. I always made my bed. Even in the jail, I made my bed, running my hands over the drab and scratchy wool blankets to make them lie as flat as possible. But this bed wasn't drab or scratchy at all; it was glowing with color. Tiny squares of colored fabric in circle patterns danced on the coverlet. I ran my hand over it as I smoothed the bedding into place. It was so soft.

My room was made of glass. I remember Martha's mother calling it a "sun porch" the night before, but I was too tired to understand what she meant. But the moment I woke up, I understood exactly why it was called that. My new room was filled with sunshine! And everywhere I looked, I saw nature. There was so much green all around me. Green grass in the yard, green leaves on the trees, green bushes rising from the ground—and a spectacular splash of yellow was wrapped around me from Mrs. Dimock's yellow roses that were blooming just outside the windows.

Inside, it was just as magical. The floor was painted a deep brown that looked like melted chocolate—nothing like the dull and dingy brown at home. There was a thick braided rug circling the middle of the floor; it felt wonderful under my bare feet. And the glass door was covered with pretty drapes that hung like flowing red flowers.

In the far corner, in a patch of warm sunlight, was a cardboard box. In it were my new clothes. I remembered Martha's mom had put them there the night before, explaining that soon I'd have my own bureau and I could keep my clothes in it, but for now, the box had to do.

I knelt by the box and gazed at the contents. Everything was tidy. There were little summer tops in one pile and shorts in another. Spotless white underpants, undershirts, and socks were all aligned in their respective stacks. I'd never seen so many new clothes. I reached inside the box and looked through all the bright colors. There were brand-new red tennis shoes and a sailor hat, orange pedal pushers, a blue accordion skirt, a pretty green sweater, and even new pajamas! I picked up a pair of bright-white socks. They were so clean, they smelled of soap. The tops were rolled down to keep each pair organized with its mate. I marveled at that. My socks at home always smelled of cigarette smoke and were rolled into tight little balls, like rocks. These were open and fresh and smelled like roses.

Carefully, I reached into the box and picked out my clothes for the day. I wanted to look my best. I wanted Martha's family to like me, so they would keep me. Brushing my hair into place, my mind racing with excited thoughts about my new home and family, I suddenly stopped. It was too quiet. Maybe I got up too early. Maybe Martha and her family weren't up yet and I'd get into trouble if I left my room before they were up. I stood by the glass French door with my hand on the glass knob, hesitating. I wanted to open the door and go out, but I was a little bit afraid. Afraid or not, I had no choice. I had to go to the bathroom. So I opened the door and noiselessly stepped into the next room. It was the living room.

I'd been there before, of course, but now it felt entirely different. Now it wasn't just Martha's house—it was *my* house. I looked across the living room and marveled at what I saw. The room seemed to stretch forever, a giant expanse of red carpet and hardwood floors. I felt as if I were living in a mansion. I couldn't believe my good fortune.

I crept up the stairs and used the bathroom. When I was done, I listened in the hallway, but I still heard no one about. Back at the foot of the stairs, I stood and listened again. Faintly, I heard a noise in the kitchen. I followed the sound, through the dining room and up to the swinging kitchen door. I could hear someone walking and opening and closing cupboards and drawers. I stood there, watching my reflection in the brass plate on the door. I was chewing my lip. What if I got in trouble for leaving my room before I was allowed? What if Martha's mom didn't want to be disturbed? But my fears were outdone by my curiosity. I had to know what was happening. I pushed the door open.

There stood Martha's mom in her pink fuzzy robe, surrounded by bowls, measuring cups, flour, oil, and other mysterious objects and ingredients. For a moment, I stared in wonder, afraid my voice wouldn't work.

A tiny "Hello, Mrs. Dimock" squeezed out of my tight throat.

She stood there for a moment, a moment that seemed forever. Then she smiled at me. "Well, Mary Zoe, I see you're up early again. Martha isn't up yet, but you're just in time to help me with the morning cornbread. Would you like to stir while I add the ingredients? You can stand on this stool and help me out. Okay?"

I climbed onto the stepstool and accepted the wooden spoon she offered me. I held the long handle of the spoon in my hand and thought of all the times Mama had told me to bring her a wooden spoon. Those weren't happy memories. But this wooden spoon was entirely different. This wooden spoon was handed to me like an award and not a weapon. I'd been rewarded by Mrs. Dimock.

"Thank you," I said. I began to stir as she added ingredients. My vision blurred. I felt my head spinning. Mrs. Dimock wanted me. I could help her. It would be okay.

As I stirred, I remembered all the times I had envied Martha for her family and home. Finally achieving my dream had taken a long time, but as I stood in the kitchen on that first day of my new life with the Dimock family, I knew that the Voice had spoken the truth. Finally, I didn't need to be afraid. Finally, it was all right. Finally, *I* was all right.

"I like this wooden spoon," I said as I stirred the cornbread. "It doesn't hurt."

"Doesn't hurt?" Mrs. Dimock laughed. "Now why in the world would a wooden spoon hurt?"

"I used to get spankings with a wooden spoon," I explained, "or sometimes a fork. It didn't hurt my bottom, but on my legs, it *did* hurt. Do you think the cornbread is stirred enough?"

I held the bowl up to Mrs. Dimock to show her, but instead of looking at the bowl, she looked at me as if I'd said something to hurt her. Her face was so sad. I immediately wondered what I'd said wrong, but before I could ask, she smiled again and took the bowl from me.

"Why, yes, I think you've done a wonderful job, Mary Zoe! You are going to be a fine helper in the kitchen! And I have a promise to make to you," she said, taking my hand in hers. "I promise you that you will never be hit with a wooden spoon or with *anything* as long as you stay here." Then she added, "I want you to know that. That is not how we punish children here."

I was relieved but a little confused. "Then how do you punish children?"

I could see her thinking.

At long last, she said, "That is a good question. Well, the first thing we do if one of the children is naughty is give them a warning. We try to talk with them, get them to understand they need to behave. And the second time they misbehave, we give them another warning. But if they are being very naughty and acting up, by the time we get to a third warning, we send them downstairs to the basement for a few minutes until they calm down and write down what they did wrong, so they understand why we're upset."

I immediately imagined being sent to the dungeon. But then Mrs. Dimock added, "But the basement isn't really scary; it's just a safe place to go for some quiet time."

I thought about it a good long minute and then said, "I think going to the basement is better than being hit by a stick."

"I agree," Mrs. Dimock said, and she lifted me from the stool and gave me a warm and loving hug that made me feel so good inside, like when my Sissy hugged me. Then she set me back down on the floor, and I watched her pour the batter into the pan.

"Did Mrs. Komoto tell you what happened?" I asked Mrs. Dimock while we put the cornbread into the oven. As happy as I was to be there, I was awfully nervous, too. What if they didn't know about Mama and wanted to send me back when they found out?

"Yes, dear," Mrs. Dimock said. "The court explained the situation to us and we thought it was best if you came here until things at home were better."

"I'm just staying here for a while," I told her, "until my mother stops taking those little round things." I knew that was why I was sent to the juvenile hall—because Mama had taken those pills. Once she stopped taking them, she would be better.

Mrs. Dimock closed the oven door, and as she set the timer, she said, "Don't worry, Mary Zoe; you can stay here as long as you need to." She was still smiling, just like the mommies on TV.

I bit my lip again and told her, "I promise I'll be good, and if you need me to do any chores or help in any way, just tell me, and I'll do it, I promise. I always keep my promises." But no sooner had I said that than I felt my face turn warm. It wasn't true, what I'd just said. I didn't *always* keep my promises, and I knew I'd better tell Mrs. Dimock the truth. "Well, sometimes I don't. Like when Mommy was sick, she made me promise not to tell Daddy we were going to California. Then Daddy asked me about it when he came to pick me up, and I had to tell him the truth—he said it would help make Mama well if I did. Boy, was she mad at me about that!"

"I know, honey, and you don't need to explain," Mrs. Dimock told me. "But I want you to know that if you ever want to talk about anything, you can always come to me. Will you promise me that, Mary Zoe? That you'll never be afraid to talk with me if you feel you need to?"

"Yes," I answered, "I promise."

All of a sudden, Martha, Jon, Larry, and Mr. Dimock all came downstairs, and the kitchen smelled of warm cornbread and maple syrup and laughter so musical that it sounded like it was coming from a house full of angels.

Still, I was worried about Mama. And I wondered if she missed me. I sure hoped so.

MARTHA AND MARY ZOE, ALKI BEACH 1962

CHAPTER 12

New Life

MY FIRST DAYS AT THE Dimocks' were a dream. All day long, Martha and I played, and I loved helping Mrs. Dimock in the kitchen; she was a wonderful cook, even better than Sissy. Every evening, we all ate together at the table, and though they said prayers before eating, they weren't long, long stories like Sissy told and our food never got cold. Mr. and Mrs. Dimock never had any fights at all, and they never yelled at anyone. Sometimes, Martha and the boys would get into a fight, but it would be over in no time and they'd be laughing again.

Mrs. Dimock was so good to me. She would brush my hair and set it in pin-curls around my face, and I looked so pretty, almost like Shirley Temple. And every night, she gave me a bubble bath, which was my absolute favorite.

"This is what I call living!" I declared one evening as I leaned into a cloud of bubbles, feeling like a pampered movie star.

Mrs. Dimock burst out laughing and said, "Why, Mary Zoe, you carry on as if you've never before had a bubble bath!"

"Never one this good!" I said, scooping a giant pile of bubbles into my hands and blowing them into the air, as Mrs. Dimock and I scooped them up playfully.

The truth that I didn't dare tell her was that the baths I was used to were lukewarm ones, in tubs that were always slimy and gross. The air would smell of mold and mildew and the cat litter box, leaving me feeling even dirtier after the baths than before. I'd never before had baths that left me feeling so beautifully clean and comforted. It truly was heaven.

Although life with the Dimocks the first few days was magical, I quickly realized that if I was going to be a part of the family, I had to do my share. So one day, I asked Mrs. Dimock, "Will you give me chores to do like the others?"

"Why, of course, Mary Zoe!" Mrs. Dimock said and then proceeded to suggest some things I could do, like clear and set the table, sweep the floors, and make my bed.

I nodded and agreed to everything she suggested, then added, "And an allowance?" I was a little bit scared asking for an allowance, but I knew that if I worked hard, I would earn it, maybe only a quarter a week, but that would buy a candy bar and a comic book and still leave me with a dime left over to save up.

"You know, Mary Zoe, I think that's an excellent idea!" Mrs. Dimock declared.

"And one more thing?" I asked, taking advantage of her generous mood.

Mrs. Dimock cocked her head and raised an eyebrow in answer.

"Is it all right if you don't call me Mary Zoe? Just Mary. The kids at my last school called me Mary Zoo and laughed at me."

"All right, Mary it is!" Mrs. Dimock agreed. "And the first thing you can do for us, Mary, is sweep up the front porch!" She handed me a broom, and I practically danced all the way to the front porch, like a regular member of the family. So from then on, I did my chores just like everybody else and even got scolded now and then for things like not settling down and going to sleep or talking out of turn at the table. One time, I rode my bicycle in the street. That was forbidden, and Mrs. Dimock sure wasn't smiling that time! And another time, Martha and I got into her daddy's shaving cream and we had so much fun playing with it—until Mr. Dimock discovered the mess we'd made. He was so mad that time I thought we might get sent to the basement, like Mrs. Dimock had described. But we just got sent to our rooms and told not to do that again.

I loved being a part of the Dimock family, and Martha and I became more than best friends—we fast became sisters. And that meant that it wasn't long before we got into some arguments, and each time we did, I was so afraid that it was the end of the world and the Dimocks would send me away for hurting Martha's feelings or doing something to make her mad. But that never happened; instead, Martha and I always ended up hugging and forgetting all about whatever it was that made us bicker.

I could tell that Martha envied all the new clothes I was getting, but she never said anything. And I envied all the beautiful things that she had. She had a big case filled with dolls from all over the world, and every time I looked at those dolls, I wished they were mine. And she had really fancy things, like a leather box full of stationery, that seemed so grown up. I wanted stationery just like that, and it wasn't long before she started tricking me into trading my own things by tempting me with her things.

"Mary, look at this," she'd say, holding out her hand. It would be something like a stone or a coin or something very common.

"So?" I'd ask.

"Do you know what this is?" she'd ask me, her eyes growing big behind her glasses.

"A rock," I'd answer—or a feather or whatever it was.

"It's protoplasm," she'd tell me, and then she'd explain all about how everything in the universe was made up of protoplasm, and the way she'd tell it, I'd be ready to trade her my belly button just to have it all for myself.

Martha was very clever. She knew just how to tug at my heart to get me to make a trade. One time, she traded me her black lacquer jewelry box for something of mine—I don't remember what it was I gave up—but a few days later, she talked me out of the jewelry box by trading it for something else I wanted. That jewelry box went back and forth between us so many times that finally Mrs. Dimock had to intervene and tell us both to stop the trading.

Martha was very smart. She also knew everything in the world. She was like a walking encyclopedia, and any question I ever had, she could answer. She skipped a grade when I got held back a grade, so even though we were only a year apart, we were three years apart in school so I really looked up to her.

As for Jon and Larry, well, they were older, almost teenagers, and they rough-housed a lot and were always up to something outside or in the garage. They were never mean to me, but I soon discovered having brothers wasn't nearly as fun as having sisters.

A big part of living in a house with a pastor was, of course, learning about religion. I was used to church because sometimes Sissy would take me, and I was used to Sissy reading from the Bible, but I wasn't used to church being such a big part of my life. I knew I had to get used to it if I was going to live with the Dimocks. Still, it was pretty new for me, and I wasn't quite sure where I stood on the matter. So one day, I decided to set things straight with Mrs. Dimock.

"I'm the type of person who finds it hard to believe in God," I explained, "because you can't see him and I don't hear him answer when I pray to him." I didn't mention to her about the Voice, because I'd only heard it that once and wasn't sure where it came from. Whatever it was, I had a powerful sense that it wasn't something I should tell anybody about, not even Mrs. Dimock. As for believing in God, I figured if I discussed the matter rationally with her, Mrs. Dimock would understand my doubts. And, true to her nature, she was very understanding.

"God doesn't answer our prayers in the way we expect," she explained. "God answers our prayers in his own way."

I thought about it for a minute and nodded, though I wasn't entirely convinced.

Then she added, "Besides, he likes a bit of mystery, Mary, to teach us to figure things out for ourselves."

"Like Nancy Drew?" I asked her.

She chuckled. "Well, not exactly, but he does like to talk in riddles and codes!" Then she rubbed my head and told me not to worry about it, but it left me even more perplexed at what this God thing was all about.

The thing was, as big as religion was in the Dimock home, they didn't really talk about God all that much. They talked more about politics and civil rights and what they could do to help people. I wasn't there very long before I realized that I wasn't the only one they were helping. Mr. Dimock worked until really late at night on his sermons or ministering to people (that was what he called it), and Mrs. Dimock worked all day fixing meals and cleaning the house and delivering things to people in the neighborhood, like cakes and pots of soup and clothes she'd collected for people who were sick or out of work. If anyone in the neighborhood was having any problems, it seemed that the Dimocks went right to work doing whatever they could to help them. And they were very concerned about the way Negroes—that's the word that was used back then—were treated. Mr. Dimock said that all God's children should be honored and that meant *everyone* no matter what color their skin was.

I liked that kind of a God, so I didn't mind learning more about him. But it wasn't easy. And the Dimocks could tell. They were concerned that I needed to know more about the Bible.

"But I already do," I explained. "My Sissy would read from the Bible every night at suppertime when Mama wasn't around."

Mrs. Dimock smiled, like she always did, but it was clear I wasn't getting off the hook. "That's very good," she said, "but if you learn the Bible yourself, you will always find comfort in its words. So let's learn a few prayers just to get you started."

I thought learning prayers would be easy enough, so I agreed. Well, let me tell you. It was hard work. I had to memorize and memorize and memorize, and it was way harder than school. But finally, I got one down.

"Whew!" I said after Mrs. Dimock congratulated me and told me we were done for the day. "That was hard work!"

For some reason Mrs. Dimock laughed when I said that, but I decided not to ask why. I sure didn't want to let her know I was still confused, or I might have to learn another prayer before I could run off and play. So I just laughed right back, like I got the joke, even if I didn't.

And just like I'd done at home, every night at bedtime, I always said my prayers. "Now I lay me down to sleep, I pray the Lord my soul to keep," I'd recite as Mr. and Mrs. Dimock looked on. "And bless Mama, Daddy, Sissy, and Martha and Mr. and Mrs. Dimock, and help me to be a good girl. And thank you for this wonderful family that's taking such good care of me. Amen." Almost every time, right after I said, "Amen," I remembered who I'd forgotten, so I'd have to tack on a PS to my prayer.

"And bless even the brothers," I'd add. Then I'd crawl into bed, and Mrs. Dimock would tuck me in and give me a kiss, just like Sissy used to do.

I sure missed Sissy. And I missed Mama and Daddy. But I was afraid if I told the Dimocks how much I missed my family, they might be hurt. Worse, they might even send me back, and I certainly didn't want that. But it didn't stop me from missing them and worrying about Mama.

The court said that I could see Mama every weekend. The first few weekends when she came to get me, she was all dressed up and bought me lots of presents. She bought me stuffed animals and coloring books and even pretty clothes. She was super nice to me and like a completely different Mama. And best of all, we started going back to the Admiral Theater to watch our matinees.

We usually dressed up to go to the movies. Mama would put on a tailored suit with heels, and she'd carry her alligator bag. She looked so slim and chic, I was so proud to be seen walking down California Avenue with her. She reminded me of Grace Kelly.

Mama always insisted that we have the "best seats of the house," which were in the upstairs balcony. They were atop a grand sweep of red carpet. and from there, I could scan the entire theater. I would gaze in wonder at the center chandelier of wrought iron and gold glass, which was surrounded by the images of the Zodiac. I knew I was Aquarius, since I was born in February, so my image was a Water Bearer. I loved that ceiling. I loved the swell of music and the way the lights turned the theater curtain a deep shade of gold. I felt safe in the theater because the hours there meant I could be someone else. I didn't have to be afraid. The fear only came when the movie was over. That's when my headaches always started, during the walk out of the darkness of the theater into the bright light of day. That was when I'd have to say good-bye to Mama and go back to the Dimocks.

It wasn't that I didn't like being at the Dimocks; I loved living with them. But I knew that going back there made Mama unhappy. And that made me feel like I'd done something wrong, no matter how good I tried to be. I really hated feeling like that, even if I couldn't imagine going back to Mama's.

The nightmares always came right after I'd seen Mama. One night, I had a dream that I was trying to rescue my friends from dynamite, but Mama was too close to save so she blew up. Then I was lying down with some other family members—I don't know who, I just knew they were my family—and I saw someone with one eye coming toward me. I was horrified, and as they got closer, I saw that it was Mama. Mama poked at me and said she wouldn't stop, that she'd keep on bothering me. Then suddenly, I was in the Dimocks' home, setting the table, when Mama jumped over the table. I jumped away, but Mama touched me and I shivered at her touch since she was supposed to have blown up.

That dream scared me so much that I got out of bed, grabbed my little doll, walked through the dark house and up the stairs, and woke up Mrs. Dimock. She came downstairs and read me a fairy story—I loved fairy stories, especially Cinderella—and then I fell asleep, sucking my thumb while Mrs. Dimock brushed her hand over my hair and sang me lullabies.

The next day, Mr. Dimock rigged up a little bell so all I had to do was pull a string and they would hear it and come to me in the night.

Mama would never have done anything like that for me. She would have screamed at me to go back to sleep or made me get up and watch a horror movie with her.

I liked the Dimocks' method better.

I'd moved to the Dimocks right when school vacation had started, so I didn't have to go to school. I liked that. It meant that I could play all day with Martha. But at the end of June, Martha had to go away to Girl Scout Camp, and I didn't like that at all.

"Why can't I go with you?" I pleaded to Martha.

"Because you're not big enough for Girl Scouts," she said. "You have to be ten years old. I'm already ten, but you're still nine years old, so you get to go to Brownies. Have you ever been a Brownie?"

I'd always wanted to go to Brownies, but Mama would never let me. "You don't want anything to do with those people," was how she explained it, but I didn't understand why. All the girls went to Brownies or Girl Scouts, why couldn't I?

I told Martha I couldn't because I didn't have a uniform.

"You can wear mine!" she said and gave me a big hug. "My mama will freshen it up for you while I'm gone!"

We jumped up and down and hugged each other, and I decided Martha could go away to Girl Scout camp without me. It would be okay.

Mrs. Dimock gave me Martha's old Brownie uniform, and it fit me perfectly. She washed and ironed it and told me I would get my own badges and pins, and then pretty soon, I'd be ready for Girl Scouts.

I put on the brown dress and the orange tie and admired myself in the mirror. I looked like a real Brownie! I'd never felt so important in all my life. But there was one thing missing—a golden pin. All the Brownies I knew had golden pins on their uniforms.

"Don't worry, Mary," Mrs. Dimock said, "You'll have one soon enough. The pins are something you have to earn, and you'll earn yours very quickly, I'm sure. If we just gave you one, it wouldn't be the same as knowing that you'd earned it."

Well, I had to agree with that, so I was happy to wait until I'd earned it. But until then, Martha would still be gone to Girl Scout Camp and I'd be all alone.

But at least I'd have Mrs. Dimock.

"I have an idea," she suggested. "How would you like to learn to sew?"

Learn to sew? With needles and scissors and patterns and pins? The smile I gave her must have split my face wide open, I was so thrilled!

Mrs. Dimock trusted me; she had faith in me that I could sew. And that was way better than Girl Scout Camp. I was ready to begin!

Mrs. Dimock got out her sewing basket and a big box filled with scraps of colorful materials cut from old clothes that Martha, Jon, and Larry used to wear. She showed me how to thread a needle, exactly how much thread to cut, and how to match the material together so the edges lined up perfectly. After having me watch her make a few stitches, she handed me the needle, thread, and fabric. I squinted, pushed the needle through the fabric, and pulled the thread all the way through, but it tangled and frustrated me so.

But instead of telling me I was stupid, like Mama used to do, Mrs. Dimock just laughed and said threads got like that sometimes, and then she showed me how to keep it from doing that.

We sewed and sewed, and pretty soon, she said I was ready to try a button. She got a shirt of Mr. Dimock's and showed me how to position the button properly, and after she got it started, she showed me how to sew it on. And I did it!

I was so proud of my work! I sewed the button on tight and couldn't believe I'd done it all by myself (although Mrs. Dimock had to tie the knot; I wasn't quite ready for that).

"Am I eager to learn?" I asked Mrs. Dimock, and again, she laughed like I'd told a joke.

So I laughed, too, and then we had a big bowl of ice cream, and that was the start of my sewing lessons.

Martha was gone for two weeks, and during that time, Mrs. Dimock spent a lot of time with me, teaching me to sew, to bake cookies, and even how to garden. But learning how to do those things wasn't nearly as difficult as learning some other things, like how to act when I got something special. One time when we were out shopping, I saw a big box of crayons—the big kind, with a crayon sharpener built right into the box. I marveled at all those colors, and I wanted them more than ever.

"Please, Mrs. Dimock, can I get these crayons?" I pleaded, smiling my very best smile so that my eyes would sparkle. They cost a dollar, which was an awful lot for crayons, but there was a whole world of color inside that box so I just had to have them.

She looked down at me from her tall height, and I could see her thinking through the problem. Then she said, "Sure, Mary, you've been a good girl, and I think you've earned these crayons, don't you?"

I was thrilled beyond belief. A whole box of crayons—sixty-four colors! It was the big box, like what they had at school. I'd never before had so many crayons, and there was nothing I liked more in the world than coloring, so when we got home, I smothered Mrs. Dimock in kisses and hugs to show her how much I appreciated them.

But something went wrong. She didn't think it was right for me to kiss her so much.

"Mary," she said, gently pushing me down, "I'm really happy that you like the crayons and I was happy to get them for you, but you don't have to go overboard and thank me so profusely!"

"What's the matter?" I asked her. "Don't you want me to show you how much I appreciate them?"

Then she looked at me for a good long time, like she was doing her thinking, then she said, "Yes, Mary, I'm really happy to know you appreciate them. But when someone gives you a gift, after you thank them, that's all you need to do. You don't need to crawl all over them and keep thanking them over and over. That's not how it's done."

I thought for a minute and then said, "But that's what Mama does."

Then she looked sad again and reached over and gave me a hug. "But that's not what you need to do here," she said. "One thank you is enough. Then, when it's your turn, you can do someone else a favor."

"Oh," I said, thinking it over. "I think I understand."

But deep down I was confused.

Wasn't showing affection how people got things?

Before I knew it, it was time to go get Martha from Girl Scout Camp. The thought of riding all the way up there—it must have been two or three hours—and coming back with a car full of girls who had all been away together at Girl Scout Camp, just didn't seem fun at all. I tried to talk my way out of it, explaining that I was used to staying home by myself, but Mrs. Dimock said that I was still too young to be left alone, and even if that was the way Mama did it, it wasn't the way it was done in the Dimock household.

"But I'll get carsick!" I pleaded, convinced that would do the trick.

"Then I'll give you some chewing gum," she replied, which she did. So we got in the car, and I rode all the way up there and back, and the chewing gum must have worked because I didn't get sick at all.

In fact, we sang songs and told stories and had a wonderful time.

But best of all, Martha was finally home!

"Come on, Mary!" Martha said, pulling me by the hand, "I can't wait to show you all the things I made at Girl Scout Camp!"

Martha and I went straight to her room, and she showed me all sorts of things she'd made out of pine cones and sticks and pebbles. It was amazing to see that so much could be made from nature, and her stories about Girl Scout Camp made me all the more excited about joining the Brownies as soon as I could.

But a few days later, when I went to visit Mama, I found out she wasn't at all excited by the idea of me joining the Brownies—at least not if I wore Martha's Brownie uniform.

"As long as you're my daughter, you won't have anything secondhand!" she said, blowing a cloud of smoke over my head. I had gotten so used to living without smoke that now when I visited Mama, the whole house smelled so bad I wanted to peel my nose right off of my face.

"But, Mama," I explained, "Martha's Brownie uniform looks brand new and it fits me perfectly! I can wear it for you next week and you'll see how nice it looks on me."

"Don't bother. I'll get you a new Brownie uniform," she said, stamping out the tail end of her cigarette.

"But, Mama, that would hurt the Dimocks' feelings. They said I could have it."

"Don't pay any attention to what the Dimocks say," she said. "It's what I say that counts." Then she sent me to the corner store to get her another carton of cigarettes.

After that, I didn't talk to Mama about the Brownies. She never got me a new uniform, but she did send me home with a big bag of clothes one day.

"Oh, dear," Mrs. Dimock said as she began pulling my old pajamas and undershirts and dresses out of the bag, "these look like they haven't been washed in months! We've got our work cut out for us!"

I could tell from Mrs. Dimock's face that she wasn't happy about the clothes, and I didn't really blame her. They were so dirty and smelly and wrinkled that I was embarrassed to bring them back. All the socks had to be thrown away because they had no mates or were too small, and some of the other things were too stained or torn to even give to the poor. But Mrs. Dimock gathered up what didn't need to be tossed and washed them real well. She used Clorox, which she said was like magic soap. And sure enough, by the time she'd finished washing them, they looked almost brand new.

"There!" Mrs. Dimock said as she arranged them in my bureau. "Don't these look lovely, now?"

"They sure do," I agreed. "My mama wants me to have nice clothes, just like she has!"

"I know she does," Mrs. Dimock said. "Your mama's trying to do her best."

"She sure is," I said, "I think she's getting better. Maybe I can go back and live with her pretty soon, if the court sees how much better she is!" I didn't want to leave the Dimocks, and I sure didn't want to hurt Mrs. Dimock's feelings, but it made me sad to see Mama hurt by all the nice things the Dimocks were doing for me. I knew Mama wanted to be a good mama like Mrs. Dimock was, but she was just sick from taking those pills. Once she stopped taking them, I knew she'd be a better Mama. And besides, Sissy used to do the washing and the ironing, so Mama just didn't know how.

"Well, we'll see how things go," Mrs. Dimock said, and then she crouched down to my height and said, "But first, I've got some exciting news!"

CHAPTER 13

A Special Visit

I WAS SO EXCITED I could hardly stand still. I jumped up and down and raced through the house the split second I heard the news.

Sissy was coming for dinner!

"Whoa!" Larry said when I knocked right into him. "Slow down, little Roadrunner!" But I didn't slow down. I leaped right straight into his arms and gave my new big brother a giant hug.

"My Sissy's coming! My Sissy's coming!" Then I wiggled back down and raced away, my mind filled with a million thoughts about cleaning my room and finding a nice dress to wear and all the things I couldn't wait to tell my Sissy. She had just graduated from high school and was still living with the Flaggs; Mama still wouldn't have anything to do with her, so I only got to talk to her on the phone sometimes. This would be her first visit since she'd moved out and I'd moved in.

"I have an idea," Mrs. Dimock said. "How would you like to make a cake?" Her eyes sparkled, and I could tell that she was almost as excited to see Sissy as I was.

"Oh, yes!" I said, jumping up and down and clapping my hands. "I've never made a cake before!"

So Mrs. Dimock got out a box of cake mix and some bowls and beaters and cake pans and taught me exactly what to do.

I followed the instructions perfectly, except for one thing. When I poured it into the first cake pan, instead of only halfway up, I poured the batter all the way to the brim.

"Oh, no!" Mrs. Dimock said. "That's too much! You only need half of that. The rest goes in the other pan."

"Oh…" I could have hit myself for not paying attention. "I'm so *stupid*!"

"Mary! Don't you ever say that you're stupid! You aren't at all stupid. That's a minor mistake, one that anyone could make."

"It is?" I asked her. I knew if I'd done that at Mama's, she would have been really mad at me for making such a mess of it.

"Yes, it's nothing we can't fix. Nobody ever learned to cook without making mistakes."

"My Sissy never makes mistakes," I corrected her.

"I'm sure she doesn't make many now, but I'll bet she's made lots of them when she was little. We all do."

"Even you?" I asked. I couldn't imagine Mrs. Dimock making such a mistake.

"Why, if I told you all the mistakes I've made, we'd never have time to get this cake baked!" Then she showed me how to take a gravy ladle and spoon the overfilled batter into another cake pan so it was all evened out.

"There," she said when she was done. "Now they're perfect!" And sure enough, they were.

Once the cakes were in the oven, we turned around to see a terrible mess. Bowls and mixing cups and broken eggshells were all over the place. But instead of getting mad at me for making such a mess, Mrs. Dimock just got a mischievous grin on her face, then handed me a beater dripping with chocolate batter and hollered for Martha to come get the other one.

Martha stopped whatever it was that she was doing and came running. Her eyes got as big as quarters when she saw the beater, and she snatched it right up.

"Yum," Martha said as we devoured our beaters. "You sure do make good cakes, Mary!"

"I like to make cakes," I declared, as I licked the beater. "Because of the fringe of benefits!"

And that made Mrs. Dimock laugh so much that after she took the beater from us, she let us have at the whole chocolaty bowl!

"I wish Sissy would visit more often!" Martha declared. "So we could have more cake!"

After the kitchen was cleaned and the cakes were cooling, we got to go outside and play. That was when Martha and I met some new kids, two boys, John and Mike.

They were really funny and nice and didn't tease me at all like boys usually did, so after a while I excused myself and ran home.

"Back so soon?" Mrs. Dimock said. "Where's Martha?"

"She's still playing," I said, out of breath and rifling through my bureau.

"For heaven's sake, Mary, what are you doing?"

"I think I have a new boyfriend!" I told her. "Either John or Mike, I don't know which one yet. Maybe both! I have to have something pretty to wear!"

Mrs. Dimock looked confused, but then she sighed heavily and suggested I change into some Bermuda shorts that she'd recently hemmed for me. I put them on and twirled in the mirror and ran back outside to play. I knew the boys would like me now!

And sure enough, they did. But I don't think they noticed my Bermuda shorts.

"That's okay," Mrs. Dimock said later. "I think you have plenty of time before you need to worry about getting boys' attention."

That wasn't what Mama used to tell me. She always said that a girl had to look good if she wanted a boy to notice.

Oh, well, I figured. I sure did have a fun day, but the most important question was, what dress should I wear to impress my Sissy? That was what really mattered!

"Mary Zoe!" Sissy cried out the moment she saw me, crouching low with her arms held wide. I threw myself at her and gave her the biggest hug of my life. "I can see you've been eating Mrs. Dimock's wonderful cooking," she said, giving my cheek a pinch. "You look healthier and happier than I've ever seen you!"

I was so proud Sissy had noticed. I was still pretty skinny, but I wasn't nearly as bony as I'd been when I first arrived. And Sissy sure had changed. Her long blond hair was all piled on top of her head real loosely, like Brigit Bardot, and her breasts had gotten as big as her waist had gotten small. She was beautiful!

"Come on, Sissy! Let me show you my room!"

Sissy laughed as I practically dragged her to the sun porch.

"And this is my bed, and this is my bureau, and these are all my new clothes!" I started opening all my dresser drawers and grabbing everything in sight to show my big sister. I had never had such a beautiful room, and now I could finally show it off.

"Oh, Mary Zoe, this is a beautiful room," Sissy said. "I think it suits you perfectly."

I beamed. "Yes, it does," I agreed. "But I don't think Mama likes it very much. She says all these windows will give me a draft."

"Well, I think it's perfect," Sissy said. "And I'm sure Mama appreciates all that the Dimocks are doing for you."

I didn't know what to say to that, since I wasn't so sure that Mama *did* appreciate my living there, but I also knew that if anyone understood, it was Sissy. She knew Mama couldn't take care of me and that the Dimocks could.

"Come on, Sissy! I have a surprise for you! Guess what I made!"

"What, Mary Zoe? What did you make?" Sissy was laughing along with me, and I knew she was as happy as I was to see each other again.

"A cake! I made you a cake! All by myself!"

"All by yourself?"

"Well, practically all by myself, but I let Mrs. Dimock help me!" I grabbed Sissy's hand and took her into the kitchen where I showed off my cake. And so began our visit. Sissy and I played checkers and Old Maid, and I told her all about my life with the Dimocks, and she told me all about her life with the Flaggs (though to be honest, it didn't sound nearly as interesting as life with the Dimocks, but at least she wasn't living with Mama, which I know made her feel better).

Mrs. Dimock had made a wonderful dinner of pot roast, potatoes, and fresh green beans from the garden. I got to say grace, which I know really impressed my Sissy (but one thing I didn't say out loud to the Lord was how thankful I was that the Dimocks didn't ask Sissy to read from the Bible! If she'd done that, I'd still be waiting for that pot roast!).

After we finished dinner, Sissy and Martha went into the kitchen to do the dishes. I didn't think it was right that Sissy should do the dishes when she was the guest, but she insisted. Then I remembered she used to live there, too, so it was probably all right.

"I'll help, too!" I announced, but Mrs. Dimock thought there were enough people in the kitchen.

"I'll tell you what, Mary," she said. "While Sissy and Martha are washing up, why don't I give you a little piano lesson?"

My eyes wobbled in their sockets. "A piano lesson? You bet!" I raced to the piano, jumped up on the seat, and uncovered the keys, ready to get started. I was so excited having Sissy there that if Mrs. Dimock had suggested teaching me how to jump out of an airplane, I'd have leaped at the chance.

But learning the piano, it turned out, wasn't something an excitable girl could master in the time it took to do the dishes.

"Oh, I'm *so* stupid!" I declared, when Mrs. Dimock showed me how to play "Chopsticks" the right way.

"Now, Mary, what have I told you about calling yourself stupid?" Mrs. Dimock chastised me. "You are no such thing; in fact, you have a real knack for playing piano. I can already tell."

"You can?" I asked, somewhat dubiously.

"I sure can," she answered. "Now let's try it again so you can show Sissy what you've learned."

Sure enough, by the time the dishes were done, I got to show off my new piano playing skills, and I felt like Liberace!

Afterward we all sat around the table and played Parcheesi. I was so excited I bounced up and down and made a funny little ritual of tossing the dice every time it was my turn.

"Mary, just throw the dice already!" Larry ordered, but I wasn't going to let him be a spoil sport, so I shook them even longer.

The only problem was figuring out what they added up to after they landed.

"You have a six and a four," Mr. Dimock said. "How many does that make?"

I had no idea.

"Three?" I asked.

"No, not three, Mary," Mr. Dimock patiently explained. "Maybe you're subtracting instead of adding. How much does six plus another four make?"

I still had no idea, but I counted each dot on the dice every time it was my turn. Sometimes I'd lose track of my counting, and sometimes Jon and Larry and even Martha would get impatient. But it was my day and my Sissy, so as far as I was concerned, they could just hold their horses.

I felt really bad whenever I captured Sissy's pawn and had to send it back, which I had to do a couple of times, but I felt even worse when *I* got captured and sent back. But by the time the game was over I didn't feel bad at all, because I was the winner! It really was a fantastic, super-lucky day.

But then Mrs. Dimock said it was time to brush my teeth and get ready for bed, and that was not what I wanted to do at all.

"Please can Sissy spend the night?" I pleaded with Mrs. Dimock in my sweetest possible voice, batting my eyes and smiling like an angel, my little hands held up in prayer.

But Mrs. Dimock wasn't that easily persuaded.

"No, Mary, she has to get home, and you have to get to bed now," she told me firmly. "It's already way past your bedtime, and your eyes are so heavy you're about to drop right here on the floor."

She didn't know what she was talking about—I could have stayed up all night!

"Mrs. D's right, Mary Zoe," Sissy said. "You need to get some sleep, and I have to get back to the Flaggs, but I'll see you very soon!"

"Then read me a bedtime story, please, Sissy, *please*!" I thought for sure she'd do it, but then she told me once again that it was getting too late and she had to go and the Dimocks agreed that Sissy could come another time and read me a bedtime story then. I couldn't believe my amazing, magical day was over, just like that.

I hugged Sissy good-bye for a long, long time, and the minute the door closed behind her, a world of tears spilled out of me. I cried and cried and cried.

"Why are you unhappy?" Mrs. Dimock asked. "You had a wonderful evening!"

"I miss my Sissy so much!" I declared through my sobs. "How would you like to be separated from *your* sister?"

In answer, Mrs. Dimock picked me up, carried me into my room, and sat on my bed with me as I blubbered out my memories of the wonderful things about my big sister. "We used to have so much fun together. We laughed all the time, and she took me to the park on Saturdays and church on Sundays. One time, she took me to the beach, and I got red as a lobster, and Sissy put a special cream on me that made the burn go away. She cooked for me and ironed my clothes and tucked me into bed and got me ready for school in the morning. She took good care of me, and when I was thirsty and wanted a drink, she'd wash me a glass so clean it sparkled like diamonds and she'd fill it with such clear water it looked like air!"

Mrs. Dimock just held me and let me cry and cry out all my memories, and then she took me to the bathroom to brush my teeth and tucked me into bed, singing me a lullaby, just like Sissy used to do.

I didn't know it then, but it would be years before I saw my Sissy again.

And she'd forgotten to tell us something very important.

CHAPTER 14

The Wedding

"Oh my goodness, Mary! What in the world has happened?" Mrs. Dimock unlocked the door and let me in, dragging my bag of things behind me.

A neighbor had called her and got her out of church, since it was Sunday morning and I didn't have a house key.

"Where's your mother?" she asked as she helped me with my things.

I started to tell her what had happened, but I couldn't stop the tears from falling down my face, as I told the whole horrible story.

I had gone to Mama's for our regular weekend visit, and at first, we had a nice time, even though I wasn't feeling well. I'd had a bad sore throat, and the doctor gave me some medicine, and I was starting to feel better. But when it was getting time for me to go to bed, Mama came into my room all dressed up and told me I was going to have a babysitter—a babysitter, on my one and only night with Mama! I should have known she'd rather go out to a party than stay home with me. I begged her not to go out.

"Mary Zoe," she said, "knock it off right now! George and I are going to this wedding whether you like it or not!" Just then, George came into the bedroom.

"Hey, kid, how ya doin'?" he said, but he didn't wait for an answer. "Zodie, have you seen my black trousers? You didn't take them to the cleaners, did you?"

"The only one I'm taking to the cleaners is you, baby," she cracked, giving him a kiss.

"Damn. I've looked high and low, and I can't find them anywhere."

"They're on the chair, the same place you hung 'em last night. They probably fell on the floor in that pile of crap you have in there," she said and turned back to me. "This isn't just any wedding, you know. Guess who's getting married?"

I had no idea who was getting married, and I really didn't care. So I didn't say anything and just crossed my arms and stared at Mama.

"Go on, guess!"

"I don't want to guess; I want you to stay and visit with me. And I don't want any stupid old babysitter!"

"Well then, I guess I'll just have to tell you. But you're to tell no one! Do you hear me? You aren't to tell a soul about it."

That got me curious enough to agree to keep the secret.

"It's Sissy's wedding. Sissy is getting married! Can you believe it?"

Sissy was getting married? No, I couldn't believe it. She'd been to visit us just two months before and hadn't said a word about getting married. How could she do that to me? And why wasn't I invited? I knew my Sissy wouldn't have a wedding without me, so I knew Mama must be lying.

"I don't believe you!" I shouted and burst into tears. Just then, George came out of the bedroom.

"Oh for Christ's sake! One of the damn cats peed all over my pants! They'd made a nest of them on the floor, and now look!" He was standing there wearing the pants, their bottoms soaked in cat pee and the rest of them covered in cat fur. Then Mama burst out laughing, and he started laughing along with her.

"Well, the first thing you need to do is get some masking tape to get that cat fur off or you'll show up looking like a Canadian fur trapper. Maybe you can throw some gasoline on 'em to kill the smell," Mama suggested. Then George wandered off.

"Anyway, stop your blubbering before the sitter gets here. The Cullen girl is coming over to watch you, and I don't want her thinking I've just given you a beating. Here, take your medicine."

"But I don't believe you! My Sissy wouldn't get married without telling me! And if she did get married, I'd be invited to the wedding!" I pressed my lips together and turned my head away, refusing the spoonful of nasty-tasting medicine that Mama held out.

"Well, apparently she is getting married and you aren't invited, so knock it off. This is an adult affair and not a place for children. If Sissy had wanted you to know she was getting married, she'd have told you. And don't you go spreading it around town; don't tell anyone, you understand? Now take this, goddammit!"

I started crying even harder when George came back into the room, holding a gas can and howling with laughter. He smelled like a gas station. "Well, I think I killed the smell of cat piss, but I hope nobody lights a match near me!"

Mama took one look at him and started laughing harder than I think I'd ever seen her laugh. "Just don't cross me tonight, darlin', or I'll be the first to do it!" she said, laughing so hard she spilled the medicine.

"Oh for crying out loud, Mary Zoe," she said when the medicine spilled. "Now look what you've done! That's just wasteful! Now I have to pour out another spoonful." She carefully measured the spoonful of medicine and pushed it into my mouth. It tasted like turpentine, but I swallowed it angrily, then turned my head away again.

I didn't know what to feel. I was stunned and hurt and furious—and disgusted. George and Mama were really going to go off to Sissy's wedding with his pants all peed on and soaked in gasoline. And why in the world was I supposed to keep my sister's wedding a secret? None of it made any sense at all.

"You wanna see a picture of the man she's marrying?" Mama asked.

I sniffled and nodded. Mama reached into her purse, pulled out her wallet, and then handed me a little tiny black-and-white negative.

"Hold it up to the light, and you can see him," she said. "Of course, the colors are all reversed; she's not marrying a colored guy, it just looks that way in the negative. I'm going to get this made up into a real picture and have it framed. But this is him."

She held the negative up to the light, and I squinted my eyes and tried to make sense of the picture. But it didn't make any sense at all.

"Isn't he handsome?" Mama asked, and I shrugged.

"I think he looks stupid!" I said and kicked all my stuffed animals off the bed. Then I felt terrible and started to cry even more.

But Mama didn't care. She and George left the room to make some drinks before the sitter arrived, and I climbed out of bed, got all my stuffed animals and kissed them and hugged them. Then I told them how sorry I was and tucked them into bed. When I was all done, I crawled into bed and cried into the pillow until I fell asleep.

I didn't wake up until early morning, when I heard Mama and George coming in. Mama and George were making an awful racket, then they went to bed and George started snoring like a semi-truck running its motor.

A couple of hours later, I tried to get Mama up.

"Mama," I said, nudging her. "It's time to get up."

"Go away. Go back to sleep," she mumbled and swatted me away.

"No, Mama, get up! It's morning. I want to hear about Sissy's wedding."

"Come on, baby. Leave Mama be; I've got a little hangover and need to sleep it off."

Thats when I did it. I'd had enough. I got a big duffle bag and packed it with my stuffed animals and PJ's and some other things, and then I wrote a note.

Dear Mother: I don't like it here. I'd rather be with the Dimocks. Love, Mary.

Then I walked all the way home to the Dimocks. And that's when the neighbor saw me pounding on the door and called Mrs. Dimock and got her out of church.

Later that day, the doorbell rang. I ran to the front room to see who it was, but as soon as I looked out the window, I saw it was Mama. I hid behind a chair where she wouldn't see me while I listened in on the conversation she had with Mrs. Dimock.

"Did my daughter come back here?" Mama asked. It was already way past lunchtime, so if a kidnapper had snatched me or I'd joined the circus after I ran away, it would have been too late for Mama to do anything to save me.

Mrs. Dimock calmly replied, "Yes, she did."

"May I talk to her, please?"

My face burned when I heard that. I didn't want to talk to her ever again!

"Well," Mrs. Dimock answered, taking her time answering, "she was pretty upset." Then she finally said, "But come inside and I'll go get her."

Then Mama came in and stood in the doorway, peering all around. She wasn't looking for me, I could tell, but was instead just checking out the Dimocks' beautiful house to see what they had and she didn't.

Mrs. Dimock called for me, and at first, I tried to hide, but she found me in about two minutes flat and made me come with her.

When I got there, I wouldn't look at her face. I just stared down at her high-heeled shoes.

"Mary Zoe, that wasn't the thing to do," she scolded me. If Mrs. Dimock wasn't there, I knew she would have been screaming at me and would have hit me with a switch or a wooden spoon, but since Mrs. Dimock was there, she was putting on a show of being polite. The real scolding would come the next time we were alone. Until then, her voice was practically musical. "You should have woken me up."

"She did," Mrs. Dimock said, coming to my defense. "You told her to go away."

"Oh," Mama said, caught in her own lies, "I'd been out at this wedding till seven o'clock this morning. I was just too tired to wake up." She sounded like she was apologizing, but then she turned to me and scolded, "Mary Zoe, I thought you were grown up enough to understand that when a person's been up all night, they're tired. I found your little note."

She stared at me as if she was expecting me to wilt. But I crossed my arms in front of myself and looked up from her shoes to her face and didn't say a word. So Mama continued scolding me sweetly in front of Mrs. Dimock.

"I don't think that was very fair," she said, like I'd hurt her.

I still didn't say anything, so she changed her voice to sound even sweeter. "Well, will you come back with me now till six o'clock and then I'll walk you home?"

I still didn't say anything.

"Why won't you talk to me, Mary Zoe?"

I still didn't answer. I was sort of liking the whole performance, because if Mrs. Dimock hadn't been there, Mama would have been beating me with a spoon by then. But since Mrs. Dimock was there, she had to behave and treat me right.

Then Mrs. Dimock spoke up. "Well, maybe we'd better keep her for the rest of the day and we can talk things over tomorrow."

Mama sure wasn't expecting that! Mama always won her fights with me because she was the grown-up. But now I had another grown-up on my side!

"Is that what you want, Mary Zoe?" Mama asked. "Do you want to talk tomorrow?"

I nodded my head and forced a fake smile onto my face, the kind that Mama used when she was pretending she liked someone she didn't like.

"Okay, then," she said, sighing loudly. And then Mama left.

As soon as the door closed, I ran to my room and threw myself on the bed, crying as hard as I'd ever cried before. When Mrs. Dimock came in, I screamed, "I wish I was dead! Why doesn't the court just kill me?" I kicked my legs and hammered my fists into the bed as hard as I could while Mrs. Dimock tried to soothe me.

I knew that once she walked out that door that Mama was crying. I was sure of it. And it was all my fault I'd hurt my own mama.

Later in the afternoon, shortly before dinner, Larry and I were riding our bikes in the neighborhood and passed Mama's house. Mama saw us and came out of the door. She called all sweet-like, "Mary Zoe, you forgot your medicine!"

I stopped my bike and went up and got it, and said, "Thank you." Then I got back on my bike and rode away with my little brown bottle of medicine. I thought it was nice of Mama to remember my medicine. Even in the worst of times, she was always good about things like that.

When I got home, I told Mrs. Dimock about it and asked her, "Should I go back and get my bunny, too?" I hadn't been able to pack all my stuffed animals into the bag, and I was worried about my bunny. He didn't like being lonely.

"Well," Mrs. Dimock considered, "do you want to go back?"

I thought about it, and the truth was, I didn't want to say I'd *never* go back. So I said, "Yes, I guess so. My mother is okay now. She's nice. I was just confused this morning. Should I call her?"

"I think that's an excellent idea," Mrs. Dimock said.

So I called Mama, and she said she'd come over the next day and we could start all over.

That made me feel so much better, and when Mrs. Dimock tucked me into bed that night, she suggested that when Mama came, I tell her how confused I was, not just about that incident, but about all my feelings.

That seemed like a good plan, and I fell asleep, happy to know I could finally tell my Mama how frustrated and confused I felt. Maybe that was Mama's problem; she just didn't understand me.

I waited for Mama all the next day, but she never came to get me. I guess she just forgot.

CHAPTER 15

Loganberry Pie

"WHY DON'T I PICK YOU up and we can go to the Chelan Café for some loganberry pie?" Mama suggested. "And then we can get you some toys and maybe even a new swimsuit at S H Kress. How's that sound, baby?"

It sounded fantastic, but it wasn't Mama's day for seeing me, and I didn't want to upset the Dimocks by breaking the rules. Besides, the court set those rules, and if we broke them, we could be in really big trouble.

"That sounds super fun, Mama, but it's only Thursday, and I can't see you until Saturday morning. That's what the court said."

"To hell with the court! If I want to see my baby, I'll see her. I don't need any damn court telling me when I can and can't see my own child!" Mama had turned so mad so suddenly, I was afraid to see her.

"No, Mama, I don't want to break any rules."

"You and your rules! It's those Dimocks, isn't it? What lies have they been telling you about me?"

"They haven't told any lies, Mama; they're not like that. They never say anything mean about you."

"I'll just bet they don't. Well you go get Margaret on the phone right now, and I'll tell her in no uncertain terms that I'm coming to get my little girl and take her out on the town whether they like it or not!"

"But, Mama, I don't want to go, not if it's not allowed."

There was a brief moment of silence, and then Mama's voice turned sweet the way it would do when she was trying to get George or one of her other husbands to do something for her that they didn't actually want to do. "I know you're a good girl, honey, but I'm not asking you to break any rules. I just want to start our weekend a little bit early; that's all. Because I have something really special planned for you—I've got a surprise for you, and I know you're going to love it."

I knew she was trying to sweet-talk me, but I was really curious, too. What was Mama's surprise? She sounded like she was really trying to make me happy and had probably gotten me something real nice.

"Well, I guess I can ask Mrs. Dimock. Maybe if she knows it's just an early weekend, she'll say okay. But I don't want to get her in any trouble with the court."

"It won't be any trouble at all, sweetie. Just tell her you miss your mommy and want to come home early. And if she says no, just cry a little bit, but don't overdo it. She won't go for it if you overdo it."

I didn't like the idea of tricking Mrs. Dimock like that, but I figured there was no harm in asking to go see my Mama. I told Mama to wait a minute, and I set down the phone and went to the kitchen where Mrs. Dimock was kneading some dough.

But when I asked her if I could go see my Mama, she said no. That's when I tried the crying, by jutting out my lower lip and squalling, "I miss my mama!"

"I know you do, Mary, and you'll see her day after tomorrow. But we have to stick to the court schedule." She seemed completely unmoved by my tears and continued to knead the dough.

So I stomped my foot made some fists and said if I couldn't go see my own mama, I would run away.

"That wouldn't be a good idea, Mary, because then you'd miss this homemade bread I'm making, and I don't think you want to miss that. It's best when it's warm from the oven, you know."

Mrs. Dimock sure was one tough nut to crack, as Mama would say.

"But Mama wants me to come *now*!" I pleaded. "She says she has a big surprise for me! And she wants to buy me new toys and ice cream sodas and take me shopping for a new swimsuit at Kress'! But you don't want me to see my mama so I can't have anything new! All I get are hand-me-downs!"

"Is that what she said?" Mrs. Dimock appeared a bit more interested, at last.

"Yes, she's waiting on the phone. She said it would be okay, that it isn't really breaking the rules; it's just starting the weekend early."

Mrs. Dimock stopped her kneading and wiped her hands on her apron. "I'll have a talk with her," she said, and I instantly regretted ever asking her. I could tell she wasn't happy.

I listened while Mrs. Dimock told Mama she couldn't see me until her visitation day and not to call again with requests like that. She said Mama was manipulating me and if she continued to do that, the court would have to step in.

That was exactly what I was afraid would happen! Oh, why had Mama even called in the first place? And worse, what if Mama wouldn't give me my surprise or take me shopping now? I ran to my room and flung myself on my bed and sobbed and sobbed.

Mrs. Dimock tried to console me a few minutes later, but I just swatted her away.

I really missed my mama. And I was so, so mad at both Mama and Mrs. Dimock for getting me into such a confusing situation. But more than anything, I wondered what Mama's surprise was and if I'd ever get to have it.

I found out soon enough, when Saturday rolled around.

"A slice of your loganberry pie for my little girl," Mama said, "à la mode. With a nice tall glass of milk. And a black coffee for me." Mama reached over and patted me on the head, while I spun around on the red vinyl stool, watching my black patent-leather Mary Janes go round and round at the end of my feet. "Now doesn't that sound good?"

"It sure does," I said, not looking up as I spun some more.

The Chelan Café was one of Mama's favorite restaurants. I never really understood why it was one of her favorite restaurants, much less why she brought me there, but it had become her favorite place to take me once I started living with the Dimocks. The Chelan Café was a diner underneath the West Seattle Bridge, an old-fashioned greasy spoon in the middle of a tangle of busy roads and railroad tracks with the shipping harbor right behind it. On the other side of the bridge was Bethlehem Steel with its giant smokestacks spewing clouds of gray dust into the air, making it hard to breathe. The diner was filled with workers from the steel plant and lots of policemen and truck drivers.

"Hey, baby," half the men all seemed to say whenever they passed by, winking at Mama or worse, stopping to stare at me and stinking of sweat, cigars, or booze. "This yer li'l girl?"

Mama would wave her cigarette like she was fanning her face, blowing the smoke from her puckered lips while she flirted right back at them.

"This is my baby girl, Mary Zoe," she'd say, tapping the ashes into a fiberglass ashtray with a dramatic flair. "Mary Zoe, sit up straight and say hello. Don't sit there like the cat's got your tongue; this nice gentleman wants to say hello."

I'd mumble out a shy "Hello," and then whoever it was would move to the end of the counter to guzzle beer or slide into a booth with some other guys to wolf down a midafternoon breakfast of fried eggs, sausage, and biscuits drenched in mud-thick gravy.

"Here's yer pie," the waitress said, setting a huge slice of pie with a melting scoop of ice cream on top, "and here's a nice tall glass of milk to wash it down!" She set the glass of milk on the counter but just as I reached for it, I accidently hit it and knocked it over, spilling the milk all over the counter.

"Oh for Christ's sake!" Mama snapped, but the waitress didn't seem fazed.

"Why there's no sense crying over spilled milk, honey! Happens all the time." She quickly snatched up a towel and wiped it away before it could drip from the counter, but Mama was furious with me, I could tell. She smiled a big fake smile at the waitress but stamped out her cigarette so hard it broke in half and then told me to get up before I ruined anything else.

"That's why I don't like taking you out," she hissed in my ear, lowering her voice so no one would hear, "You can't even drink a goddamn glass of milk. Oh, hell, just look at this!" Mama pulled at her beaded blue sweater and showed me a wet spot where some milk had splashed on it. Quickly, she grabbed my napkin and dipped it into her water glass and dabbed at her sweater, all the while making funny sounds with her breath.

I felt my face getting warm and my ears burning with embarrassment. No one was paying us any attention, but it felt like the whole world was watching.

"Mama, I'm sorry—" I started to say, but Mama cut me off.

"You're always sorry," she said in her low voice, "but then you turn around and do it again. I never should have brought you here in the first place!"

I wanted to slink down in my seat, but the best I could do was spin away from Mama, to hide my face.

"Here ya go, honey," the waitress said, putting a fresh glass of milk on the counter. Then she added, "Don't worry about it, sweetie. Weren't no harm done, t'all." Then she turned back to Mama with a big, friendly face and said, "Can I get you gals anything more? A refill on that coffee?"

"I think we'll get a booth," Mama said, her voice returning to normal, while pulling me by the arm. "She needs to sit still and stop playing around. Come on, Mary Zoe, get up!"

"You do that," the waitress said, "and I'll just bring yer pie and drinks on over."

I scrambled off the stool, and we went into a dark and smoky room, where Mama found us a booth. It had a tiny jukebox on the table with songs by Patsy Cline and Porter Wagner, but nothing I wanted to hear. I took some bites of my loganberry pie, but it didn't taste very good anymore. I just wanted to go home, and the more I thought about it, the more I realized the home I wanted to go home to was back at the Dimocks and my little room on the sun porch, where I was safe and quiet and no one would yell at me.

"Eat up," Mama said. "We've got a busy day ahead of us." Then she talked on and on about all the things we would do and see and buy and how happy I was going to be once I saw all that she had planned for me. She was returning to the happy mood she'd had when the day began, and after a while, I began to relax and started to look forward to our day once again.

"And now for some big news!" Mama announced. That was usually how she announced she'd gotten a new husband, but since she was still married to George, I had no idea what it could be.

"George and I have rented a new apartment on Queen Anne Hill. Oh, baby, it's so beautiful it'll just make you drool! It overlooks the city and you can see Puget Sound and the mountains. It's real classy, the nicest place we've ever lived. You'll see."

That got my attention! "Do I have a big bedroom?" I imagined a big, beautiful bedroom with giant windows and a great big canopy bed.

"No, it's a studio," she said.

"What's that?" I pictured a giant place where they made movies, but I knew it couldn't be that classy.

"That means it doesn't have any bedrooms, just one big room and a kitchen and bathroom."

I didn't think that would make me drool. Whoever heard of an apartment without any bedrooms?

"Then where do you sleep?"

"We have a fold-out bed; it's called a Murphy bed. It folds out of the wall." I'd seen those kinds of beds in the movies, and she was right, that *was* classy. I couldn't wait to see it!

"But where will *I* sleep?"

"You can sleep on the couch. We'll take the back cushions off. You'll see. It'll be fine."

Then Mama started talking about the upcoming World's Fair, which was coming to Seattle, but my imagination was running wild as I thought about the new apartment and what it must be like to be so luxurious but not to have any bedrooms, so I didn't hear much of what she was saying. Then, after I'd finished my loganberry pie and Mama had finished a few cups of black coffee, she reached into her alligator bag like she was getting ready to pay the bill.

"I've got something I want to show you," she said, and my eyes widened. Mama really had planned a whole day of surprises!

She pulled a hundred-dollar bill out of her wallet and leaned across the table, waving it at me the same way she'd wave her cigarette when she wanted to make a point.

"You see this hundred-dollar bill?" she asked, her face hardening ever so slightly.

"Yes," I said, feeling amazed at so much money and afraid at the same time. I could feel my throat tighten, like I'd swallowed a stone. Mama could turn on a dime, and I'd learned to pay attention to any shift in her voice or her mouth or her eyes or her posture, and I saw in her face and heard in her voice that this was one of those moments when she could snap at any instant even if I didn't spill another drop.

"This is what I have to pay that attorney every...single...*hour*...that he helps me get you back."

Then her voice got friendly again. "See how much you mean to me?"

Just then, the waitress approached, a coffeepot in her hand.

"Another refill?"

"No, thank you," Mama said, not even looking up. "We're going now. Can you bring us our check please? We have to get downtown."

"You betcha," the waitress replied, eyeing the hundred-dollar bill as she left. Mama leaned back in her seat, but her eyes had narrowed as she stared at me, waiting for my response.

"I'm sorry, Mama," I said, ready to burst into tears. "I don't want you to have to spend all that money on me! I'm so sorry, Mama!"

She put the bill away in her alligator bag and lit her cigarette. I watched her red nails tap the table and flick the ashes of her cigarette in the ashtray. "You know the only reason the Dimocks want you is because the State of Washington pays them." She blew smoke to the ceiling. "I'm your mother, and I love you. No one has to pay me to take care of you. You'll discover that blood is always thicker than water!"

The waitress came back with the check, her face all smiles. Her eyes searched around the table for the hundred. Mama opened her pocketbook, reached in, and put a five-dollar bill on the table. "You can keep the change," she told the waitress, pulling out a compact and lipstick and painting her lips a bright coral as she stared into the little round mirror. She smacked them a couple of times with an audible pop, gave me a great big smile, and said, "Come on, baby girl. Let's go shopping!"

Mama took me window shopping at the Bon Marche, and then we went to the drug store and she bought me an Etch-a-Sketch, which I'd wanted for a long, long time. Then we went to Kress Five and Dime for a new swimsuit, but Mama said they were too expensive so I didn't get one. I immediately knew the reason why, but I didn't dare say it—it was because of all the money I was costing Mama on the lawyer.

"Never mind that," she said, as we left the store ', "Once you see your surprise, you'll forget all about some silly bathing suit."

I didn't think a new bathing suit was silly at all, but I couldn't wait to find out what my surprise was. "What is it? What is it?" I begged, jumping up and down. But Mama only smiled.

"Let's get home, and you'll see," she said. "Besides, I sure could use a drink." She stopped in the middle of the busy sidewalk, reached into her alligator bag, and pulled out a golden cigarette case. Then she lit a cigarette and smiled down at me, as if evaluating me for the first time. "Okay, sweetheart, let's go see your surprise." We walked rapidly down the street, her high heels making a sharp click-clacking sound as I hurried to keep up, all the way to the car. She wasn't driving the red Fiat anymore. After I left, she'd started driving a '52 Buick convertible; it was ten years old, but it felt like a Cadillac and Mama looked like a movie star in it, complete with the scarf tied under her chin and her eyes hidden behind oversized cat-eyed sunglasses.

And like a movie star, she was far away. She drove toward Queen Anne Hill, not saying a word, her eyes fixed on the road. She seemed lost in some faraway place, as if a million thoughts were passing through her head and she didn't have space for any conversation.

So we rode in silence, while I turned the knobs on my new Etch-a-Sketch, wondering what my surprise was going to be and how many more hundred-dollar bills I was going to cost Mama by living with the Dimocks.

The apartment was, as Mama said, simply beautiful. The moment we stepped into the lobby of the old brick building, I was in awe. It looked like something out of Park Avenue, wherever that was, with fancy moldings and beautiful hardwood and mirrors that glistened like crystal. We took an elevator up to her floor, and walking down the hallway, I felt like we were at a fancy hotel. And once inside the apartment, I was shocked—it was not just beautiful; it was immaculate. Mama had never cleaned up anything for as long as I'd been alive; after Sissy left, I just got used to the garbage and clutter and filth, even though I couldn't stand it. But now that I was gone, it was as if Mama had turned into a completely different person. There was no clutter, no filth, no garbage, no dishes, not even any dog fur. Since the fire that had killed all our dogs and birds, Mama was down to only two cats, Jimmy Brown and Missy, and the apartment just sparkled.

It had wood floors and glass French doors, and it was filled with sunshine. The picture windows were so big that even though the apartment was the smallest apartment I'd ever seen, it didn't feel that way at all. It was filled with light, and we could see the whole Puget Sound and the Olympic mountains from the window (and later, at night, we could see the whole city lit up like a Christmas display).

I looked around and saw that Mama even had new furniture. It was still Early American, a style I didn't care for at all, but that was what Mama liked. There was a new couch and chairs, and she'd polished her coffee table until it shined. I was dumbstruck.

"Mama! This is beautiful!" I gushed. I wanted to move in right away—except for the not having a bedroom part. The Dimocks' house was beautiful and cozy, but this place was downright posh!

"And wait'll you see what we got you!" Mama and George stood side-by-side, George's arm around Mama's waist with something big behind them. They were smiling like little kids and were almost as excited as I was. Then George reached around and offered me a great big package as big as me, all wrapped up in colorful paper with a great big giant bow.

"Here you go, kid," he said. "Don't say we never gave ya anything!"

"George!" Mama scolded, giving him a swift but playful swat, "Don't present it to her like that! Go ahead, open it up, honey! George, come on. Fix me a drink, will you?"

"In a minute, in a minute! Let's see how she likes it!"

I couldn't recall when I'd seen them getting along so well, and I couldn't wait to tear open the package. It was way too big for me to hold, much less carry, so I just tore it open right then and there on the floor, and my mouth dropped open when I saw it. It was a giant doll almost as tall as I was, with beautiful blond hair just like mine and a pink party dress that was the prettiest dress I'd ever seen on a doll. I stared and stared for several seconds, completely mesmerized and thrilled. This was my very own absolutely spectacular doll!

"Well, what do you think?" Mama asked. "Do you like her?"

"*Like* her?" I answered. "I *love* her! Oh, Mama and Daddy, thank you, thank you, *thank* you!" I wrestled my new doll out of the box that imprisoned her as fast as I could and held her and hugged her and danced with her all through the apartment. She was even better than Chatty Cathy!

The whole weekend was magical, even if my new doll and I had to sleep on the couch. Mama and George hardly fought at all, and we played card games together and Mama colored with me and even did some arts and crafts and showed me how to make my Etch-a-Sketch transparent by scribbling all across it until I could see right into it. I'd never had so much fun with Mama, and she never once got sick.

When it was time to go, I was almost sad to say good-bye. But I missed the Dimocks and there really was no room in the apartment to play in, so as fun as the weekend was, I was ready to go home. Still, I couldn't help but wonder why Mama never lived like that when she had me, and why once I was gone she started living like a rich movie star. It just wasn't fair; it wasn't fair at all.

I packed everything up in my little bag and started to get my new doll ready for the ride home.

"Come on; let's brush your hair," I said, brushing her nylon hair with the little plastic brush that came with her. "I want you to look nice for the Dimocks!"

"Oh, no, Mary Zoe," Mama said, overhearing me. "You can't take her to the Dimocks. She stays here so you can play with her when you visit."

"But I want her to come home with me!" I pleaded. "I'll take good care of her, Mama, and I promise to bring her back when I visit!"

"No, Mary Zoe!" Mama said, turning mad. "I said no. I didn't buy her just so you could take her over to those people's house. If they want you to have such a nice doll like that, they can go out and buy you one. After all, they get paid plenty for taking care of you!"

I didn't know what to say. No one had ever said anything about the Dimocks wanting me just because they got paid to do it. The tears started to fill my eyes, but I wiped them away and held on to my dolly.

"Come on, Mary Zoe. Let's get going. I haven't got all day." Mama pulled my doll out of my hands and tossed her on the couch. "You can play with her next time. I wouldn't even have to take her away if you weren't living with those Dimocks. Now let's go!"

We got in the car, and Mama drove me back to the Dimocks, reminding me all the way of how much I was missing by living with the Dimocks. By the time we got there, I didn't know what to think. All I knew was, things had changed.

CHAPTER 16

Rocky Days

EVERYTHING WENT WRONG WHEN I walked back through that door. At first, everything was okay and everyone said it was great to see me. I helped Mrs. Dimock in the kitchen, and we had a nice lunch, just like any return from a visit with Mama. But this time, everything just got more and more frustrating with every hour that passed. It seemed nothing was going right. I couldn't even brush my own hair; it just got all snarly and messy until finally I threw my hairbrush across the room in frustration.

"I can't do anything right!" I screamed and threw myself on the floor, kicking and wailing. Mrs. Dimock tried to comfort me, but she frustrated me, too. She didn't know how to brush my hair the way my Mama did, and I was so mad at her for even trying.

Then she wanted to give me a piano lesson, but that was another disaster. I finally blew up when no matter how hard I tried, I couldn't get my music piece right. Then, on top of it all, when I asked if I could go swimming, Mrs. Dimock said I couldn't do that because there was no one else swimming and she was too busy to keep an eye on me. I was so mad I threw a temper tantrum that I knew would scare her halfway to heaven.

"I hate you!" I screamed. "You never let me do anything I want to do! You're hateful!"

Mrs. Dimock was not happy to hear that, and she immediately sent me to my room. A few minutes later, she came into the room, sat down, and asked me what had happened over the weekend to make me so upset.

"Nothing happened!" I retorted, furious that she would automatically assume something was wrong with visiting my own mother. "Except that I had a *heavenly* time! And now that I'm back, it seems that nothing I do is right and you really don't even want me."

"Now, Mary, that's not true at all, and you know that," she said firmly. Mrs. Dimock never got mad or lost her temper, but I could tell she wasn't pleased with me.

"Then why did you want me?" I asked her, though I already knew the reason. Because she was paid by the state to want me. "You could have had any child. What made you choose me?"

"We knew you had no home to go to," she said, "and we wanted to give you a safe home."

"But I could have stayed at the youth center." The more I thought about it, the better the youth center seemed. At least there I wouldn't have been tricked into thinking I was wanted when the truth was I was just a way to make money.

"Yes, you could have stayed at the youth center. But that wouldn't have been very fun, would it?"

I thought about it for a while and realized she was right. "No, I guess not," I said, resigned to my fate. And then Mrs. Dimock said I could go outside and play. But even that was no fun, and eventually, I went back inside where there was nothing to do.

It was an awful Sunday and made even worse after dinner when *Disney* wasn't on and instead there was some stupid program with President Kennedy going on and on that the Dimocks thought was mesmerizing. I thought it was boring and ended up telling everyone how stupid he sounded until even Mr. Dimock was mad at me, and worse, pretty soon, Martha was talking back at me.

"Why don't you go on back to your mother's if she's so special?" she said, and then I burst into tears, ran to my room, and threw myself on my bed. I knew I couldn't go back to Mama's, no matter how much I wanted to. She didn't even have a bed for me anymore, and besides, the court wouldn't let me go. If only Mama hadn't driven to that motel and drank all that booze and almost died! If she hadn't done any of that, I'd be home with my own mama and there would be no youth center and no court and I never would have had to go to jail.

I cried as loud as I could until Mrs. Dimock came into my room. I thought for sure she was going to punish me and send me to the basement, but instead, she just sat on the edge of the bed and asked me what was the matter and why I was so upset.

"Oh, I wish I was never born!" I cried to her. "Why did my mother have to ruin my life?"

She pulled me up and hugged me close, while rubbing my back with her hand. I loved Mrs. Dimock's hugs; they reminded me of Sissy's.

"Don't you think such awful thoughts," she scolded me softly. "God wanted you to be born, Mary Zoe, and even though your mama has some troubles, she hasn't ruined your life. You have a wonderful life, and it will just keep getting better, I promise." She held me and rocked me until I finally fell asleep, sucking my thumb like a tiny baby.

But things didn't seem to get any better as the weeks went on. Mama kept calling and reminding me that it wasn't right for me to be living at the Dimocks, and each time she called, she told me about something new and wonderful in her life—something new and wonderful that I was missing. And she promised me all sorts of presents when I came back, as long as she could still afford it what with all she had to pay the lawyers. Then she'd ask me about living with the Dimocks and tell me that they weren't treating me right, not the way a real mother would treat her daughter.

"Remember, blood is thicker than water, which is why I will always treat you better than those people ever will. They're just putting on a show for Mrs. Komoto, but when push comes to shove, you'd better believe they'll put their own kids ahead of you and never love you the way I do."

The more I thought about it, the more I realized Mama was probably right. Even though the Dimocks were really nice to me, it seemed that I always had chores to do or I was always getting scolded for putting my feet on the slats under the dining room chairs, or putting my elbows on the table or talking out of turn at dinner, or not finishing my chores.

One time I got in so much trouble for talking with my mouth full that I really did get sent to the basement. The rule was that we got three warnings before being sent to the basement. Jon and Larry got sent there a few times because they wouldn't settle down, but I never thought Mrs. Dimock would send me down there. But she sure did, and all I did was talk with my mouth full of food and not pay attention to the warnings.

Well, let me just say that it was really scary. Once that door was shut, I was terrified. I sat on the basement stairs as close to the door as I could, looking down that scary stairway. I'd been in the basement many times before, when Mrs. Dimock was down there doing the laundry or Mr. Dimock or the boys were tinkering with something. But it looked a lot different from the top of the stairs with the door firmly closed.

The basement was dark with weak, watery light filtering through the skinny windows. The wooden poles that held the house up looked like prisoners had probably been chained to them for horrible tortures. The whole basement was nothing but concrete and spider webs, but there was a bathroom on one end, and on the opposite end, there was a little room that had been turned into something like a bedroom (a room for prisoners, no doubt). It had a little window in the door, and I had never seen an inside door with a window before. When I first saw it, I thought it was so curious but crouched at the top of the stairs looking down as I endured my punishment, I realized that window was probably for watching their prisoners. I prayed I wouldn't have to use the toilet, because I'd seen it in the daytime and I knew that it growled and made scary noises and it was filled—just filled—with huge spiders. For the longest time, I was so scared of those spiders that I'd cringe just at the sight of a daddy longlegs, until Mrs. Dimock read me *Charlotte's Web*, which made me feel a lot better about spiders.

There was also a work bench with lots of tools and an area where Mrs. Dimock hung the clean laundry to dry. I never saw someone hang laundry before; Mama went to the Laundromat, and our clothes came back wrapped in blue paper.

I looked down those stairs and stared at the clothes hanging on the folding drying rack, but they didn't look like clothes at all. They looked more like ghosts. I had never been more terrified in my life, and I kept telling myself that it was only Mr. Dimock's shirts and not to be afraid.

Well, that day, I had to write out what I had done wrong at the table before I could come out. Sitting as close to the door as possible, I made my list on the notebook paper Mrs. Dimock had given me. I was very careful not to make any mistakes. I hated to make a mistake, and this time, especially, I was afraid. If I made too many mistakes, maybe the Dimocks wouldn't like me and send me back to Mama. I loved Mama, but I didn't want to go back—not then, at any rate.

By the time Mr. Dimock came to get me, I ran to him and hugged him around his legs, since he was so tall that was as far as I could reach. He picked me up and held me close, and then Mrs. Dimock came to get me. She read what I wrote, and I told her how sorry I was, and she said she was proud of me and I'd learned my lesson. Then she let me go play.

I knew they didn't really keep prisoners down in that basement, but for a little while, it seemed that way. Still, Mama never sent me to any dark and scary old basement. And I never had to worry about getting punished for table manners at Mama's. It didn't matter if I talked with my mouth full or put my feet on the chair slats at home or my elbows on the table or talked out of turn or didn't do any chores at all, just as long as I took care of Mama. And I liked taking care of Mama; after all, she was my real mama and what kind of a girl wouldn't want to take care of her own mama when she got sick?

I was starting to see that living with the Dimocks was getting to be harder than living with Mama had ever been. It was just rules, rules, rules. And having brothers and sisters wasn't exactly easy either. For one thing, the boys teased me all the time, calling me Chicken of the Sea because I was scared of swimming in Puget Sound. And I wasn't allowed to ride Martha's bike, and I didn't think that was fair at all. She had a nice new bike, and all I had was a yucky old used one.

One day, when Martha wasn't at home, I begged Mrs. Dimock to let me ride her bike, but she absolutely refused so I got so mad. I started throwing rocks at my old bike, and then I pushed it over and let it crash on the pavement so it would be so smashed up they'd *have* to get me a new one. Of course, that upset Mrs. Dimock, and I got sent to my room, but eventually, she came in and sat down with me.

"I have an idea," she said. "Why don't you wash your bike and get it nice and shiny so it looks like new? If you take good care of the bike that you have now, maybe someday soon you can get a new one. But first you have to show that you will take care of the one you have."

That made a lot of sense to me, so I grabbed a bucket and some rags and ran outside where I washed it so clean it shined like new. Then I laced ribbon through the spokes so it made pretty colors when I pedaled, and after a while, I wasn't so upset about the bike and kind of liked it, in fact.

But I kept getting upset about a lot of other things, and whenever I saw Mama and Daddy George at their fancy new apartment where I got to play with my new doll, Mama would be sure to remind me that I'd never have as many nice new things as long as I lived with the Dimocks. Mama bought me pretty new dresses and lots of toys and arts and crafts kits that we could do together. One time, she bought me a mosaic of two Indian goddesses. It had gold tiles, crushed glass, and golden cords, and I thought it was the most beautiful thing I'd ever seen. We would work on it together during my visits, and she'd set it aside for the week so we could finish it when I came back. I just loved doing that mosaic with Mama!

And she took me to the movies just like we used to do when I was real little, and after the movies, we'd always go out for pie or ice cream. She was a changed Mama, I could tell, and she wasn't taking so many pills or drinking as much as she used to, so I started to like being with my real mama.

Also when I went back home to the Dimocks, not only did I have all those chores to do, but they also sent me to bed really early, like eight thirty when it was still real light out. That didn't seem fair at all, and I'd tell Mrs. Dimock that I had no bedtime at Mama's, but she didn't care about that.

"Well, that's not how we do things here," she'd say. "Here, you have a bedtime."

It just didn't seem fair at all. Before I had to stay up all night long at Mama's and never get any sleep, and then I had to go to sleep so early at the Dimocks' that I felt like I was being punished. I just couldn't win for losing.

One time, I got so mad I tried to run away. Mrs. Dimock had told me to get ready for bed, and no matter how much I pleaded, she wouldn't let me stay up any later or watch any more TV. So I went to my room and took my pillowcase off my pillow and filled it with some clothes and started to sneak outside to run away, but Mr. Dimock caught me.

I was so ashamed that I got caught that I told them I deserved to be punished. "I've been in jail," I cried. "No one puts a child in jail unless they deserve it. I'm evil inside."

"No, you're not evil, Mary," Mr. Dimock said. "You're a good girl, and God loves you."

"I don't believe in God!" I screamed, thinking it would hurt him.

But it didn't. He just said that it was okay if I didn't believe in God, but God believed in me.

Once school started, things really got rough. I was put into fourth grade at Alki Elementary, but I had no idea what they were talking about. The math was way too hard for me, and even the reading was difficult. The harder I tried to make sense of it, the more the kids made fun of me. They laughed at me and told me I was stupid, and the teachers kept telling me I should have learned those things in third grade. But I'd missed so much of the third grade because Mama was always sending me away or taking me out of school so often that the teachers decided I had to do third grade all over again. The kids sure made fun of me then.

I was so miserable. They mocked me and teased me and the minute school got out and I had to walk home, they really picked on me and called me names. They said I was stupid and that I was a slob. But Mama had taught me that if people like how you look they'll treat you real nice, so I figured out a solution.

"Please can I have some fancy dresses to wear to school?" I begged Mrs. Dimock. "And pointy shoes and a stick-out slip so the boys will notice and like me?"

"I don't think you need the boys to notice you for you to have friends," Mrs. Dimock replied. "And you don't need to wear fancy dresses or any of that other stuff to school. We'll just be sure you look a little neater with what you have."

That didn't seem to be much of a solution at all as far as I was concerned, and when I told Mama about it, she agreed.

"If you lived with me, you'd have all the fancy dresses you wanted," she said. "And I'd let you wear a stick-out slip; after all, that's what gets the boys' attention!" She winked and showed me how to walk with one foot in front of the other so my hips wiggled, and that made me walk so funny that Mama and I laughed and laughed.

I knew Mama was telling the truth about buying me new dresses because she was buying herself lots of new dresses, so she and George obviously had the money. One day, she had a beautiful new gold lamé dress with pointy high heels, and another time, she got a gorgeous yellow wool coat with a mink collar that looked like something Audrey Hepburn would wear.

"It's from Neiman Marcus," she told me, and though I didn't know what that was, the way she said it, I knew it was fancy. She opened it up and showed me the beautiful lining and a label with big cursive letters on it that she let me touch once I showed her my hands weren't dirty.

"George has figured out a system," she explained, "when he goes to the races. He's been on a winning streak ever since. If you came back home, you'd have clothes like these, too, but as long as we have to pay the lawyers, I'm afraid there's not much more that we can do for you."

Back at the Dimocks', it was just jumpers and tennis shoes and plain old pleated skirts. No boys noticed me, and not many girls wanted to play with me. Worst of all, Martha stopped wanting to play with me.

"You can't always follow me everywhere," she said. "You need to make your own friends, Mary!" She was my best friend and my new sister, but even she didn't want me, so I just accepted that I was someone no one could ever love. We started fighting so much that Mrs. Dimock made us change our seats at the table so we weren't next to each other. Martha and the brothers said I was acting like a baby, and pretty soon, Mama made me see that that was what they *really* thought of me, and the proof was what Mrs. Dimock packed in my lunch.

One of the things I loved was little jars of Gerber baby food. I especially loved the peaches, pears, and custard, and sometimes, for a special treat, Mrs. Dimock would pack a jar in my lunch box. But when I told Mama about that, she got mad.

"They must think you're a baby!" she said. "That's why they give it to you. I would never put baby food in your lunch box!"

After that, I didn't like it so much, so I asked Mrs. Dimock to stop. She did, but the truth was, I really missed it.

Then, right before Halloween, I went to visit Mama, and she had another surprise.

"Go on, open it!" she said.

I opened the big box and didn't know what to say. It was a fairy queen costume, a really expensive one.

The only problem was, I didn't want to be a fairy queen, but I couldn't tell Mama that.

"Well? What do you think?" she said. "Isn't it beautiful?"

I pulled it out of the box and pretended I loved it, but secretly, I was really disappointed. I wished that Mama had asked me before deciding what I'd be for Halloween, but it was too late. I had to be a stupid old fairy queen.

The night before Halloween, when I was trying on my costume, no matter how hard I tried, I couldn't get the costume to feel right and I got so frustrated I threw it on the floor and screamed, "I don't *want* to be a fairy queen!"

"Okay," Mrs. Dimock said. "How about if you're a gypsy, like Martha?"

"But what will I tell Mama? She'll be hurt if I don't wear the costume she got for me!"

"Mary, you need to learn how to be more honest with your mother," she said. "You're so afraid of hurting her feelings that you end up hurting yourself. I've seen you do this time and time again, and that's not fair to you or your mama."

"It isn't?"

"No; how can she know how to take care of you if you aren't honest with her about your feelings?"

That made a lot of sense, and the truth was, I really did want to be a gypsy and dress up like Martha so we'd look like twins. So Mrs. Dimock got some colorful clothes and costume jewelry and made me into a gypsy.

The following night, just as we were getting ready to go out trick-or-treating, Mama called and asked me how I looked in my fairy queen costume.

"Well, Mama," I said, taking the honest approach, "last night, I decided I wanted to be a gypsy, so I'm going as a gypsy, just like Martha!"

"After all that money I spent?"

Mama was biting mad. *So much for being honest,* I thought. I tried to reassure her that I'd wear the costume for play, but she was so mad I finally started to cry and handed the phone to Mrs. Dimock. Mrs. Dimock talked to her for a while and then hung up. I could practically see the smoke rising from the phone; I knew Mama was that mad. It ruined my whole Halloween, and I went trick-or-treating as a miserable gypsy who couldn't do anything right.

CHAPTER 17
Meat Grinder

It was decided by Mrs. Komoto that my visits with Mama had to be shorter—no more staying overnight and no more showering me with presents. For some reason, Mrs. Komoto didn't like Mama buying me all those things, and she said that the Dimocks would buy me my clothes. Mama sure wasn't happy about that.

"Do the Dimocks ever talk about Mrs. Komoto?" Mama asked me.

I told her the Dimocks rarely mentioned her.

"Hmm, well, isn't that interesting?"

I told Mama I didn't know if it was interesting or not, and Mama explained that the Dimocks and Mrs. Komoto were in on it together, trying to keep us apart.

When we did see each other, the first thing Mama would ask me was, "How did your week go?" But the minute I started telling her about all the things I did with Martha and the Dimocks, she'd snap, "I don't want to hear about them and their churchy bullshit! They're only in our lives because they're nosy and want money!"

If I tried to defend the Dimocks, it only made Mama madder. "Just remember," she'd point out, "Mrs. Dimock didn't make you; I did, all by my lonesome. And what have I taught you about that?"

"Uhh..." I had no idea what Mama had taught me about that.

"It means that blood is thicker than water!"

Every time she'd say that, I'd think about all the blood that spilled out of Mama that New Year's Eve and wish it had been only water.

Pretty soon, the visits weren't fun anymore. It became more and more difficult to find things to talk about that wouldn't make Mama mad. Mama started getting mad at me a lot, just like she used to do, and if I talked back or said the wrong thing, she'd slap me and say mean things. Mama had been nice to me for a while, but she still had a wicked temper that no amount of nice could cure. She said she could damn well slap me around if she wanted and no one would care, because she was my mama and had a right to discipline me.

"I'll tell Mrs. Komoto!" I screamed, but Mama just laughed.

"You do that, honey!" she scoffed. "And see how far it gets you. Let me tell you, Mrs. Komoto doesn't give a damn about you. To her, you're just more paperwork. And if you go whining to her that your mama slapped you for talking back, I'll let her know that as far as I'm concerned, she and the Dimocks can have you! I'm sick and tired of your constant crying and carrying on about how badly I treat you. Look at all I've done for you! And what thanks do I get in return? Huh? You go bellyaching to the Dimocks, and now you can't even spend the night here and I'm not allowed to buy you the pretty dresses I wanted to buy you. So don't blame me if you aren't having any fun anymore. This whole thing is your doing, missy, not mine!"

I thought about what Mama said and realized she was right. I couldn't spend the night with her anymore because I was the one acting up, not Mama. It was my temper tantrums that got Mama in trouble. But it was Mama who was being mean; that much I knew. It wasn't right for her to slap me, even if she was my own mama. Mrs. Dimock never slapped her children. Why did my mama have to slap me?

So instead of talking like we used to, we'd go shopping for arts and crafts at the Piggly Wiggly or sometimes we'd go to the movies. We used to have so much fun at the movies, whispering back and forth. But more and more, she started keeping her thoughts to herself in the darkness of the theater. We'd sit in the section where smoking was allowed, so that Mama could smoke. I remember watching the red end of her cigarette arc in a perpetual motion from the armrest to her mouth. She would chain-smoke throughout the whole movie, her legs crossed while they kept up a rapid trembling, as if she was impatiently tapping her toe. That was a habit she developed when she was standing and looking down on me, tapping her toe, tap, tap, tap, her pointy high heels making it clear to me that she was upset about something. She especially did it those times she brought out the hundred-dollar bill, something she started doing a lot, in case I didn't get it the first time.

There was no doubt about it; the heavenly days with Mama were over, and before long, she and George were back to screaming at each other, and the beautiful Queen

Anne apartment was filthy and dark. The winter rain had returned so the sky was always wet and gray, and Mama didn't open the curtains half the time, trapping the smoke inside.

When I'd go home, I'd tell the Dimocks I had a great time, but they knew better. For one thing, I always had a headache. For another, I was always so unhappy. Mrs. Dimock let me know that I could talk to her about anything that bothered me but that she wouldn't make me talk about anything that I didn't want to share. That made me feel a lot better and actually made it easier to share things. So pretty soon, I started talking to Mrs. Dimock about other things that bothered me, like David Walz and my grandpa. She would listen to me and hold me, and let me suck my thumb while she rocked me like a little baby.

One night, after I told her some of the things that David Walz had done, I had a dream that I was playing in the basement with Martha and the brothers and we came upstairs to watch TV. I was sitting on Mrs. Dimock's lap watching a cooking show, and a girl on the TV was making a ham sandwich. In my dream, I was the girl on the TV, even though I was also watching the TV, because that's just the way dreams are. All of the sudden, I watched as the girl put me through the meat grinder with a bunch of lettuce and cheese. Then she took out some bread made from human skin with teeth ground up for decoration and made a sandwich out of me between two slices. Then she stuffed me back into human shape like a sausage, but there were marks all over me from where I was stitched together, with my eyes sticking out and my teeth all funny. It was such a terrible dream.

Later, when I told Mrs. Dimock about it, she explained that maybe I felt like I was being put through a grinder by all the things I was remembering and that maybe I felt I was caught between two families.

"Yes," I agreed. "That's probably right. It does feel like that sometimes."

Mrs. Dimock said I didn't need to talk about any of it if I didn't want and reminded me again that if I ever did want to talk about it, I could always come to her.

Then she wrote it all down in her diary. She was keeping a diary about me, and sometimes, I'd see her writing in it at the end of the day, but she wouldn't let me see it. She told me it helped her to understand me and to see how much I was changing.

Sometimes, I felt like I wasn't changing for the better but for the worse. Maybe that was why Mama was so upset with me. Maybe she thought I was turning out to be no good, like the husbands she'd get rid of.

It was Saturday, and Mama was late again. I sat in a wooden chair in the front hall, swinging my legs anxiously. I chewed a fingernail and thought back. Had I done anything to make her mad? What if she didn't show up again? Didn't she want to see me? I was even wearing a new dress she had bought me. It was lime-green organdy with white spots and a matching jacket. It was lovely. But it itched. It left a red rash on my skin at the neck and arms. It wasn't my favorite dress, but I thought it might make Mama happy if she saw me wearing it.

I tried everything to make Mama happy, but it seemed that instead, all I did was make her mad. I thought about the hundred-dollar bills she'd wag at me, telling me how I was costing her so much money she couldn't afford to even buy food. I thought about how mad she got every time I mentioned the Dimocks and how somehow this whole thing was my fault and I never should have called the motel manager when Mama fell on the floor. She said she would have eventually woken up, since she always did. Why couldn't I have left well enough alone? I was only trying to help her; I didn't know it would cost her so much money and make her so unhappy.

Our visits were always like that, I thought, as I sat in the scratchy dress. Somehow, she always mentioned the money she was spending to get me back and how the Dimocks were only using me for the money they got out of it. Over and over, she continued to remind me that "blood is always thicker than water." I wanted to believe her, but Mrs. Dimock was so good to me, and I really loved Martha. And I was starting to love Mr. Dimock and even the boys. Mr. Dimock had started giving me horsey rides on his shoulders every time I got a math problem right, and I was getting more and more horsey rides these days, thanks to getting smarter. I really loved the Dimocks, and I could tell that they loved me, no matter what Mama said. But I didn't dare argue with Mama.

She was really late. I began to worry. Maybe she wasn't coming. As my worries grew, I stopped thinking about the bad times and how unhappy I made Mama and started remembering the good times. Sometimes, Mama would buy me toys after we stopped at the café for pie. Once, she bought me a Barbie doll with bouffant white hair, pink lips, and the bluest eyes. She was lovely. I spent hours dressing and undressing her with those tiny little dresses and shoes. She even had matching purses. A new doll always smelled so good.

I stood up and walked to the window to see if Mama was coming up the walkway. It was empty. I sat back down and waited—and waited—checking the window every few seconds, but each time, I saw she still wasn't there. It was obvious she wasn't coming for me. I was confused and in a way, relieved. Not going out with Mama meant I wouldn't have a headache when I came home.

Mrs. Dimock entered the hall and placed her hand on my shoulder. "I'm sorry, Mary, but it looks as if your mother missed her chance for a visit with you this week. Go and change out of that dress and come help me prepare dinner. Okay?"

I looked up at her kind brown eyes, and I knew in my heart she didn't like me just for the money.

"Sure, I'll help," I answered, as I walked to my glass bedroom. I knew that Mama was wrong; blood wasn't thicker than water. Sometimes water won.

True to Mrs. Dimock's promise when I first moved in, since Martha had gone away to Girl Scout camp, I'd enrolled in Brownies. I loved putting on my uniform, and I'd even gotten a gold pin just like she said I would. But it wasn't always fun—sometimes, the other girls picked on me, and they could be real mean. But Mrs. Dimock urged me to stick with it, and after a while, they let up. I was glad about that because Brownies could be a lot of fun. We did all sorts of arts and crafts and went on some really fun field trips, and got to meet all kinds of interesting people.

One of people we met was a Japanese woman who had a collection of Japanese dolls. We got to go to her house and see them in the tall glass cases. I'd never seen anything so beautiful in all my life. After seeing those dolls, I became fascinated by all things Japanese. I sought out anything I could find about Japan or Japanese art, and

Mrs. Dimock even took Martha and me to the International District in downtown Seattle to learn more about the Japanese.

One evening, Martha and I decided to dress up as geisha girls and put on a dance for Martha's parents. Mrs. Dimock got us a big box full of old dresses and fabrics and scarves, and things, and we went to Martha's room to get started. But try as I might, no matter what I did, I just couldn't get the costume right, and finally, I fled to my room in tears.

I don't know what came over me, but I threw a terrible fit and started knocking over chairs, tables, even my dolls, screaming and carrying on something awful. It didn't take long for Mrs. Dimock to come running, and when she saw what I had done, I thought she'd throw me out right then and there.

But she didn't.

"Well," she said, not at all happy, but not angry either, "you must've been mad."

"I felt like breaking this picture!" I said, holding up a photo of me and Mama, "and this window!" I pointed to the nearest window and held up a stuffed animal I was ready to hurl through the glass.

"Come here," she said, sitting on the side of my bed. She reached her arms out to me and I went to her, reluctantly. I was still furious and worked into such a state that I couldn't calm down, but Mrs. Dimock pulled me up onto her lap and held me close. "I wonder why you feel so mad?" she asked.

"I don't know," I answered, so frustrated I felt like tearing off my own head and throwing it through the window. I wiggled and squirmed to get down, until she finally set me back down with a sigh.

"Do you want me to go out for a minute?" she asked. "So you can calm down?"

In answer, I threw my hairbrush across the room so hard that it broke right in half. But still, Mrs. Dimock didn't throw me out. She didn't even punish me. She just took me by the hand and led me to her room, where she held and soothed me, trying to calm me down. She even tried finger games to take my mind off my rage, but the minute I'd find myself playing along, I'd lash out once again, pummeling whatever was in sight—a blanked, a pillow, whatever I could grab hold of.

"I can't do *anything* without flubbing it!" I screamed. "Even being a Japanese woman!"

"Oh? Is that what this is all about?" she asked me.

I nodded.

"Now, Mary Zoe," she said, "that's not true at all. Being a Japanese woman is very difficult; being any kind of a woman is difficult. And you can do so many things right I don't know where to begin."

"No, I can't," I answered, bound and determined to be upset.

"Yes, you can," she responded.

"Like what?"

"Like make beautiful art and take care of people and make us laugh and be happy and...let's see." She cocked her head and wrinkled up her mouth, putting one finger next to her chin as she thought. "Oh, yes, and you are an excellent cooking assistant and a hard worker, and you sing beautifully and you are a very enchanting performer!"

My heart warmed to hear Mrs. Dimock saying such nice things about me, and I let her get me into my pajamas and read me some comic books. Then she went downstairs and straightened up my room and tucked me into bed, and kissed me good night.

It was a wonderful end to a frustrating day. But it wasn't long before I was upset again, and this time, I was going to do something about it. I was going to run away.

It all started with a dance. Martha and I had decided to put on a dance for the Dimocks. Mrs. Dimock had said such nice things about my dancing that I wanted to make her proud.

So we practiced and practiced until we had it down perfect, but just as we started our performance, Martha twisted her foot.

"Owww!" she cried, crumpling onto the floor and rubbing her ankle.

Mrs. Dimock hurried to her and felt it closely. She declared that it had been twisted and there'd be no more dancing.

"She's spoiled the whole show!" I wailed. "Now we can't have any fun! I wish she'd broken her leg!" Then I ran to my room, threw myself on my bed, and cried into my pillow.

Pretty soon, Mrs. Dimock came to my room.

"Why don't you watch *The Flintstones*?" she suggested.

"It's just stupid old reruns," I said, sitting up and wiping my nose with the Kleenex she'd handed me. "But 77 Sunset Strip is on! I can watch that!" I loved watching *77 Sunset Strip*!

"No," she replied. "You can't watch that. It's not appropriate."

"Why not? It won't hurt me. It's just a detective show."

"It might give you nightmares."

"It won't give me nightmares! That's what I *want* to watch. I can't ever watch what I want to watch here. And I can't have any fun at all, now that stupid old Martha had to twist her stupid old foot."

Mrs. Dimock didn't say anything. She just got up and started to leave the room.

"You aren't listening to me," I mumbled to her back.

She stopped and turned toward me. "Well, you're just complaining and I'm getting tired of it. Come upstairs and talk calmly about it if you want. Otherwise, I'm leaving."

Then she walked out and just left me there, all alone.

After a while, when I could tell she wasn't coming back, I went upstairs and sat down next to her.

"When I lived with my mother, she let me watch anything I wanted," I told her.

"Well, it isn't that way here," she said.

There was no point in arguing. I wasn't going to get my way. The only thing to do was run away.

The next day, after more frustrating efforts to get things done and nothing turning out right, my mind was definitely made up. "I'm running away, and there's nothing you can do to stop me!" I declared.

"Why do you want to run away?" Mrs. Dimock asked me. "Aren't you happy here?"

"There are too many rules!" I said. "And I can't do anything right, and nobody wants to play with me!"

Mrs. Dimock thought it over, then said, "I think you're right. Running away is a good idea."

"It is?" I asked, bewildered. "You mean you *want* me to run away? You don't want me here?"

"Oh, yes, of course we want you here," she said. "But it sounds as if you are very frustrated and need to do something about it. Why don't I help you pack, and you can have a planned runaway."

"What's a planned runaway?"

"That's where you run away but not too far. Just someplace nearby where we know you're safe. And then you come back after a little while."

That sounded like a perfect solution, so Mrs. Dimock helped me pack my pillowcase full of stuffed animals, a change of clothes (just in case), and a snack. Then she gave me a hug good-bye, and I ran away to as far in the backyard as possible and ate my snack.

Then I went back home.

Running away is sometimes the best solution, I discovered. Just as long as you don't run too far.

Mary Zoe at Christmas 1962

CHAPTER 18

Satan

THE HALLWAY WAS DIM AND the floor was a deep polished red. I had been in that hallway before. It was always the same. I walked softly in my bare feet, my nightgown flapping around my legs. I was being drawn down the hall against my will. I knew that the room at the end of the hall held the demon, but I couldn't stop the movement down the hall.

Standing in front of a large desk, I watched in dread as the tall swivel chair slowly rotated toward me. The minute the chair was facing me, I was gazing at the terrible man. He had blood all over his face and sharp, razor-like teeth. He jumped up from behind the desk and reached for me with claw hands. I ran from him, screaming. As I ran, I could feel his claws just missing my nightgown. I knew that someday he'd catch me, and I would die as he squeezed the life out of me. I ran panting and the claws came closer, until I felt a sharp claw grab ahold of my shoulder and screaming as loud as I could, I awoke.

It was always the same dream. Petrified, I hid under the covers of my bed in the glass sunroom. Reaching out from under the covers, I searched for the twine at the head of my bed, the twine that led to the upstairs bell. Finally, after what seemed a very long time, my searching fingers met the string, and I pulled with all my strength. I heard the little brass bell ring in the stairwell and the sound travel upward to the Dimocks' room. Then I waited, still hiding under the covers. I didn't want the monster to get my hand. I knew I was safe under the sheet.

Soon, I heard the rustle of a robe as my door opened and Mrs. Dimock slipped into my room. Sitting on the side of the bed, she patted my back, "What woke you this time, Mary?"

"That same nightmare," I answered from under the covers. "Mrs. Dimock, could you hold me, like a baby?"

"Sure," she said. "Climb on my lap."

I was so cold from the nightmare. As she adjusted her back along the headboard of my bed, I crawled into her lap for the comfort of warmth. Curling in her lap, with my head on her shoulder, I began to suck my thumb. She pulled a blanket around me and rocked me, humming, "Hush, Little Baby Don't You Cry." As she finished humming the song, she patted my back and continued to rock me in her lap.

"I wish you were my mama," I whispered. "Is it okay if I call you Mommy? It can be our secret. Mama doesn't need to know."

"Hmm," she answered. "I usually don't approve of secrets; I find that honesty works best. But I think in this case, you may call me Mommy, if you'd like."

"Yes, I would." The patting and rocking continued in companionable silence. "Why can't I live here for the rest of my life? I like it here."

"Mary, dear, we've discussed this before. The decision of where you live is up to the court. They want to make sure your mother is well enough to take care of you; that's why you have the weekend visitations."

"But I don't like them!" I protested.

"Well, your mother has problems inside herself. There are certain things that she can't do for you because she doesn't have enough security in herself. But you'll just have to grow up a little bit by yourself and learn to face life without having someone personally comfort you all the time. You'll have to be a big girl."

"I know I'm supposed to love my mama, but I think I love you more, Mommy." Yawning, I asked, "Could you tell me the story of the pink cloud?"

"Sure," she answered with a smile in her voice. "Climb back into bed, and I'll tell you all about it." So Mommy spun the story of the pink fluffy cloud that settled on my bed and carried me away to an enchanted land of fairies and nymphs. Off glided the pink cloud bearing me to an emerald glen with a sparkling creek, where birds sang and fairies slept in the flowers. All the while, her hand patted my back. As my eyes closed, I knew I loved my foster family and that I didn't want to leave, no matter what the court said.

I'd been with the Dimocks nearly a year when Mama gave me the news—she and George were leaving the Queen Anne apartment and moving back to Alki, not very far from us and right around the corner from the church where Mr. Dimock was the pastor.

"So we can see each other more often," she said.

"But we still need Mrs. Komoto's permission," I said.

"To hell with Mrs. Komoto and her damn permission! I'll see my own kid when I damn well want to!"

"Mama, you know that will only get us in trouble. Please, Mama, I don't want to get in trouble with Mrs. Komoto."

Mama backed down and once again turned syrupy-sweet. But I knew her sweetness was just an act, like when she was trying to get someone to do something for her. Growing up with Mama taught me the difference between Mama being real and Mama being fake. And no doubt about it, the charm she was showering on me and the outside world was Mama being fake.

The new house was dark and messy and terribly small. Mama was drinking a lot and taking her pills again. The visits weren't very fun at all, but Mama must have sweet-talked Mrs. Komoto because I started spending the night again. At first, I liked that, but it didn't last long. In the mornings, I wouldn't see Mama because she wouldn't wake up until it was time to take me home. I'd have to fend for myself until she got up.

I'd rummage around in the cupboards for something to eat, but there usually wasn't much. I'd find some cold cereal or raw oatmeal, and that would have to suffice. Sometimes, I found Saltines and I'd eat them with some butter. I set up a little play kitchen in the master bedroom where I slept. Mama and George slept on the floor in the living room, so I couldn't play out there or watch TV; I had to stay in the back room, until Mama was up and had her coffee. I spent a lot of time waiting for Mama to get up. So with the little doll dishes in the play kitchen, I would pretend to cook the oatmeal, and then I'd eat it raw right off the plastic play plate.

Besides the play kitchen, I had a baby doll I put in real baby clothes. I fed her with a tiny play milk bottle, but then I'd get bored with her and dress up the cats. Jimmy Brown was Mama's Siamese tomcat, and I liked to put him in my baby clothes and feed him real milk from my play bottle. Needless to say, he resented playing dress-up, so I'd get lots of milk on his face.

One day, when Jimmy Brown and I had had a particularly messy altercation and I wanted to make amends, I took him to the bathroom to bathe him. I figured it was the nice thing to do since I got him all milky and all. Besides, I'd never seen anyone give him a bath so I thought I'd do him a favor. Lucky for me, Jimmy Brown was a gentle soul so although he didn't like the bath one bit, he never once scratched me. I soaped him up and rinsed him real well, and when I took him out of the bathtub, he looked so pathetic and funny. I got a towel to dry him, but he ran off into the front room and must have woken up Mama.

"What have you done to my purebred Siamese cat?" she screamed, so furious you'd think I'd painted him blue. "Are you trying to kill him?"

She snatched the towel out of my hands and briskly wiped him down, then glared at me with a look that scared me clear through to my bones. When she was finished but still not speaking to me, she lit a cigarette. Squinting at me through the smoke, she asked, "Don't you know that cats give themselves baths all the time? With their tongues?"

Yuck, I thought. But I didn't dare say that. "No, I didn't," I answered, my head hanging down.

"For Christ's sake! Do I have to teach you everything?"

I didn't answer, and kept my head down. After a few more puffs on her cigarette, she continued, "That's how God made them, so they can be independent."

I looked up and wiped my eyes with the back of my hand. But Mama wasn't finished.

"Don't you ever do that again! You were cruel."

I didn't mean to be cruel. I thought I was being good. But before I could say anything, she added, "How could you be so stupid?"

"I'm sorry, Mama!" I cried, but it didn't do any good. Mama just told me to get my things and she was taking me back to the Dimocks before I did any more damage.

The days were getting worse and worse, but just when I thought Mama couldn't get any meaner, she'd suddenly get nicer. She'd take me out to movies or lunch like we used to do, and she'd do arts and crafts with me and even play jacks with me, beating me every time. That was one of my fondest memories, Mama laughing happily while she snatched up the last of the jacks, beating me once again. She was having real fun, laughing real laughs. But then, from out of the blue, she'd get mean again.

During one of my visits, after we spent some time on the waterfront having a marvelous time, Mama suggested we go to a fancy seafood restaurant. We walked in all la-de-da, like two rich ladies on their way to a social luncheon. I felt all grown up and fancy as we were seated and the waiter handed us two menus the size of French doors. Mama ordered a Crab Louis salad and we were having so much fun that I wanted to be just like Mama, so I said that was what I wanted, too.

"If you order it, you eat it," she said with a broad but funny smile.

"I will!" I promised.

When the salads came, I couldn't believe how big they were, but they looked really, really good with lots of crab and hard-boiled eggs and a big bowl of thick orange dressing that I poured all over the salad. I took my first bite, and it was absolutely delicious!

"How do you like it?" Mama asked, her tone more serious than friendly.

"I love it!" I said and took a few more big bites.

We ate and ate, while I guzzled Shirley Temples and Mama had gin and tonics. By the time Mama finished her salad, I was really slowing down. I was so full already, but I still had three-quarters of my Crab Louis salad to finish. I struggled with the mountain of greens and crab as Mama lit up a cigarette and smoked, watching me through the slits of her eyes. Finally, she signaled the waiter to box it up so we could take it home with us.

I was so relieved! All the way home, I felt carsick because I'd eaten so much, and I was so thankful Mama let me box it up to go. But when we got home, I could tell Mama still wasn't happy. As she set the to-go box on the counter, she peered down at me and said, "And now you're going to finish it."

"Mama! I can't eat any more! Please, Mama, I feel so sick!"

"You ordered it; you'll eat it," she said, heaping it onto a bowl. Her high heels furiously tapped the linoleum, as she handed me the bowl and a fork. "All of it!"

I sat down at the table, and Mama sat across from me, smoking, drinking, and talking on the phone, casting angry glances my way as I sat in my corner poking at the shellfish and praying that I could get it all down. It took me a long time to finish, but she didn't stop glancing at me and she didn't get up until I'd cleaned my plate.

"All right, now you're excused and can get ready for bed." She stamped out her cigarette and pointed the way to the back bedroom where I slept. But before I could get there, I dashed to the bathroom and threw up in the toilet. I heard Mama's high heels coming up behind me. Crying over the toilet bowl, I said, "I'm sorry!" Mama didn't say anything. She just held my hair back. When I was finished throwing up, she wiped my mouth.

"There, now; that's better. Now you know better than to waste expensive food. Don't order it if you can't eat it. Now brush your teeth, take your bath, and go to bed."

Mama went off to watch her TV show, and I gave myself a lukewarm bath, went in the front room, kissed her good night, and crawled into bed alone, wishing Sissy were there to tuck me in. Why was Mama so nice to me and so mean to me at the same time? I didn't know the answer; all I knew was I wanted to go home.

"She's a creep! I don't want to go back to her!" I stomped my feet and swore to Mommy Dimock that I'd never go back. "And she dislikes you, you know." Since Mommy never said a mean word about Mama, I thought maybe if I told her the truth about how Mama felt about *her*, then she'd be on my side. "And I don't like it. *You're* the one that's taking care of me, and she ought to be grateful!"

"I know you're upset," she calmly responded, "but I promise you you'll feel differently soon. I know you love your mama."

"*Love* her? I don't love her—I *hate* her!" I couldn't believe I'd just said that, but I had. And even worse, it was the truth.

"Imagine me hating my own mother! She's the one who made me—I ought to like her. But I don't. I don't even feel as though I belong in that family. I belong in this family, with you, Mommy."

Mommy looked at me with such love and sadness in her eyes. She took me in her lap and asked me what had upset me so.

"Sometimes when I go to my mother's, they have a nice house and everything and I think I would like to go back to her and that she's normal. But other times I think I want to stay here. I don't know *what* do to! I feel all twisted up, like this!" I twisted my hands to show Mommy how I felt. "And I have to put on a polite face even though it curdles my insides!" Mommy held me close while I cried, then I wiped my tears away and said, "Oh, why am I even worrying about this? It's not up to me. It's up to the court and you." I looked up at her, hoping she would magically announce that I could stay with her and Daddy forever and ever.

"We'll see how things go," she replied, stroking my hair. "God will watch over you and do what's best."

I wondered if God was watching over Mama and doing what was best for her. It sure didn't look that way to me, but I kept my thoughts to myself.

One of the thoughts I kept to myself was about Grandpa Jerre. He was back. Sometimes, I'd hear Mama on the phone to him telling him she couldn't see him because "the baby" was over that weekend. I began to wonder if she moved back to Alki to be closer to me or to be closer to him. Either way, I could tell by their phone calls that they were back to going off together, and I just prayed he wouldn't come over. Unfortunately, my prayers weren't always answered.

When he did come over, he wouldn't say anything to me; he'd just shoot me his dirty looks, and Mama would send me outside. Since I wasn't allowed back in until he left, I'd take long walks on Alki Beach. I got used to my time alone.

Then one day, Mama told me she had another big surprise for me. I wondered if it was another doll, and if it was, could I bring her home to the Dimocks'? Mama still didn't let me bring my other dolly home to the Dimocks, so I never gave her a name. But maybe if Mama gave me another doll, I could bring the other one back home.

Mama took me up to the junction where we got ice cream sodas and coloring books and laughed and talked just like we used to when I first started living at the Dimocks. She even took me shopping and bought me a pretty new stick-out slip with lace on the bottom and a beautiful dress to go with it. It was a wonderful day, and when it got close to suppertime, Mama said we had to go home. By home, she meant to her house, where my surprise was waiting.

"Unless you want to stop at the bar for some drinks? I sure could use a Manhattan!"

I knew Mama was kidding, but my face turned red.

"Come on, kid!" Mama gave me a playful slap on the shoulder. "Since when are you embarrassed by a little joke? I thought I raised you to be tougher than that!"

"I'm not embarrassed," I said, "But Mama, you shouldn't be going to bars. It's not right."

"Oh for Christ's sake! What are the Dimocks telling you now? I suppose they're telling you I'm some drunken, Godless heathen."

"No, Mama, they haven't said anything like that, whatever that is." I could feel Mama turning mad again, and I sure didn't want her to get mad. We were having so much fun. Why couldn't it stay that way at least until bedtime?

"A heathen is someone who doesn't go to church," she explained. "Someone who's not religious. People like those Dimocks think anyone who doesn't think like them is going straight to hell. Well, let me tell you—"

"No, Mama! The Dimocks don't say anything like that! They believe in Jesus; that's all! They're good people, and they're teaching me good things, like manners and math and piano and the Bible!"

"Oh, I'm sure they're teaching you all about the Bible, all right!"

"Mama, please can we stop talking about the Dimocks and just go home and let me see the special surprise?"

Mama relaxed and agreed it was time for my surprise. Whatever it was, it was going to be good, I could tell, because she was almost as excited as I was.

"You're going to love it; that's all I'll say."

"Is it a doll?" I asked.

"No, it's not a doll."

"Is it a new bike!?"

"No, I'm not buying you any bike, not until you come back to live with me. Then I'll get you the nicest Schwinn you've ever seen. But it *is* something you've always wanted!"

I thought about all the things I'd always wanted and still couldn't figure out what it was. I pretty much had all the toys I ever wanted except for a new bike. It was a safe house and a normal Mama that I wanted, but I doubted that was her surprise.

When we got back to the house, Mama made me wait outside while she went in and helped George get it ready. Then she came out on the porch and told me to come inside.

"Hurry up! Come on! It won't wait all day!" Mama was smiling such a big, happy smile that I ran up the porch steps as fast as I could and burst through the door. George was standing in the living room with a great big box the size of a TV set in front of him, and he was smiling, too.

"Hurry!" he said, as eager as Mama for me to open it. "Open it up!"

I opened the box, and my mouth literally fell open. Inside was a tiny little puppy with big brown eyes, looking right up at me!

"He's your very own," Mama said, "and he's a rare breed so you take good care of him. He's a long-haired German shepherd."

I pulled him out of the box and petted his long, silky golden fur. He had dark-brown spots, floppy-tipped ears, and a face that melted my heart, with a big brown beauty mark on his left cheek.

"I love him!" I cried, cuddling my new puppy, as he scampered all over me. He was so excited, he scratched my face with his claws, but I didn't care at all. I kissed his beauty mark and rubbed my nose against his nose.

"And he's going to grow up to be really big," George said, "just look at those paws!"

He had paws almost as big as his little head, and they were climbing all over me.

"I think I'll name him Hercules!" I said. "Because he's going to be big and strong! Or what's a good hero's name? He's my puppy hero!" I was giddy with happiness as my new little puppy played with me. Mama was right—this was a wonderful surprise and something I'd always wanted. A puppy of my very own! "Wait'll I tell the Dimocks! Even they don't have a puppy!"

"Wait'll you tell them his name!" Mama said.

"But I haven't decided on his name yet!" I said.

"No, but I have," she answered.

"But he's *my* puppy! I get to name him!"

"You get to take care of him, but I paid for him, and let me tell you, he cost a pretty penny. A dog like that doesn't come cheap!"

"I know, Mama. I can tell he's really expensive!"

"You bet he is, and don't you forget—those Dimocks could never afford a breed like this."

"I know, Mama," I agreed.

"So since I've paid for him, I name him. And you're going to have to call him the name I've given him." Her voice was so stern, I knew there was no point in arguing.

"Okay," I shrugged. "What's his name?"

"Satan!" Mama declared, laughing devilishly. And from that day on, my dog's name was Satan, but there couldn't have been a more inappropriate name in the world, because he was just an angel.

"I never had such a wonderful time in my life!" I announced as soon as I got home after getting my new puppy. "We went for sodas and shopping, and when I went back to Mama's, I had the best surprise of my life! I got a puppy! A pure-breed puppy that was really expensive!" I was babbling with excitement but couldn't wait to go outside and play. "Hurry! I want to go play with my friends!"

"Slow down!" Mrs. Dimock laughed. "First, let's get you unpacked, and then you can play outside until dinner's ready."

She carried my things into my room and started to unpack them.

"What's this? Another slip?" she asked, holding up my new stick-out slip and admiring it.

"Yes, Mama bought it for me," I said, snatching it from her hands. Then I pulled my new dress out of my suitcase and held it up against me so she could see how pretty it looked on me.

"Don't you think this is a pretty dress?" I asked, twirling around as I held it to my shoulders.

"Yes," she answered. "But I'm puzzled about it. Your mother isn't supposed to be buying you clothes now. The welfare people are paying for your clothes."

"But I needed an extra dress," I said, angry that she would criticize Mama for being so nice. "She picked it out just for me!"

"Well, that's nice, and it's all right if it doesn't happen too often. But I don't think Mrs. Komoto will be very happy about it if your parents buy extra clothes for you when they should be saving the money up for other things they need."

"You're just jealous because my mother's richer than you are!" I blurted. "You could never afford such a beautiful slip or especially a purebred puppy!" There was a scornful tone to my voice, I knew, but I just didn't think it was fair that Mama got treated so badly after all she had done for me. And as wonderful as Mommy Dimock was, she just didn't have Mama's classy tastes. I could never imagine Mommy Dimock driving a big fancy convertible like a movie star, the way Mama did or wearing the fancy suits and dresses Mama wore. I wanted her to know that she just wasn't being fair to Mama.

"And my mother's kind; in fact, she's so kind it's pitiful!" I wanted Mrs. Dimock to know that my Mama was nice to me and that Mommy Dimock just didn't understand that; that was why she let me say those mean things about Mama. She didn't *want* me to love my mama! Blood *was* thicker than water; I was just taking a long time to figure that out.

Mrs. Dimock didn't say anything; she just helped me unpack my things and listened while I told her all about my new puppy. She hardly even flinched when I told her his name; she just asked if that was what Mama named him and sort of shook her head and rolled her eyes, just a teeny bit.

"It's because he'll be so fierce and deadly," I explained. "That's why he's named that."

"I see," she said.

Then I ran outside, but just as I reached the door, I turned back and said, "Oh, and I'm going to call you Mom Dimock or Mrs. Dimock from now on!" Then I bolted outside, thrilled I had such a wonderful mama—and adorable puppy.

After dinner and the *Disney* show, it was time for bed, and I sure was ready for it. "Oh, I've never been so tired in my life!" I exclaimed to Mommy Dimock. "I want my bed!" I started to undress, and as I did, I remembered all the fun I'd had at Mama's and wished I had Satan to sleep with. I already missed my puppy, and I'd only had him for two days.

"I kind of like the idea of going back with my mother now," I said. "She's going to give me a playhouse, a real good one." Mama and George had promised me that when I moved back, not only would I have my own puppy and a brand-new Schwinn bicycle, but they'd even get me a playhouse for the backyard.

"That's really nice, Mary," Mommy Dimock said. But as she turned down the covers for me to climb into my own bed, I was so happy to get into my own bed that I confessed, "Mommy, I had to sleep in their big bed again, and I don't really like it." I stretched my toes all the way into my sheets and felt the crisp, clean sheets caress me.

"But it's a nice big bed," she said, pulling the covers up close to my chin just the way I liked it. "What's not to like about it?"

"The sheets aren't nice like this. I had just an electric blanket and a spread that was torn up where Satan chewed it. I wish I could take *this* pillow and some of your sheets when I stay over there. Can I, Mommy? Please?"

"Now, Mary, you know it's not appropriate to take the sheets and pillow off your bed. When you visit someone, you take what is provided. When your mother and stepfather get their finances worked out, they will no doubt buy you some new sheets and blankets."

I mumbled an agreement, but then just before Mommy was going to kiss me good night, I realized how every bone in my body was aching. "Mommy," I said, "my neck hurts, and my head hurts, and even my calves hurt!"

"That's because you've had such a busy weekend," she said, "but you'll feel better tomorrow."

"I don't think so," I told her. "I feel awful, like I'm going to throw up."

Mommy massaged my back while I sucked my thumb, and I felt better, but just before I fell asleep, I told one more confession.

"I had a bath last night," I said.

"Good," she answered.

"And I almost froze!"

"Why? Wasn't it warm enough?"

"No, and their bathroom was cold," I said. "I like my baths here better." Then I fell into a deep, happy sleep, feeling so safe and loved and cozy. It was good to be home.

CHAPTER 19

The Court Decides

NOT LONG AFTER ZODIE AND George moved back to Alki, the fires started up again. Mama was always starting fires when she'd fall asleep with a burning cigarette. And they always seemed to get stamped out by someone just in the nick of time. Mama never seemed to mind, but I was so scared that one day they'd burn the house down, maybe even with us inside it.

One time when I went to see her, her hand was burned so bad it was just a black claw.

"Oh, it's not as bad as it looks," she said, laughing at her own injury. "I caught the mattress on fire and woke up in time to stamp it out. I rubbed some butter on it; it'll be fine. Besides, we got a new bed out of it!" I'd seen Mama get more upset over a chipped fingernail than such a terrible burn. Mama thought it was funny, but I didn't. I thought it was scary and wondered if her hand would ever get better.

Before I could say anything more, Satan came bounding toward me and nearly knocked me down. He was getting so big, and he loved me more and more each weekend. He slept with me at the foot of my bed each night and woke me up by licking my face each morning. The truth was, I looked forward to my visits not so much to see Mama and Daddy George anymore, but to see Satan, who kept me company when Mama was with Grandpa Jerre or fighting with George or sleeping through the morning. I never felt alone when I had Satan to keep me company.

But the more I got used to living with the Dimocks and seeing Mama only on weekends, the more careful I had to be about what came out of my mouth. One time, when I was visiting Mama, I accidently referred to the Dimocks as Mom and Dad, and boy did I regret it!

"Why do you call *them* that?" Mama demanded, her face all twisted in anger.

"I don't know," I stammered. "It was an accident. I didn't mean to. I'm sorry."

"You'd damn well better be sorry, because they're not your mother or father. George and I are, and don't you forget it, young lady!"

Mama sure didn't forget it. The rest of the weekend was awful, and two or three times, I got slapped or hit with the belt for something wrong I did that I didn't realize was wrong. It was a terrible weekend.

When I got home, I told Mommy, "I'd better stop calling you 'Mommy,' because Mama will get jealous."

"Okay, I understand," she answered.

"But maybe I can still call you that sometimes," I said. I didn't want to stop calling Mommy and Daddy, Mommy and Daddy. I didn't even think of Mama as Mama anymore; I had started to think of her more just as Zodie. But I didn't dare let her know that.

"I think that's a fine idea!" Mommy answered. "You can call me Mommy or Mom whenever you want, and if you don't, that's okay. Just as long as you know that in our hearts we love you like our own daughter." Mommy gave me a great big kiss and a hug, and when I went to bed that night, I told her she and Daddy were my real parents, no matter what Mama thought.

The next day, when I went to school, I found a little note in my lunch box. "Dear Mary, Hello! I love you, Mom."

I'd never had a note in my lunch box before, and I was so thrilled. I asked Mommy to do that every day. And she did. Zodie rarely even made my lunch, much less left a note inside it. I knew I wanted to stay with the Dimocks for the rest of my life. But I also knew that Zodie was working hard at charming Mrs. Komoto into thinking everything was better and that she was clean and sober. She switched from drinking scotch or gin to drinking vodka, so no one would notice the smell. She cleaned the house from top to bottom whenever Mrs. Komoto was coming for a visit, and if the visits were unexpected and the house was dark and messy, she just didn't answer the door. She was sweet as molasses on the telephone whenever she spoke to Mrs. Komoto or the Dimocks. Of course, the Dimocks weren't fooled, but I knew Mrs. Komoto probably would be.

The only thing I could do was wait and see. And what I saw was that while Zodie was drinking more than ever, she was also nicer than I'd ever known her to be whenever adults were around and in a way, more unpredictable than ever. By the end of my first year with the Dimocks, Zodie had changed so much that I knew deep in my soul I was in danger.

The school year had ended, and I was passed to the fourth grade—again. But first, I had to go to summer school. I wasn't happy about that. Mr. Dimock had worked real hard with me to help me with my arithmetic and reading, and I was catching up, but the teachers said I still needed more school. But aside from summer school, I was thrilled. It was my second summer with the Dimocks, and what a summer it promised to be—the World's Fair had come to Seattle! It was all anyone talked about, and they'd practically built a whole city around it. They even built a monorail that was straight out of the future, like something you'd see on *The Jetsons*! The whole theme was about science and the future, and all kinds of movie stars were coming to see it—they even said President Kennedy was coming, but then he cancelled on account of what they said was a bad cold but turned out to be the Cuban Missile Crisis.

We were all so excited on the day we got to go. Mr. and Mrs. Dimock and the boys and Martha and I all went together, and there were millions of people there, more people than I'd ever seen in my life.

"Now you boys stick with me," Mr. Dimock instructed, "and you girls go with Mom." We did as they said and listened patiently to all the instructions for not getting lost and obeying the rules and meeting up again at a designated spot at a designated time. There seemed to be an awful lot of rules we had to follow, but I didn't care, just as long as we were there!

One of the first things I noticed was that all the men were wearing green felt fedoras with a jaunty feather on the left side. They looked like a cross between Robin Hood and the Rat Pack, and when Mr. Dimock put one on, we laughed and laughed at how silly he looked, but he wore it as proudly as anyone there.

First, we got to ride on the Monorail. It was so clean and smooth that it felt like we were flying over rooftops and sailing over the traffic. I got to see modern art at the World of Art and eat foreign food at the Food Circus and drink my first Orange Julius. But best of all was the Coliseum. It was a huge glass building with silver boxes suspended way overhead, and there was a clear bubble filled with people that lifted them into the air! I watched fascinated and scared as my turn approached. Up and up the bubble elevators went heading toward the silver boxes. But when they came back down, they were empty! *What happened to the people inside?* I wondered.

"Don't worry; they're just going to another exhibit," Mom said, but I was still confused and nervous. How did she know for sure? She'd never gone into the silver boxes before either. But I knew Mom wouldn't lie to me, so if she wasn't worried, I knew I shouldn't be either. Martha and I looked at each other, and Martha shrugged, so I decided to act nonchalant like she did.

But when it was our turn and we got inside the Bubbleator, I couldn't pretend any longer. I held onto the railing with both my hands as the clear bubble climbed higher and higher. I could see the whole fair on the ground below, swirling with crowds of people and little green hats like funny bugs moving through the crowds. Then the elevator stopped, and the doors opened for us to go into the silver boxes. I was so scared that my heart was about to explode when suddenly I saw what was in them—it was a big, amazing movie theater that we walked through, like a walking tour of the future! No wonder no one ever came down in the Bubbleator. They all walked down a futuristic walkway of shiny silver, like nothing we had on earth.

By the end of the long and miraculous day, just when we'd run out of tickets and had to go home, Mom found another ticket for the Fairway lying on the ground. I began jumping up and down, begging and pleading for another ride, and then Martha joined in with me. I worked my persistence up to a pretty good pitch, certain that our mom would give in, when instead she angrily snapped, "Enough! We are *going home*!"

I felt as if she'd socked me in the stomach. I couldn't breathe. My head felt dizzy. I had made her mad. I was sorry beyond words. I wanted to hide from shame. There had to be something very bad about me to make Mom angry. She never had a cross word for anyone before, not Mr. Dimock, not Martha, not even Jon or Larry.

It was me she was mad at.

I was quiet after that.

I rang the bell at 6:30 in the morning, trembling from my nightmare, the tears streaming down my face. In my dream, I had taken my Chatty Cathy doll to school and was on my way home, carrying her in my arms. She was so big and heavy, but I was her mama, so I had to be careful with her.

I walked and walked but couldn't find home, no matter where I went. Everything was different. I walked and walked some more. Soon, it was getting dark. Finally, I stopped at my friend Gay's house. I set Chatty Cathy down and knocked on the door, but when Gay's mother came to the door, she yelled to her husband, "George, get that tramp out of here!" Then they threw me out into the dark night.

"Hunting for home?" Mommy asked, when I tearfully told her my terrible dream.

"Yep," I answered. "That's the title of it."

Another school year had started, and since I was finally in the fourth grade, I'd soon be ready for Girl Scouts. I could hardly wait. Everything was going so well; the kids had stopped bullying me, I was doing better in school, and I was even getting used to all the rules I had to remember since living with the Dimocks.

They had remodeled the basement and turned it into a rec room with lots of lights, a wooden floor, and a white drop-down ceiling. Mom had put a trunk of old costumes in there and Martha and I would play dress-up. They even got a Ping-Pong table, and Martha and I would play against Jon and Larry for hours. The scary basement wasn't so scary anymore, and no one got sent down there. There were no more spiders, no more ghosts, and no more torture rooms. It was just a room full of fun and family.

But I knew my family days might end at any moment. Mrs. Komoto was impressed with all the "progress" Mama had made, and she explained that the courts didn't like to keep families separated, so I might be able to go home soon. I thought that was funny, considering she might take me from the only real family I'd ever known in order to send me to a home I'd never lived in, but it wasn't funny enough to make me laugh.

It made me want to cry.

"Looks like I won't be staying here the rest of my life after all," I told Mrs. Dimock.

"Maybe not," she said, "but we'll see what the court decides."

But I did have to admit that there was a big part of me that loved the idea of going back to Mama and George and Satan and the cats. After all, she was my real mama. And she promised me lots of wonderful things like a playhouse and a new bicycle when I came back. But mostly, I was excited about going back because I loved spending time with Mama when she was normal; she always made me laugh, and I felt so fancy when we went out.

But as enticing as it was, deep down, I knew that Mama was only putting on an act and she'd stop performing it the minute I got back home. I knew I wouldn't have any more fun evenings with the family in the rec room or weekend trips to the beach or afternoons in the kitchen with Mom. We even got to go camping, and I knew that was something Mama would never do in a thousand years. The fact was, I'd become so settled in my new life that I'd just assumed it would last forever. But with every phone call or visit from Mrs. Komoto, I worried that maybe I wouldn't get to stay with the Dimocks after all. Worst, I worried that maybe I *should* stay with the Dimocks, but that wouldn't matter to Mrs. Komoto. Mama had dazzled her with her charm, and there wasn't much I could say or do to change that.

I was in a terrible turmoil not knowing what was going to happen. The only thing I knew for sure was that Mama was going to keep drinking and taking those pills and seeing Grandpa Jerre, and hitting me when she got mad and leaving me alone when she got drunk, and I knew she'd keep starting fires.

That was all that I knew, and it made me sick, so sick I started throwing up and having sore throats and headaches so bad it felt like my skull was shrinking and squeezing my brains like Play-Doh. I became so sick so often I started missing school again and even missing Brownies.

"Maybe something's really wrong with me, like on *Dr. Kildaire*," I suggested to Mommy. "I might have a rare blood disease and can't be cured!"

"I don't think you have a rare blood disease," she assured me, wiping my forehead with a cool cloth. "But I do think you are under an awful lot of stress and your body is paying the price."

"Well, that's ridiculous," I answered. "I don't want to pay *anything* for all that stress!"

I knew that Mrs. Dimock was right; I was so stressed from the possibility of leaving the safety of their home and returning to Mama that I felt like I was being hit with hammers. So when my tummy started really hurting and I started vomiting a lot, I just figured it was more stress.

But it wasn't.

It was my day for visiting Mama, and even though I wasn't feeling well, Mama was taking me to the movies and I didn't want to miss that. It was a warm and sunny day, so we drove with the top down on Mama's '52 Buick. But as soon as the cartoons were over and the movie started, I had to go to the bathroom. I was so sick I just stayed there in the movie theater bathroom until Mama finally came looking for me. She asked me where it hurt, poked my belly, and felt my head with the back of her hand and took me straight to ER.

"You could have appendicitis," she said. "I never should have left you with those Dimocks."

I felt too sick to say anything back, even though Mama never actually left me with the Dimocks.

It turned out that I didn't have appendicitis. What I did have, though, was infected lymph nodes, and they were inflamed.

"She's had to have had this for some time," the doctors said, "for it to get this bad."

"This proves the Dimocks haven't been taking good care of you!" Mama said. "When Mrs. Komoto hears about this, that will be the end of that!"

"Mama, please don't get the Dimocks in trouble!" I pleaded. "They didn't know I was that sick. I've been sick so much ever since I moved there that they just didn't realize!"

But it did no good. Mama was furious, and when the Dimocks rushed to the hospital and were terribly worried, Mama was thrilled. She had proof they were the bad parents, and she and George were the good ones. Then I felt really awful. It was only a matter of time, I knew, before I'd be going back to Mama's.

I woke up trembling, shaking with fear. It was another nightmare. I reached for the string to ring the bell, but I couldn't find it. Then I remembered. I wasn't in my glass bedroom. I was at Mama's. I got out of bed and went into front room and tried to wake Mama up, but she wouldn't wake up. Then I went to George and shook him, and he popped up like a jack-in-the-box.

"What's wrong? What is it?" he said, looking around the room.

I was weeping, my dream had scared me so much. "It's me, Daddy. I had a bad dream."

"Oh, is that all?" he said. "I thought something was wrong. Don't wake me up like that unless it's something important."

"But it is important, Daddy. I'm scared. Can I sleep with you and Mama?" I didn't even remember what I'd been dreaming, I just knew that I didn't want to be left alone.

"No, you go back to bed, we need to get some sleep," he said. Then he plopped back down in bed, and before I'd even left the front room, he was snoring.

In the morning, Mama was mad at me. George had told her about me waking him up.

"You can't go around waking people up because you've had a bad dream," she said.

"But I was crying," I explained.

"Why were you crying?" she asked. "What was so bad about your dream that it made you cry?"

"I don't know," I answered. "I was just real sad."

"This has to stop," she said firmly, "This could develop into a kind of sickness. Don't do It again."

When I was back home with the Dimocks, I told Mommy about what had happened. She stroked my head like a kitten, and kissed me, which made me feel better.

Then she wrote it down in her diary. I saw her writing, but she said she was just making notes and not to give it another thought.

But I thought about it a lot. What would happen the next time I had a bad dream at Zodie's? If I couldn't tell her about my bad dreams, how could I tell her about any of my feelings?

I was so glad I had Mommy to talk to. I could tell her anything, even if she did write it down later. That was okay, I decided.

"I have some good news for you," Mrs. Komoto said, peering over her glasses with a strange smile. "It looks like you'll be going home soon!"

I wanted to tell her that I was already home, but she wouldn't understand. Instead, I said, "But I love the Dimocks. I'm not sure I'm ready just yet to leave."

"I know they've been good foster parents to you," she went on. "But your mother has made many changes and I'm very impressed with how far she's come in this short time."

It didn't seem short to me at all. It was October 1962, and I'd been with the Dimocks almost a year and a half, and Mama hadn't changed as far as I could tell.

But she'd persuaded Mrs. Komoto that the past was the past. And she'd persuaded me that the past was probably going to be my future.

"If I go to stay with my mother, it'll wreck me!" I cried into Mrs. Dimock's arms. "I'm only ten years old!"

"I know, honey. I know," she said, stroking my back. But there was nothing she could do.

The court had rendered its decision. I would return to Mama and Daddy George and not even have scheduled visits with the Dimocks. I could only see the Dimocks if Mama said I could. And I had a sinking feeling that Mama wouldn't let me.

The day of my final packing was especially difficult. I felt like I was being thrown to the wolves. Mommy told me I could call anytime I wanted, and if there was ever an emergency, she'd come in a hurry. She pushed my pillow into my arms, the pillow I'd asked to take with me to Mama's, but she'd never let me take. Now she'd gifted it to me, so that when I became frightened, I could stroke the smooth pillow and remember my sweet family.

I smiled at them. I'd always remember their love.

Daddy George had packed all my boxes into the trunk of the Buick. Sitting in the backseat, holding my pillow and my Barbie doll suitcase, I turned and waved good-bye to Martha, Mommy, and Daddy Dimock. My throat felt tight, but my eyes were dry. Mama would be mad if I cried. I was going back for good. When the car turned the corner and I could no longer see my lost family, I turned around to face the back of Zodie's head.

Her words floated back to me along the wispy trail of her cigarette smoke. "It's going to be a whole lot better now, Mary Zoe. You'll see."

I wanted so hard to believe her, but in my heart, I didn't. I knew in my soul that it was going to be bad.

I just had no idea it would be horrifying.

Part Three

Zodie in kitchen 1963

CHAPTER 20

Home Sweet Home

I FELT A HURRICANE OF emotions as I walked up the steps to Zodie's duplex. This time, I would not be going home on Sunday morning. The sunny world of the Dimock house was no longer my refuge; the court had decided that it was not my home. Instead, this dark, mud-colored house where George and Zodie lived would be my home. I was defeated, and yet in some strange way, I felt a certain comfort. For one thing, I was at last home with my own mother. The finality of the court's decision, however imperfect it may have been, gave me a sense of peace. I would no longer be tormented with worry over what the court would decide or who would become my parents or if I was hurting Zodie's feelings. The decision had been made, and I'd been returned to my own mother. It was the right thing to do, after all.

But it also felt so wrong. It felt wrong to be walking up those steps into a home that wasn't mine and into a life I knew could only hurt me. The darkness of the porch, half-buried in dead leaves and debris and enveloped in gloom, pulled me into a darkness all my own. I knew that whatever it was that awaited me behind those doors would be frightening and confusing. Most of all, I knew that Sissy wouldn't be there to protect me; I hadn't heard from her since she'd gotten married. When I walked through that door, I knew that I'd be all alone.

The door opened, and Satan lunged at me, draping his big puppy paws on my chest. He looked at me in adoration, and I swore he had a goofy smile on his face. I dropped to my knees and hugged him tight. God and Satan would protect me. God would be my father, and Satan would be my friend. I laughed inside at the irony of such a loving puppy having such an awful name, but I couldn't have been more relieved to know that my giant loving puppy was thrilled to see me.

"Welcome home, kid," Daddy George said with a warm smile as he lugged my boxes back to the only bedroom. Just then, Mama's Siamese cats, Missy and Jimmy Brown, greeted me by rubbing their slim bodies against my legs, eager for attention. I reached down and stroked their silky fur, comforted all the more in the knowledge that they loved me, too. Then two more cats appeared, eager for attention. They were up to four cats and a dog. How in the world they would manage to keep them alive baffled me, but I figured that since I was back, I'd be the one in charge of taking care of them.

Rising up from petting the kitties, I took in the house. Just as when I moved into the Dimocks', I saw their house anew, so did I see George and Zodie's latest house as if for the first time. The living room looked even smaller than I'd remembered it from my visits. The hardwood floors were covered in dust, and the dull beige walls felt drained of life. There were twin beds in the living room, which hadn't been there before. Zodie had tried to make them up like daybeds, by adding matching bedspreads and jewel-toned pillows, but they still looked like twin beds to me and conspicuously out of place in the living room. Zodie's prized coffee table glistened from a recent polishing, and her lighter and ashtray were poised upon it, ready and waiting. The windows were covered with sheer white curtains where Zodie had tried to hide the mold on the windowsills. But the sheer fabric did little to conceal the mold or the moisture that clung to the glass like steam—the house was so poorly insulated that just the heat from our bodies was all it took to fog up the windows.

And everything smelled of cigarette smoke.

"I could use a gin and tonic." Zodie strode into the dining room, her heels making that unmistakable click-clacking sound that marked her arrival. She tossed her suit jacket over the back of a chair, revealing a sleeveless, striped top to go with her wool pencil skirt. I was shocked to realize how thin she'd become; her collarbone and shoulders practically poked through her skin. I watched as she went to the kitchen to fix herself a drink, the cats in close pursuit. My eyes followed her into the kitchen, worriedly, but there was nothing I could do about Zodie so I headed toward my room.

Entering the bedroom was even more depressing. Empty beige walls closed in on me, bringing back memories of the juvenile detention center. In place of jailhouse cots, there was a lone double bed, which took up most of the room. It was Zodie's bed; the one she'd set on fire, though the mattress had been replaced. It had a black headboard and footboard and four tall spindle posts rising from each corner. It was so different from the brightly colored bed in my glass bedroom at the Dimocks' home. The whole room felt dreary and sad.

I placed my little suitcase on the bed, playfully batting Satan away as I did so. He was so eager to play, but first I wanted to get settled in. I crossed to the old dresser and started to put my clothes away when I noticed a sad pair of eyes staring back at me in the mirror. They were my own eyes, so defeated and old that I didn't even recognize them at first. Turning from my image, I hung my coat in the closet and set up my doll crib for my big golden-haired dolly, the one that Zodie had bought for me. Because I was so short and thin myself, the doll was almost my size. I hoisted her in my arms and laid her in her crib. Then I kissed her on the forehead, just like Mrs. Dimock used to kiss me, and I went to the kitchen to be with Mama.

The kitchen was a very small galley kitchen with an old white refrigerator, dull harvest-gold Formica countertops, and a tiny gas stove. There was nothing decorating the white walls of the kitchen, except for ancient food splatters and stains. Dirty dishes were piled high in the sink, and a cat was on the counter, drinking water straight from the dirty dishes.

There was one window in the kitchen, and Zodie's dark dining table and three chairs sat in front of it. She had covered the table with a lace tablecloth, but that, too, was tattered and worn with coffee stains and holes. Zodie was seated at the table, cigarette in one hand, the other holding a gin and tonic. She was talking on the phone, the receiver wedged between her shoulder and her ear.

She was talking to Grandpa Jerre, drinking and laughing and swinging her crossed legs with a single high-heeled shoe dangling off her toes.

"Well, I finally got the baby back!" she declared victoriously, nodding to me and pointing with her chin toward the dirty dishes. And so my new life began, and it was clear that it would be just like my old life.

I batted the cat off the counter and turned to the pile of dishes, squirted them with dish soap, and started the hot water, as Zodie launched into a rant on the phone about the courts and the Dimocks and how they'd learned not to mess with her.

As the water ran, images of the Dimocks' kitchen flashed through my mind, but it hurt too much to let my thoughts go there. I closed my eyes and willed the memories of the Dimocks out of my head. No one could know. The shining light of the life that was supposed to be had become a burning flame inside my heart. I didn't know what was going to happen. All I knew was that I had to live long enough to get that flame back. As the warm, soapy water flowed over my hands, I realized that no matter what was going to happen, I had to survive. I needed to take charge, like Gale had done. I had to be vigilant.

Zodie was gesturing from the table, her empty glass suspended in midair. I walked over to her and took it so I could refill it with some fresh ice. Glancing down at the table, I noticed the marks left from when the Chinese man exploded, and I winced to remember that awful night. After I got Zodie her ice, I returned to the sink and finished washing up the dishes.

As much as Zodie had been on her best behavior when I was living at the Dimocks, it wasn't something she could sustain for long. Within days, she and George were right back at it, drinking and smoking and fighting like never before. Having had a taste of a different life, of adults who didn't fight, their screaming felt more frightening and disturbing than ever before. Before I'd lived with the Dimocks, their screams were all I knew, so I'd learned to tune them out. But now they terrified me. It wasn't a normal way to live. It wasn't safe.

Those first few nights, I would bury my head under my pillow or hug Satan closely as they screamed the most horrible things to each other, the smell of burning cigarettes and sounds of glasses clinking and bottles being dropped in the trash reminding me of the past I'd once escaped but had been returned to for my future.

A few blocks away, there was a family who had some children and a tree house, and I made a point to get to know them on my very first day back. They seemed so normal that I hoped they'd be like the Dimocks to me, even though I knew no one could ever replace the Dimocks. But it gave me someone to play with at first and a place to escape to when Zodie and George started screaming. And when I couldn't escape to their house, I went back to escaping in front of the TV, where families were happy and homes were safe.

I'd been there less than a week when I awoke in the night and knew something was wrong. The lights were all on, but the house was eerily silent, except for the TV. I crept out of the bedroom, and there in the living room were Zodie and George, fast asleep. They had left the lights and TV on, and the smell of cigarette smoke was strong. I turned off the TV, checked the ashtrays, and turned out the lights. All seemed to be safe.

As I walked back to my room in the dark, I heard the Voice.

"Run! Fire!"

I was suddenly drenched in a chill. I knew the Voice wasn't real, but I also knew it was warning me of something that *was* very real. It was telling me that Zodie would start a fire again. And I was certain that she would. I just knew it. We'd already had so many fires, and Zodie dropped her cigarettes onto her bedding so often it was a wonder there weren't more. Fires were very real in our lives. They were very possible, and they terrified me half to death. So whatever the Voice was—real or not—the bottom line was that there would be another fire.

I quickly got dressed and put my big dolly in the bed so she'd look like me sleeping beneath the covers. I covered her up with my blankets, gave her one last good-night kiss, and slipped out of the house and into the cold, dark night.

I ran directly to the household with the tree house. I beat on the door and cried for help.

"Please! Help me! Help me!" I cried at the closed door until finally the mother came to the door.

"Who's out there?" she asked from behind the closed door, her voice more angry than curious.

"It's me, Mary Zoe. Please let me in! I'm so scared!"

She opened the door and peered down at me. At first, she was clearly upset and didn't want to let me in. She wanted me to go away.

"Mary Zoe, you shouldn't be here at this hour of the night. You go home now! Do you hear me?"

"Please let me in, please! I'm in danger! Please let me in and call my foster parents."

She paused but then relented and let me inside the door. But still she wasn't happy. I pleaded to be allowed to stay and asked if she would please, please call the Dimocks.

"All right," she said, not happy. "I'll call them in the morning. But you need to be quiet and go to sleep. I'll make up a bed on the sofa, but first thing in the morning, you'll need to work things out with your family and go home."

I fell asleep on the couch while watching a tank full of fish swim back and forth, back and forth, back and forth. They say that fish can't remember more than the last few seconds of their lives. Each time they swim from one end of their tank to the other, it's a brand-new experience. I fell asleep wishing I could forget as easily. Maybe then I wouldn't be so afraid if I didn't know what was coming because I couldn't remember what I'd lived through before.

The next day, the Dimocks came for me, and shortly after, so did Zodie. They all kept asking me why I ran away in the dead of night. But I couldn't answer. I couldn't tell them that I was afraid of fire and believed that Zodie and George would burn me alive. I knew I'd sound crazy if I said that. Besides, I heard the Voice tell me to leave, and I knew if I told them I heard a voice they'd really think I was crazy and then I'd be in real trouble. I knew what they said about people who heard voices, so I kept my mouth shut.

"I had a terrible dream," was all I could say. I looked up at Mrs. Dimock and spoke the truth with my eyes. I could tell that she understood that it wasn't just a bad dream that had sent me fleeing in the night. Her eyes told me that she loved me and wanted to take me home with her and Mr. Dimock.

I looked up at Mr. Dimock, and his eyes said the same.

"I apologize for Mary Zoe," Zodie said firmly. "She hasn't been behaving ever since she came home." She cast a cold glance at the Dimocks. "But you can be sure it won't happen again. Will it, Mary Zoe?"

I hung my head in shame. "No," I said softly.

I had thought that the Dimocks would help me and take me back, but now that Zodie was there, I realized that they couldn't help me. No one could. I belonged to Zodie. She could do anything she wanted to me. Mr. and Mrs. Dimock each gave me a hug good-bye.

"We love you, Mary Zoe," Mrs. Dimock whispered in my ear, hugging me close.

And then they left.

Zodie took me by the hand, and we went home.

On the short drive back, Zodie was very quiet. When she pulled into the drive, instead of getting out, she shut off the engine, lit a cigarette, and turned to me. "You were pretty clever to put that doll in your bed. We didn't figure it out until George went in and threw the covers off!" She chuckled slightly, took a drag on her cigarette, and blew it out like steam from a boiling teakettle. Then the chuckle faded, and her voice grew cold. "You are never to run away again," she ordered. "If you do, I'll handle it personally." She tapped her cigarette into the little ashtray on the dashboard. "You'll wait until your daddy gets home. You hear me?" I heard her.

I was resigned to the fact that Daddy George would spank me for running away. And sure enough, he did. He had me lie across the bed, and he spanked me hard. Just a few smacks, much less than when Mama spanked me. But it stung even worse than Mama's sticks; my only consolation was that I hadn't had to take my pants down. When it was all over, I wiped my face, and the incident was not spoken of again.

Still, I was confused. I had heard the Voice tell me to run, but there had been no fire the night I ran away and I just got into worse trouble. Then why had I heard the Voice? I didn't understand and was so embarrassed I'd run away for nothing. But I still believed the Voice. There would be a fire.

In the meantime, all I could do was wait for it to come.

The days were grueling, but I wanted to be a good girl and do what I should and not do anything to upset Zodie. I wanted to please her, to show her how smart and good I was, and I hoped she'd be happy. So I stayed on my best behavior. But everything had changed. She didn't take me out anymore and she didn't buy me presents anymore and we hardly ever did any arts and crafts. She just seemed to have forgotten all about those things once she had me back.

Every day, I remembered a better life, a beautiful life that was closed off from me because of the court's decision. The pain of that loss would become so severe sometimes that I'd double over with burning pain.

And the only thing that seemed to ease the pain was comforting myself with food.

I began to overeat, just to stop the pain. There was never much food around the house, but I always found something. Once I ate crackers and butter for my breakfast and lunch while I waited for Zodie to wake up and drive to the store. I waited a lot. Zodie would sleep through most of the day and wouldn't wake up until just before George came home. It was rare that I'd find her lucid when I got home from school. On those rare days when she was sober, she'd bustle around doing the wash, making her bed, and even fixing dinner, so all would seem normal to George when he got home. But it wasn't normal.

Most of the time, she was too messed up to get out of bed, so I just did what had to be done. I cleaned the house, washed the dishes, emptied the litter boxes, fed the cats and dog, and tried to cook whatever food was available so that when George got home, he wouldn't know the truth about how Zodie spent her days. And as I did the housework, I'd remember what it was like at Martha's house and try my best to recreate that life with what I had to work with.

Alone in the kitchen, I tried to make cookies, but all I could remember was flour, sugar, butter, and cinnamon. I couldn't remember anything else, so I made goo, a kind of paste, and I'd eat that. It would stop the pain in my stomach for a while. But the ache always returned, and I would search through the kitchen for something more to stop it, anything to bring me comfort.

I had also been calling Martha on the sly for weeks, when Zodie was asleep. During the chitchat, she would ask me about what I was doing for fun.

"What are you doing this summer?"

"Nothing. Just taking care of Mama."

"Nothing more? You have to be doing *something*!" She sounded incredulous.

"Nope."

And so it went, phone call after phone call. I still wanted Martha, Mom and Dad, and that wonderful, loving life back. But the closest I could get to it were my memories and my secret calls to my best friend who'd become my second sister. She was my link to a real life, a safe life. I could tell her anything.

But I couldn't tell her about life with Zodie, not how bad it really was. When it came to Zodie, I learned to keep my mouth shut and put on my best performance.

"How's it going?" Martha would ask.

"Oh, you know," I'd answer. "I miss you."

A few months after moving back with Zodie, she dropped me off at her girlfriend's house and disappeared. She was off for another one of her benders. I knew better than to ask any questions, so I just sat in front of their TV set and did my best to remain invisible. A few days later, Zodie returned to pick me up.

"Well, baby, you'll never believe what happened," she said once we got in the car. I was afraid to find out.

"What?" I asked.

"Your bed burned up!" she answered, then howled in laughter. "Good thing you weren't home. You were lucky I sent you away."

"Wh-what happened?" I said, starting to cry, though I knew exactly what had happened. "Is Satan okay? Satan wasn't in there, was he?"

"No, Satan's fine, all the cats are fine. But your mattress is gone and all the bedding. You'll have to sleep on the box springs. We were lucky to save those, but we don't have the money to buy another mattress. We'd only had that one a year, you know. Oh, well, what's one more thing to lose?" Then she unrolled her window and flicked her cigarette into the sky.

"All my bedding? What about my pillow, the one the Dimocks gave me?"

"That's gone. It's all gone. But we'll get you a new one, kiddo, and I found you a couple of old blankets."

Swallowing back my sobs, I grieved for the pillow I'd loved so much, my last link to the Dimocks. When we got home, Zodie used ironing stripping to attach mattress ticking over the blackened skeleton of the bedsprings. And I slept on those box springs from then on.

CHAPTER 21

The Devil Returns

I'D ONLY BEEN BACK A few months when my world grew darker than ever before. I came home from school one day to find David Walz in the kitchen, his hands all over Zodie. The sight of him paralyzed me, and I stood there, trembling and frozen, as Zodie pushed his hands off her and straightened her clothes. He turned around, and the moment his stone-colored eyes hit mine, I fled to my room but not before catching a glimpse of his sinister smile.

I couldn't believe he was back. I sat on the edge of my bed, shaking and sweating, my heart beating so hard I thought it would explode then and there. I threw my head into my hands and wept, my whole body shaking in fear and defeat. She had brought him back into our lives, and I knew it would be next to impossible to get him out again. He would be back.

A little while later, there was a knock on the bedroom door and Zodie strode in, her lipstick long gone and her hair still a mess. I could practically smell him on her.

"Now, baby, what was that all about? Was that any way to greet your stepdaddy?"

"He's *not* my stepfather," I replied. "George is. Mama, why did you have to let him come back?"

"We just ran into each other, is all," she said lightly, inspecting herself in my mirror. "Oh, I look a mess, don't I? You see, I was taking a nap when he came by." Her feeble excuses sounded pathetic, and all I could think of was *why*? Why had my own mama let such a horrible man into our house? She knew what he had done to me, and still, she let him back in.

"I hate him."

"Well, that's no way to talk about someone who's supported us and taken good care of us. David was always good to us and gave us such a nice life. We haven't lived as well since."

I continued to shake, furious that she would put the pleasure of his income ahead of the horrors of his actions.

"Mama, *please* don't let him come back!" I pleaded. "*Please!* You know if Daddy catches him, he's going to be really mad. Mama, please don't let David Walz come back!"

She looked at me as if I was begging for the impossible. Shaking her head, she walked out the door, saying, "You just don't know anything about the real world, Mary Zoe, but one of these days, you'll wake up."

Then she was gone.

David Walz began coming over more and more often after that. At first, when I'd see his car in the drive, I'd wait outside or go to a friend's house until he was gone. But sometimes he'd show up after I got home, and he and Zodie would start drinking. Then I would go outside or straight to my room until he left.

After a while, he'd stay longer and longer until it wasn't long before I might as well have been invisible; they'd just carry on together in Zodie's bedroom, the same way that Zodie and Grandpa Jerre would carry on when I got sent outside.

One time, I came out of my room to find them on the sofa, both naked with David Walz on top of Mama. They were having sex, I could tell. It was a horrible sight, and I couldn't get the image out of my head no matter how much I tried to cry it out.

I knew if Daddy George ever caught them, there'd be hell to pay (as Mama would say). I started feeling bad for not telling Daddy George what was going on, but I knew if I told I'd be in big trouble with Zodie, so again, I kept my mouth shut. Eventually, though, I came to realize that George suspected something was going on.

Once when George walked me to the store along Alki Beach, a ferocious little Chihuahua came running up to us, yapping and snapping its little jaws. I tried to make friends with it, but it tried to bite me.

Daddy George pulled me away, swearing, "Leave that Goddamn dog alone!" I was stunned at his reaction. Daddy George loved animals, and I never knew a dog he didn't adore, but he just yanked me away from that little Chihuahua as if I'd tried to pet a rattlesnake. "He's just like David Walz—little, cowardly, vicious and he'd pee on your foot out of spite!"

I couldn't believe his reaction. It was unheard of. I had my own reasons for not liking David Walz, but I didn't know he had any.

I had to ask, so I whispered, "Do you hate him?"

"Yes," he whispered back. He said it so quietly and coldly that it chilled my blood.

That was all he ever said about David Walz. I could see that the mere thought of him put Daddy George in a rage—and put me in utter terror.

I had prayed that David Walz would leave me alone, but it did no good. Once he started hanging around longer and longer, it wasn't long before Zodie would pass out before he left, and I'd be left alone with him. That's when he started touching me again.

I was eleven years old and just starting to develop. I hated the changes in my body, the hair between my legs, and my small budding breasts. I didn't want to look like Zodie. The only thing I could do to control the changes in my body was to eat. If I ate enough, I would gain enough weight to hide the changes in my body, but no matter how much I gained, it wasn't enough to keep David Walz away.

He'd pull my panties down and prod the fine hair between my legs until I shut off my mind and went to another place in my head. But I don't want to talk about that. Besides, mostly I've forgotten. Except for the time Mama was right there in the room, holding onto the dresser, swaying back and forth because she couldn't keep her balance while David Walz held me down on the bed and touched me in all those wrong ways.

My stomach was sick, and I wanted to vomit in his face. But Mama just kept swaying back and forth, like she was dancing to her own melody while I whimpered and begged for her to help me.

"Just be a good girl," she mumbled. "Daddy David isn't doing anything to hurt you. Oh for Christsakes, this bottle's empty already."

One way or another, I had to get out.

CHAPTER 22

Escape

NOT LONG AFTER I RETURNED, we had to move because the neighbors complained about the animals. Zodie and George had continued collecting more cats and dogs, and with each additional animal, the smell got worse and worse until the neighbors couldn't take it any longer. And so we moved. And we moved again. Eventually, we had to leave West Seattle altogether, because the landlords there wouldn't rent to us. George found us a house on the north side of the city, and we settled in there, and again, I settled into a new school. I had moved eleven times since first grade, so I was getting used to it. What I wasn't getting used to was Zodie.

She would get better, and then she'd get worse. Once in a while, she'd spend some time with me, playing board games or doing arts and crafts, laughing and happy, and then she'd sink into days of drinking and taking pills, not getting out of bed until it was time for George to come home. Then after weeks of hangovers and blackouts, she'd rise from the bed cursing and laughing, ready to battle the world.

But I'd learned that the grandiose, devil-may-care Zodie was never a new mama. Even though each time she'd start to be fun and hysterically funny and I'd think my mama was getting better, turning into a normal, happy mama, it would be followed by a crumpled, incompetent, "ill" Zodie. It never failed. And each time the inevitable crash came, I was left to pick up the pieces.

And each time, I wondered how the Dimocks were and wished I could go back there.

There was one good thing about moving to the other side of the city, and that was that I never saw David Walz again. But I knew he could come back at any moment, so I still didn't feel safe. Besides, Grandpa Jerre did come around, and while

I trusted Mama to keep him away from me, I couldn't ever shake that feeling he gave me when he came by. He still gave me the evil eye each time he saw me, and I knew that was no way for a grandpa to look at a little girl. So I kept a close eye on Grandpa Jerre and watched out for the return of David Walz.

A year after I'd moved back, George and Zodie gave me the news that they were breaking up and I was going back to the youth center. George had been going to the racetracks and blowing his paycheck, and Zodie had been running around with David Walz and Grandpa Jerre, so they were fighting all the time. One time, he bet our grocery money on a New Year's football game, and we watched that game on pins and needles because if he lost, it meant we'd be eating soda crackers for a week. But he won so everybody cheered.

Zodie loved the races, too, so she really didn't mind him gambling on the horses, but it just got to be something she could throw back at him when he complained about her running around with other guys. The truth was, I never really paid much attention to the details. All I knew was they were breaking up and I was going to the youth center.

I didn't mind really. Life was probably better in the youth center than at home, anyway. This cycle had happened so many times before. They fought. I ended up being in the way, unwanted, and then sent to someone's house until they made up. And now here they both were, giving me the big news, yet again, that their marriage was over.

"You won't be there long, baby," Zodie explained, pouring herself another scotch and water. "It's better this way; you'll see."

If they thought I would wail and beg them to stay together, they were wrong. Instead, I heaved a heavy, disinterested sigh and strummed my index finger against my lips signaling "Here we go again," as I'd seen my friends do at school.

All of a sudden, George erupted and charged me. In a flash, he had me hanging from my heels while he beat me mercilessly. Bursts of searing pain shot through my back and buttocks. I couldn't ward off the blows; my hands were useless against his attack. My arms were too slow to stop him because he held me upside down. He was a strong man, and I was only eleven. Fear turned my stomach to ice, as my screams filled the tiny house. Then suddenly, he let go of my ankles, and I crashed into the chair below me. But the beating wasn't over. He lunged at me and started hitting me, harder and harder.

Through my terror, I saw Mama jump on his back, trying to pull him off of me. But it was no use; he just shrugged her off as if she was a fly, and then he hung me upside down again. Scrambling over furniture, Mama threw herself on him, scratching and biting until he released me again to fight with Mama. Her fingernails raked his face, while his huge hands began to squeeze her neck. Mama writhed on the couch and dug her hands into Daddy's eyes. Daddy George had never hurt me before, but now I knew he was raging and that he would kill Mama and me if he got the chance.

A knock at the door broke their death stance. He threw her across the couch and stalked to the door. The light from the street shone full on his face and the black bloody tracks from Zodie's nails glistened. It was Lynn, my girlfriend who lived down the block.

"Can Mary Zoe play?" Lynn asked him.

"No!" George shouted and slammed the door. He turned to me. I ran into my bedroom and leaned against the closed door. I didn't care if they killed each other, if only they'd leave me alone. When I heard their fight continuing in the living room and knew I was momentarily safe, I undressed. Ugly red welts were rising like waves all along my back, legs, and buttocks and the pain was excruciating. Gingerly, I put on my nightgown and crawled into bed, pulling my blankets gently around me. I hurt so much. Crying, I swore then and there that I'd never let a man touch me. Then, through my sobs, I heard my door open, and I looked up. Daddy George loomed huge in the doorway. I froze.

He took a step toward me, and I instantly drew back, hiding my face behind the sheet, only my eyes remained uncovered.

"I'm sorry," he said softly. "I shouldn't've beat ya. It was only I was so mad at your ma. It's gonna be all right. You don't have to go to the youth center." He closed the door gently.

Pain welled up and choked me. "I *want* to go to the Youth Center!" I screamed silently. "I want out!"

But I didn't get out. Zodie and George got drunk instead and decided to stay together. And to cement their continuing bond, they got a new puppy. And another one. And another.

By 1965, the passing of time had not been kind to Zodie. She looked haggard and even skinnier than before. She had let her looks go. She no longer scrutinized her face for stray imperfections, plucking here, moisturizing there. Her hair was no longer pretty and blond with pin curls. It hung in greasy brown and blond strings in front of her face.

"Come on, Mama," I'd say, trying to coax her to eat something, anything. "I made you some chicken noodle soup. Please eat it."

After a few sips, she'd push it away and go back to bed or open up another bottle.

She spiraled deeper and deeper into her personal darkness. No matter what I cooked, washed, or cleaned, Zodie took no interest. She refused to do anything with me—no shopping, no TV shows, no arts and crafts. Nothing brought her better self around anymore; it was as if her spirit had been vanquished. She lay in bed, covered by cats, saying she was better off dead. That always frightened me, and she knew it, but still, she said it.

"If I die," she'd say, "you'll be all alone."

I never knew what to think of such words.

One morning, I got up to use the bathroom and found Zodie curled around the toilet, cuddling the base as if it were a pillow. Finding her there was hardly novel, so I just reached out and shook her shoulder. "Hey, Mama, don't you want to get up and go to bed?" She lifted her head off the floor, and I saw that one side of her hair was wet.

"Wha?" she mumbled, confused. "I'm not in bed?"

"No, Mama, you are definitely not in bed." With that, I heaved her up and dragged her to her bed. Tucking her in, I smoothed her hair.

"Give me the phone, Mary Zoe. I have to make a call."

I handed her the phone and walked to the bathroom. When I came out, I heard what she was doing. She was setting up her Will. She thought she was dying.

"You can't stay with George," she told me, "not after I'm dead. You'll have to go to my mother's."

"But, Mama, you're not going to die," I said, half-scared and half-bored. I wasn't sure if something really was wrong with Zodie or this was just another one of her dramas. But the prospect of going to California to stay with Nana thrilled me.

"Yes, baby, I am. I'm dying, and I know it. You're going to have to go to Nana's. I have to focus on writing my Will."

Overjoyed, I ran to my room and began to pick out the clothes I would pack in my little suitcase. I had a chance! I was getting away from Zodie!

On the flight to California to see my grandmother, I was filled with excitement. I was going to live with my Nana! I could barely contain my nerves as I sat in the window seat, brushing cracker crumbs off my best party dress. Mama said she wanted me to make a good impression, so I had on my good clothes. I even had on my new training bra, which George had taken me to buy (since Zodie was too sick to take me). Secretly, I gave myself a hug. I felt so grown up. I had curves. The very same curves that I tried to conceal from David Walz, gave me such pleasure once he was gone.

A nervous giggle squeaked past my tight throat. Glancing at my seatmate, I was mortified to see he had heard me giggle. He smiled at me and returned to reading his college textbook. Hastily, I looked back to the window. Yes, I was going to try to make a good impression on Nana. I knew I would. After all, I wasn't a little kid anymore; I knew how to behave. I resolved that I'd be so good that she would want to keep me. Maybe this time, Mama really was dying, I thought as I rested my head near the window to watch the clouds. I remembered when I was little and looked out the airplane windows on my way to Nana's or Daddy Johnny's, and I would wonder if I threw a gift out of the airplane window and it landed on a cloud, if God would pick it up. The memory tickled me as my eyes closed.

Abruptly, the college student shook me awake. He said we were landing, and I had slept through most of the flight. I must have been worn out, he said. I nodded. I was tired. Mama had kept me up all night.

Just as she had done with Sissy so many times before, on the night before I left for Nana's, she had dragged me out of bed demanding, "You don't think I'm a good mother, do you?" It wasn't the first time. Whenever she did that, I would protest that she was a good mother, and eventually, she'd let me go back to sleep.

But this time, eager to go see Nana and provoked beyond my patience, I had agreed with her, just so she'd let me go back to bed.

"Waddya mean I'm not a good mother? Don't you love me anymore?"

"For Christ sake, Zodie, let the kid go to bed," George bellowed. Then they went at it and started screaming at each other, while I sneaked back to bed.

It was the same old pattern. The only difference was this time I was flying away.

Yawning while straightening my party dress and adjusting my plastic hair band to pull back my long hair, I took a deep breath and marched off the plane with the other passengers. That was when it hit me. Would I recognize Nana? Would she recognize me, now that I was a big girl? I remembered seeing Nana when I was about six. She filled up a room. She pounded Mama's piano and sang. It was as if she took all the oxygen out of the room, she was that powerful. Bigger than life size was how I remembered her. I didn't see her very much, so I used to get her confused with Bette Davis and Tallulah Bankhead, the movie actresses being more real to me than she was. My heart started to pound, and I felt a thin veil of sweat begin to cool my skin as I worried that I might not know my own grandma at all.

But as I rounded the bend to exit the plane, there she was! Nana, standing tall in a tailored beige suit, her golden hair arching over one side of her forehead and a blood-red smile painted on her lips. She stood with her arms spread open wide, waiting for me!

I ran to her but stumbled on the ramp and thumped right into her, knocking us both off balance. "Hi, Nana," I mumbled as I found my footing.

Nana continued to smile at me, but her smile didn't reach her clear blue eyes. Her eyes looked as strange as I'd remembered them, surrounded by thin, auburn arches she had penciled in place of her real eyebrows. Holding me at arm's length, she said, "My, what a sight you are!" Her penciled-eyebrows were raised to an alarming level. "That hair and that dress!" she cried, and I suddenly felt ashamed of the pretty outfit I'd been so proud of. "We'll fix that right now," she declared.

Grabbing my arm, she strode into the terminal with me running to keep up. She paused, as she gave her attention to the terminal traffic, and then she turned and assessed my appearance once again, as a general would view the troops. "Yes, that dress has got to go! And we must do something about your skin!" She sniffed. "You aren't beautiful like your Uncle Tucker's children, Sean or Tanya, but with a little help, you'll do." We got to her car, and she drove on in silence as I tried to disappear.

Everything about me was already so wrong.

Entering her apartment, I made my first mistake. A gentleman held the door open for us. Nana glided by him, but I stared. No one had ever opened a door for me before. I was amazed. Was it because I was a big girl now?

Farther down the hall and out of the man's sight, Nana grabbed my arm and shook me. "What are you doing? Are you trying to invite him to our apartment? Are you going to be just like your mother, Zodie?"

Shocked and puzzled, my eyes burned with unshed tears. "I'm sorry, Nana. I didn't mean to be bad. I just never saw anyone open a door for me before."

She released her grip and stared at me. "We'll have to work on your manners too." Then she turned and strode away, leaving me to hang my head and follow her into her apartment.

Living with Nana the next few weeks was like trying to keep up with a force of nature. Everything gave way before her. Changes came so rapidly, they made my head swim. She wanted to change everything about me. We'd only been there one day when she told me to get in the car because we had an appointment.

"Mary Zoe," she said, "you have a horse's face. It's too long for hair past your shoulders. Your face will look better with a haircut."

Then she took me to a beauty salon, and they cut off all my hair.

Nana got rid of all my clothes, including my pretty dresses and even my training bra, saying, "You're too young to need something like this." She bought me two tastefully tailored dresses, sensible school shoes, and all white cotton undershirts and panties and brilliant white socks.

"Now you look appropriate for your age," she sniffed.

I didn't tell her that I liked the clothes she got rid of. I just did as I was told and tried to avoid Nana's expressive sniffs of displeasure.

A few days later, Nana told me that she wanted me to go to a private, very exclusive school, but I could only get in if I passed an entrance exam. I was terrified. If I didn't pass the exam, then Nana would be mad at me. I tugged at my hair all day, trying to remember what I was supposed to study. My stomach burned, and my head ached, but fortunately, I passed the entrance exam. Unfortunately, my score was too low, so they put me in a younger grade.

"It's because those schools in Seattle are inferior," Nana said. "That's why you're behind. Tucker's children have never been behind, like you are." I could tell I'd disappointed her with my score, so I vowed to work as hard as I could to catch up and not disappoint her.

"The only reason the headmistress had let you enroll was because I've taught you how to behave," Nana said. "You were the only girl who had stood when she entered the room, and that's the only reason you were admitted. Because of what I've taught you."

When the headmistress had entered the room, I had automatically stood, and apparently, that had impressed her.

I didn't tell Nana that the only reason I did that was because I watched enough movies to know that a student stood when the headmistress entered. It wasn't Nana who'd taught me. It was Shirley Temple.

But Nana was right about that making an impression. On the day I started school, the headmistress introduced me by announcing that of all the students at the school, I was the only one who stood when she entered without being told to rise.

Great, I thought to myself, as I saw the heated looks directed my way. "Just great," I mumbled as I sat down in class, the new kid yet again. And sure enough, from that day on, I studied alone. I ate my lunches alone. And I stood up alone.

At night, Nana would have me sing while she played the piano. She said with training, my voice could be good. She promised we'd work on that daily. And we did. Those sessions were tough, and I could feel the tension in my shoulders as I worried about missing a note. I was relieved when Nana would forget to drill me in my music lessons and she would tell me stories instead. She told me all about her exploits on stage with the opera in New York and how she trained to hit high C over C. Nana was very proud of her stage experience, and she told me at length what it was like to sing at Carnegie Hall. She explained that she had been known for her beauty, grace, and voice, but that she had to leave the opera when she got pregnant with Zodie, which she made clear was a huge disappointment.

"But now I'm one of the best real estate brokers in the Oakland area," she said, "and that's nothing to sneeze at, let me tell you. I've worked hard to get where I am, and I'm as smart as any man, don't you forget it."

I didn't doubt it. Nana had a lovely apartment and so many nice things in it because she did work hard and was probably even smarter than any man. Nana *was* smart. And she was strong. She told me stories of raising Uncle Tucker alone, because her husband had left her and Zodie didn't help her at all.

"That mother of yours has never been any good," she'd sniff, "always carrying on like a no-good whore. She stole my last husband, Roger. I'm sure I told you about that," she'd say, over and over again. "I caught him looking at her like she was his dessert, and let me tell you, I knew then and there that she was nothing but trouble. That's why I threw her out, you know, because I wasn't about to let her have my man. A lady has to be tough, I'm telling you, because men will try to ruin our lives if we let them. You hear me?"

After I'd finish my homework, she'd work on my table manners or make me walk with a book on my head. "A lady must have good posture!" she'd drill into me. And every night before prayers, she would have me sit on the floor with my head resting against her knees as she put medicine on my skin to cure my acne. I'd watch her smoky topaz ring flash in the light as her hand dipped from the jar to my face. Her ring fascinated me.

"It's terribly expensive," Nana would say, showing it off to me. "Maybe when I'm dead, I'll leave it to you," she'd say, admiring it on her hand. "Unless I leave it to Tucker. But I'm not leaving it to your mother. She doesn't deserve such an expensive ring, as much as she'd love to get her hands on it."

Nana loved jewelry. She always wore the best of everything and had the best of everything, and she was going to teach me to be the best. Like her. So as much as I winced at her put-downs, I listened. I wanted to be a proper lady.

One sunny day, Nana said we were going to visit Uncle Tucker and Aunt Licha and my cousins, Tanya and Sean. I could hardly remember Uncle Tucker, so I was nervous to make a good impression. When we entered his foyer, Uncle Tucker stood tall and blond. As he was introduced to me, we shook hands. The white gloves I was wearing were beginning to make my hands sweat, but I held a smile on my face as I met my aunt and cousins. They didn't have to dress up like me, I noticed. They looked like regular kids. I was puzzled about why I had to be so different. But I kept my mouth shut.

Aunt Licha was a petite Mexican woman with lovely brown hair that showed red highlights in the California sunlight. She wore exquisite jewelry and perfect makeup, and I thought she was absolutely beautiful. She reminded me of my sister, Gale, so I warmed up to her right away.

But Nana wasn't very nice to Aunt Licha, so I was careful not to let Nana know how much I liked her. I must have done well because when we left, Nana said I had done that so well that it was time to practice my manners at a local hotel for tea.

I had never seen anything quite so grand as this hotel in San Francisco. I sat bolt upright in the wing-back chair and although my feet didn't touch the floor, I managed to keep my napkin in my lap. The tea tasted terrible, but the cookies were good. I was helping myself to more cookies when Nana frowned at me and hissed in a low voice, "You're too fat now; you've got to watch what you're eating." Ashamed, I put my hand back in my lap. I made no other mistakes that day. Nana was pleased.

A few weeks later, when Nana picked me up from school, she was very angry. She explained to me that she had been in correspondence with the Dimock family regarding my home life with Zodie. She was not pleased. And she mistrusted Mr. Dimock intensely.

"The only reason those people wanted to keep you was because the state paid them to have you, you know," she said. "It's a good thing you're out of there." Then she sniffed and added, "Always remember, blood is thicker than water."

I listened to her drone on and on, sounding more like Zodie with every sentence. Of course, I didn't dare disagree, or point out that Zodie had said the same thing. Nana would be furious if I ever compared her to Zodie. I tried my best to ignore her, to let her words buzz through the air without notice, but then she said something that caught my attention.

"And since they're coming to California, they want to see you," she said.

The Dimocks were coming to California!

"Oh, Nana, please can I see them?" I begged. I saw right away that she wasn't pleased at all that I wanted to see them, so I quickly added, "I mean Martha. Please can I see Martha, Nana, please?"

Nana grumbled some more about how awful the Dimocks were and what a bad influence on me they'd been, but eventually she did agree to allow a visit between Martha, Mrs. Dimock, and me. But, Nana said, if my manners were even slightly off, I'd be punished.

"We'll show those Dimocks what sort of class we are," she said, sniffing with a perverse pleasure. "I think they'll get the message."

Nana arranged the meeting in the lobby of a local hotel. I was dressed in my freshly pressed blue tailored dress, with purse, white gloves, and a bad case of nerves. Nana was dressed splendidly with her smoky topaz ring flashing as she applied shiny red lipstick to her lips while we waited for our visitors. She smacked her lips together, making a popping sound.

"There! That's perfect," she announced. She turned and looked me up and down. "But that hair will never do. Come here; let me fix it."

She spun me around and began brushing my hair so hard I thought my head would fall off. Then she jabbed some barrettes into my hairline so tightly they hurt, and finally, she said that I looked much better.

"All right, let's go show those Dimocks who they're up against," she declared, strangely delighted with herself.

I prayed Nana wouldn't embarrass me in front of the Dimocks, but I knew the odds were stacked against me.

I gasped when I saw Martha. It was all I could do not to run to her and throw my arms around her. My eyes filled with joyful tears as I watched them approach. Smiling bravely, I held out my hand and shook hands with both of them. But before I could say a word, Nana took over the entire conversation. I remained mute as a statue by the fireplace. I was terrified to open my mouth, for fear I'd be punished for my bad manners. So I just stood still through the entire twenty-minute visit, shifting my weight from foot to foot.

When they left, Martha looked back at me with a puzzled frown and I knew I'd disappointed her. But Nana was very pleased. I had made no mistakes. "Children should be seen and not heard," she said as we left.

My heart hurt, but I just said, "Yes, Nana."

Weeks passed, and Zodie didn't die. But she didn't send for me either. My life with Nana was looking more and more like it would be permanent. Then, finally, Nana said I was ready to meet some of her dearest friends, people who had even known Zodie as a young woman.

"Fortunately, I've been able to live down your mother's legacy of shame by my own decent living," Nana said, "but that doesn't mean that I can live down yours if you follow in your mother's footsteps, so you just mind your manners, do you hear me?" She sighed heavily, then added, "But you just might turn out all right, now that you're away from her and under my direction."

As she navigated the turns of the road, she explained to me that her friends were very important to her and members of her church. It was an honor, she explained, to be invited to their Sunday brunch. As I listened to her tell me how honored I was to be invited, my nerves became strained. Even though this wasn't a formal affair, I knew

I had better be careful. Nana further explained that everyone at the party knew that Zodie slept around.

"Your mother's nothing but a whore." She sniffed. "My husband Roger ran away from me because of her, you know that, don't you?"

Yes, Nana, I wanted to say. *You've told me this a thousand times.* But I kept my mouth shut.

"It's all her fault that Roger left me. She used her sex appeal to ruin my life!" Nana spit the words out as she raced the car up the hill of a very posh neighborhood. She was so mad that I thought she'd smash right into a mailbox or maybe even run over a child riding a bike on the quiet street.

As I tried to make sense of it all, it occurred to me that if Mama was a whore, who had raised Mama? Who had robbed Mama of her childhood? Who taught her about men and sex too early? The lights came on in my mind. It all came down to Nana and Grandfather Jerre. *They* had made the mistakes, not me. And it was Zodie she was mad at, not me. So, all I had to do was live down the fact I was Zodie's child and perhaps Nana would forget the past and like me. At least I had a chance. I tried to calm myself as the car rounded the last bend of the hill. "Please, God," I whispered, "let me do this without any mistakes, so Nana will like me."

She pulled into the drive of a large house and turned off the engine. She took a deep breath and forced a tight smile onto her face, then said, "Now remember what I've taught you."

"Yes, Nana," I said, nodding obediently. What I didn't add was, "You've taught me more than you'll ever know."

At first, the afternoon went smoothly. There was laughter and light conversation. The spring sun was warm, and the patio rapidly heated up. Everyone had shed extra layers, and the host served us in his sleeveless tank top. But in my hot blue school dress, I had nothing to peel off. The sweat trickled down from under my arms, and my back grew damp with sweat. I spoke when it was appropriate and kept my hands in my lap. I did everything possible to behave and not make Nana hate me.

And I almost made it. But after a light meal, I was still hungry as the host passed by me offering more muffins. I didn't have to be asked twice and reached out to snare a muffin, but then I heard Nana's voice in my head "You're too fat. Don't eat that extra muffin!" So as rapidly as I put my hand out for a muffin, I put my hand back in my lap even quicker. The host gave me a startled look and checked his stride but continued carrying the tray away. About an hour later, as we climbed the stairs to get our sweaters and purses to leave, Nana asked me why I had reached out so suddenly. What had I wanted?

Oh no! I thought. *If I tell her I wanted another muffin, I'll be in trouble.* So taking a deep breath, I answered, "Nothing, Nana."

The ride back to Nana's apartment dripped with icy silence. I didn't know what I had done, but Nana's knuckles were white on the steering wheel. My heart beat faster and faster as the silence grew louder and louder. Then, as soon as the apartment door closed behind me, she grabbed a handful of my hair and pulled my face around to face her.

"The host and hostess told me never to bring you again! You're just like your mother, aren't you? You were reaching to touch that man, weren't you? You were reaching out to run your fingers in his chest hair, weren't you? *Weren't you*?" She punctuated each question with a quick rap of my head on the door frame.

"No, Nana!" I wailed as she hit my head into the doorframe again. "I just wanted another muffin, but I knew you wouldn't like me to eat more because I'm fat! Please, Nana, please, I'm sorry. I made a mistake."

"You sure as hell did," she snarled, and after one more tug on my hair, she settled in her favorite chair and picked up the phone. I ran from the room to splash cold water on my face. I could hear her on the phone talking long-distance to Zodie, telling her what a horrible child I was. But what she was saying was a lie! I didn't do anything bad, my mind protested. Suddenly, I realized that she was throwing me away, just like she had done with Mama. I'd behaved so well, done everything she'd told me, and still she didn't want me. She was sending me back. Back to Zodie. I dropped to my knees praying, "Please, God, don't let her send me back." I cried until I had no tears left and was just a puddle on the bathroom floor.

That night, right before dinner, she explained that I was to go home the following day. I was wearing a long robe that Nana had insisted I put on, but it was too big for me and I had to lift it up when I walked. We were standing in the dining room, where the table had been set for one final meal, with her best china and crystal goblets.

"You're mother's not dying, and since you're so much like her, it would be better for all of us if you lived with her instead," she said, glaring at me as she carefully straightened the silver.

I stepped back from Nana's angry face and tripped on the long robe and went sprawling into the dining table. Horrified, I watched one of the crystal goblets totter and slowly crash to the floor between my outstretched hands. I sat on the floor by the shattered crystal and wept, the goblet smashed, just like my hopes.

I had ruined everything. Nana didn't want me. I was going back to Zodie because I was too much like her. It hadn't been really that good a place to stay, but still, it was better than home. I thought I'd have a chance at a good life, but now it was over, all because I couldn't please her. I was Zodie's child, and there was nothing to be done about that unforgiveable fact.

I'd had one more chance at a better life, and once again, I was being sent back to my life with Zodie—and straight to the most terrifying experience of my life.

CHAPTER 23

Driving in the Dark

IT RAINED THE DAY THAT Daddy George picked me up at the airport. He stood at the gate alone. "Mama isn't here?" I asked, stating the obvious.

"Nah, she couldn't make it. She's waiting for you at the house." Silently, we gathered my luggage and walked to the car. "I like your haircut, Mary Zoe," he said to me just before getting in the car.

"Thank you," I said in a barely audible voice. I hesitated, bracing myself for riding in our car. After experiencing a clean house and car for a few months, climbing into the Buick was grim. The car that had once been so luxurious, no longer turned heads when it sailed down the street. After a few years in the hands of Zodie and George, it was worn and filthy. The upholstery was ripped, the windows were gray with dog nose smudges, and there were dings and scratches from headlight to taillight. When the car door swung open, a cloud of reeking cigarette smoke and the stench of dog pee hit me. Trying not to wrinkle my nose, I settled into the car and watched the rain splatter on the windshield. Even a Seattle downpour couldn't clear the leaves, dead bugs, and dirt from the grimy glass.

"How's Mama?" I asked as George drove.

"Oh, she's a little bit better." He paused before adding, "Pretty much the same, really." He turned to me and smiled a sad smile. "I'm glad you're home, Mary Zoe." Knowing what he *wasn't* telling me, I knew that I wasn't so glad to be home. All I felt was sick and afraid.

"Me too," I said to George.

He turned on the radio and we rode the rest of the way home, listening to the songs of Patsy Cline.

I thought I'd be prepared for what I found, but I was not. Walking through the door, the stench of animals was overwhelming. I could no longer count how many there were, but it was obvious that with me gone, no one had been cleaning up after them.

And yes, Zodie was better, if better meant she was out of bed. She was propped up on the sofa surrounded by crumpled fast-food bags, cigarette butts, empty medicine bottles, scotch bottles, and howling cats. From the looks of her, she had been parked there for quite a while. I had my work cut out for me, I thought. I ran to my room and deposited my bags when I heard, "Come here and give me a kiss!"

"Okay, I'll be right there, Nana," I hollered back. There was silence. Horrified, I realized I had called Zodie Nana. I hurried to the living room and approached Zodie timidly. "I'm sorry, Mama," died on my lips. Zodie had her scotch in one hand and a cigarette in the other—and pure fury on her face.

"No, I am not your grandmother," she said through clenched teeth. "Is that clear?" Looking me over, she said she liked the haircut but that I was wearing a stupid dress. "Go change. I don't want to see any of her things. Then you can feed these cats and get dinner started."

I was definitely back. Nothing had changed in the time I'd been gone. She had just moved her location from the bed to the couch.

Weeks passed, and then months, but not much improved. Zodie began to come back to life, but it was a strange, unsettling kind of life. She was drinking constantly, and when she wasn't drinking, she was passed out or sleeping or in a rage. I never knew what to expect, except the unexpected.

And the unexpected hit with a wallop when I was twelve years old. It was a hot summer night, and I was getting ready for bed. I'd just brushed my teeth when Zodie took it into her head to drive over the mountains to Wenatchee, to "take a vacation." She was always getting it into her head to do something reckless at the drop of a hat. Usually, it meant that she wanted to move. She was impulsive in all aspects of her life, in her love for me and her love of her needs. I had learned early on that if I did not address her needs immediately, her temper could be as spontaneous as her love. So I always tried to please her when she got a wild hair to do something impulsive, and this looked to be one of those times. I stood watching helplessly as she threw our clothes in the backseat.

"Get in the car!" she demanded.

I looked at her tight mouth and weaving stance and knew that she wasn't just drinking. She was on something. *Yes,* I thought to myself, *this is going to be very bad.* But maybe, just maybe, I could get her to see reason. I had to try.

"But, Mama," I pleaded, "shouldn't we wait for Daddy George? It's really late. Shouldn't we wait until morning?"

"Don't be such a worrywart," she said, her voice so jocular it made me nervous. "I can do it." She slid into the car, fumbling with the keys. "We'll have fun!"

"Sure," I answered faintly, stepping into the car as if seating myself in an electric chair to await my execution. I sat. My stomach clenched, and I was afraid that I might get sick in the Buick's big front seat as Zodie threw the car into reverse and stepped on the gas.

I don't remember much about the first part of the trip, except I kept watching her to make sure she was still awake and that she stayed on the road. Zodie loved to drive, and she did it without hesitation, no matter how messed up she was. Any suggestion that she was too "ill" to drive, her euphemism for smashed, did nothing to make her reconsider. Instead, it was an insulting challenge to her skill as a superior driver, so she'd be all the more determined to prove her accuser wrong. Nothing stopped her. In one particularly bad incident, she scraped the hubcaps along the guardrails of the Alaskan Way viaduct. Horrified, I watched her wrestle the wheel as the car rebounded into traffic. I closed my eyes and prayed, slipping into the accident position that had been drilled into me by George. I dropped to the seat and floor of the Buick. Horns blared, but there wasn't any accident. Zodie always got where she was going. So traveling to Wenatchee at night was just the sort of chance she'd take to have a good time, and I had no choice but to go along.

It seemed to take a couple of lifetimes to get away from the city during that midnight trip across the state of Washington. The dark pressed on my eyes as I strained to watch her and the flashing white striping on the highway. The contrast of the dark night, the flashing white lines, and the green reflection of the dashboard in Mama's glasses made my eyes ache.

When we were deep in the mountains, Mama pulled over to the shoulder of the highway and stopped the engine. "I'm going to have a seizure. Move over."

"Seizure" was Mama's code word for passing out. I'd long ago learned not to challenge her on her choice of words. If she said she was ill when I knew she was drunk or wasted on pills, then I agreed that she was ill. And if she said she was about to have a seizure when she was about to pass out, I accommodated her. I always accommodated Zodie.

I slid over to give her some room, and she slumped over in the front seat, her head on my lap. We sat that way for a long time. Trucks roared by, and the car would rock with the wind through the convertible top. Then the roar would fade and there'd be such quiet I could hear the clock tick in the dash. I was filled with fear and dread and just wanted to be home in my own bed, even if it was just a hard box springs with a couple of flimsy blankets.

When she finally lifted her face, I couldn't see her eyes, just her glasses reflecting the green glow of the dashboard clock.

"You're gonna have to drive us the rest of the way," she slurred. "I can't do it."

I felt cold all over, and ice pooled in my stomach. "Mama, I don't know how to drive! I don't know where to go! Please don't make me do this!"

Zodie just shrugged. "We all have to do things we don't want to do," she said, as if she were telling me to take out the trash. "That's life. Now get out and get behind the wheel. I'll talk you through it."

I walked around the '52 Buick and climbed behind the wheel, terrified to do as she said, but even more terrified to defy her. By the time I got into the driver's seat, Zodie was slumped over in the passenger seat, having her "seizure."

The car was enormous. I was too little to see over the steering wheel so I had to peer between it and the dashboard to see the road. The shiny hood of the Buick seemed to stretch forever. I had no idea what to do, but I knew I had to do it. There was no way out. My habit of catering to Zodie ran deep. It never crossed my mind to say, "That's okay, Mama. We'll just sleep here." My Mama needed me to help her, and my job was to do what she told me to do. Besides, the risk of crossing Zodie was greater than the risk of driving the car.

Zodie mumbled incomprehensible instructions that floated into my ears through a roar in my head. Somehow, I got the car started. Gripping the wheel with both hands, I scooted myself to the edge of the seat so I could reach the pedals. I could barely reach them with my toes. I was petrified with fear as I pulled the car onto the highway. My chest was so tight I could barely breathe, so I panted. My mouth turned bone dry, and my eyes stung with the strain to see. Sweat dripped down my back, and I could smell my own fear as the perspiration soaked me. My hands were slippery with sweat, so I had to grab even tighter to keep the big wheel and the giant car going in the right direction.

Blinding headlights tore at my eyes as trucks and cars passed me, their horns blaring. Mama was directing me, telling me to push down on the gas pedal, slow down with the brake, but soon her directions grew fainter, until finally she dozed off. I drove on, watching the darkness and the flashing white line as if that line would take me straight to our destination.

After a while, my shoulders began to shake and my hands started to tingle from the grip I had on the wheel. It seemed that I had been driving for hours. All I saw was black and white, black and white. The black of the darkness, the white ribbon of the guiding line. I felt I was in an unending nightmare and I couldn't wake up. My shoulders and neck ached so badly from all the tension they contained, but the only thing I could do was keep going.

Then, in the gray distance of the Buick's headlights, I saw a bridge. I gasped. I hated bridges. There was a floating bridge at home, and everyone knew that people could fall through its hole and drown. This bridge didn't seem to have a hole in it, but it was more than I could handle, and I started to cry.

"Don't be such a baby," Mama ordered, roused from her sleep. But I couldn't stop, the tears started to pour from me.

"Keep going!" she ordered, so I did, certain that we'd be killed. The gray girders surrounded me, and I drove as if paralyzed until eventually they flashed by. I'd gone over the bridge.

That horrible night seemed to go on forever as I drove on with my eyes glued to the white line. My stomach rolled with nausea, and I was afraid I'd be sick while driving. What would happen if I threw up while I was driving? The thought tormented me as my stomach churned. I begged my body not to get sick and drove on, every inch holding me in a state of utter terror as I sat, literally, on the edge of my seat, barely able to reach the gas pedal. I drove like that for hours, my body pleading for sleep but my eyes opened wide in terror.

Then, just when I thought I couldn't take another second of it, I found myself in the center of a living hell. The night sky seemed to have been swallowed up in darkness, and the road twisted and turned more and more. We were driving through the mountains. I gripped the wheel even tighter, praying I wouldn't drive us off of a mountain but certain that I would.

After many hours and ever so slowly, the black night turned to a soft gray. As the sky lightened, Mama started to stir.

"It's okay, baby doll," she said, still not rising, "We're out of the mountains. We're getting close to Wenatchee." A few minutes later, she sat up. I could see her eyes! Maybe now she'd take over and drive! Relief washed over me like a cooling breeze. My mama would drive the rest of the way!

But suddenly, there were cars and trucks all around me. I was in city traffic. There were stoplights and parked cars and so much to watch out for, and it had all happened so suddenly. I'd driven straight into a blizzard of color, noise, and fear. I couldn't possibly stop the car so Mama could drive because there were too many cars in the way. I felt as if we were pushed along by the other cars and had no control of the car at all. Panic pounding in my throat, I tried to keep the car in my lane.

"I know the hotel's around here somewhere," Mama mumbled, fumbling for her cigarettes and seeming to be oblivious to my panic. Lighting a cigarette, she added, "There should be a parking lot right around here..."

My head was screaming in fear, and her words seemed so far away and unreal. Why wasn't she helping me? Couldn't she see what was happening? Couldn't she see how terrified I was?

"There, there it is!" she blurted, waving her cigarette like a pointer. "Turn here." I didn't know what to do, the cars were pushing me faster and faster, when suddenly, Zodie's voice turned mad and she screamed, "Right now!"

My arms barely responded. I was a frightened stick figure attached to a steering wheel. Everything slowed down, like a slow-motion film. I watched a lady in the car directly in front of me, her mouth making an "O" from horror as I came racing straight toward her. But of the two of us, I was sure my face looked more frightened than hers.

Somehow, the huge wheel turned, and I got the car onto the side road without hitting the lady. But before I could even congratulate myself for not killing anyone, Zodie grabbed my arm and shouted, "Turn again, *now*!"

But I couldn't see where to turn. All I could see was what was between the dash and the steering wheel. Grabbing at the wheel, Zodie tugged and we spun into an alley. It was away from the traffic, but there was a bunch of construction straight ahead.

"Stop!" she ordered. But I couldn't move. There were too many sensations all at once, and my feet felt nailed to the floor. "Look out!" she screamed.

The car stopped with a crunching sound. I'd hit something, but I couldn't see it. The paralysis melted away, and all I felt was dread. I had failed Mama. She had told me to drive, not to have an accident. Now I was in for it.

I watched a construction man lean on his shovel and laugh. "Hey, you! You've hit my concrete block! Whaddya think you're doing, honey?" He and the other construction men laughed.

I watched as Mama turned to me, her eyes blazing with anger. "How could you be so stupid?" She placed her hand on the dash to steady herself, and I stared at her red polished fingernails as she leaned across the seat to me. "You were doing so well, and now you've gone and wrecked the car! What were you thinking?" Throwing her hands in the air, she said, "What the hell am I going to tell your father?" Glaring, she pushed me and spat, "Just get out! Get out! I have to do everything, goddammit!"

I climbed out and watched as Mama drove the car into the hotel parking lot. The chrome bumper seemed crumpled and growled as the tire rubbed against it. The construction man looked at me, dropped his eyes, and stopped laughing. He began digging. I was invisible.

I stood alone in the alley, wet, nauseous, and trembling. "How could you be so stupid, stupid, stupid," kept pounding in my head. I had tried my best, but it still wasn't good enough. But at least I was alive.

CHAPTER 24

Prize Winner

IT WASN'T LONG BEFORE WE had to move again. This time, we got a house on the north side of the city in a little cul-de-sac right across from Aunt Charlotte, who'd moved out of her trailer and was now living in a nice house. Aunt Charlotte was a big woman, almost as tall as George, with bright, bleached-blond hair that framed her full face in soft curls. She had a missing front tooth and a booming, husky laugh, and she sure laughed a lot.

She laughed even harder as she told me stories of her life as a "carnie." For years, Aunt Charlotte, her husband, and their daughter, Denise, ran carnivals. They had incredible stories that always ended up with me laughing helplessly, grabbing my stomach in fits of hilarity.

Aunt Charlotte was a colorful character. She favored brightly colored stretch pants and colorful tops, which showcased her wide hips. In contrast, my cousin Denise was tall and thin with long dark hair, very square white teeth, and a wide and pretty smile. Denise liked denim and country music. She was a runner, a fast runner, and I wished that I could run like her. If I could, maybe I could run back to West Seattle and live with the Dimocks again, but I knew that was just a silly dream and the best I could hope for was spending time with my aunt and cousin.

I stayed there as often as I could because Aunt Charlotte listened to me tell stories of my life with Zodie and the happy memories I had of living with the Dimock family. Aunt Charlotte didn't say mean things about the Dimocks, the way Zodie and Nana had. Instead, she tried to help however she could. I had the feeling that that was why George moved us there. Charlotte helped us both survive Zodie.

Once when George and Zodie were yelling at each other in Aunt Charlotte's kitchen, Aunt Charlotte grabbed Denise and me and ran outside, dragging us both by the arms. She opened her car door and shoved us quickly inside. "Now don't open the doors for anyone but me," she warned. "I'll try and settle things down." With that, she spun around and ran back into the house.

Denise and I sat in complete silence as we watched the mime show through the living room window, as George and Zodie battled each other like a couple of mud wrestlers. Aunt Charlotte marched right in between them and separated George from Zodie. Then she hid Zodie in the carport's storage closet. George ran all over the house looking for Zodie but settled down when Aunt Charlotte began speaking to him earnestly. He seemed to be calming down when Zodie suddenly climbed out of the storage shed and George saw her. He ran and grabbed Zodie, dragging her into the living room where he beat her head into the floor, again and again and again, right in front of the picture window.

Unable to tear my eyes off the silent violence, I felt Denise's hand on my shoulder, as she reached to make sure the door was locked.

"I didn't know it was that bad," she said.

"Yeah, they do this all the time." I closed my eyes and rested my forehead on the cool glass of the car window. I just couldn't watch anymore. Somehow, Aunt Charlotte got them to stop fighting and finally got us out of the car and gave me a hug.

Aunt Charlotte understood what it was like for me, so she gave me hugs whenever she could. I didn't get hugs from Zodie, so the ones I got from Aunt Charlotte were all the more special. They reminded me of Mrs. Dimock's hugs, but I kept that thought to myself.

I knew I had to reach the Dimocks. I wasn't sure what I would tell them, but I knew I needed their help. So with the help of Aunt Charlotte, I finally got Mr. Dimock on the phone and it was arranged that he would meet me at Aunt Charlotte's house to talk.

I sat on the brown slipcover of Aunt Charlotte's sofa, and for the first time, I noticed that her entire living room was brown. She had a brown rug, brown table, brown TV, and even a huge brown retriever named Sebastian. Only the walls were white. Aunt Charlotte was such a colorful figure that somehow I'd been totally unaware of the drab rooms she lived in. But the darkness of my life had finally caught up to me, and now not even Aunt Charlotte's kaleidoscopic personality could bring color to my world. But where the color had been drained, hope had returned. Mr. Dimock was coming to see me!

My heart fluttered with excitement when the doorbell rang. I hadn't seen any of the Dimocks in ages. I was so excited but also so nervous. I wasn't even sure what it was that I wanted to say. I just knew I needed to see Mr. Dimock, that he might be the only one in the whole wide world who could help me at that moment.

Aunt Charlotte let Mr. Dimock in the front door and then said she had an errand to run and would be back in ten minutes.

He was so tall and thin, but not quite as tall as I'd remembered him. Although I'd become taller, in my mind, it was Mr. Dimock who had become smaller, but not at all less majestic. Here was a man who could help me—and would help me, I just knew it.

Mr. Dimock sat down next to me, gave my shoulders a hug, and then leaned away to take a good look at me. "My, what a long face you have. What's going on?"

"Oh, Mr. Dimock, it's been so bad ever since I came back from Nana's! Mama is sick all the time now!" I hung my head and let the tears fall. Softly, I said, "I feel so alone."

"You are not alone, you know that." His face was so gentle and full of love, I knew in an instant that he was right. I wasn't alone.

"I have to tell you something, Mr. Dimock, and please don't laugh."

"I won't laugh, Mary Zoe " he said, "I promise. What is it?"

Whispering, I told him, "I hear God talk to me. I heard him that night at the youth center when I was little. I've heard him since then, too." I gripped his hand and suddenly panicked—what if Mr. Dimock thought I was crazy? "You have to believe me!" I added. "I'm not crazy! I hear a voice that tells me not to be afraid."

"Do you believe it is God in that voice, Mary Zoe?" His face was serious; he didn't look at me like I was crazy at all.

"Yes."

"Then you hear him." He paused, collecting his thoughts. "Hearing God comfort you, why does it make you so unhappy?"

"I'm not unhappy because I've heard the Voice," I explained. "I'm unhappy because it's been *so long* since I've heard it! I'm sure God has forgotten me. Everyone else has."

Placing his hand atop my clutched hands, he, too, spoke softly, "Do you really believe that God has given up on you, Mary Zoe?"

"Yes, sir."

"But don't you know that God knows everything about you? He knows every hair on your head. He hasn't given up on you at all; I know He has a plan for you."

"But he left me with Mama!" I insisted. "The court took me away from you, and now I'm stuck with Mama!"

"That's true, but I'm certain he has great plans for you. Just don't give up."

And so it went for the entire visit, me protesting that the Voice had abandoned me and wailing that God left me alone with Mama, and Mr. Dimock countering all of my arguments with a vision of hope and healing. I tried to believe. But I just wasn't convinced that God believed in me.

Shortly after Aunt Charlotte returned, Mr. Dimock said he had to leave and gave me a big hug good-bye.

"Don't despair, Mary Zoe," he whispered. "God is watching over you."

Watching Mr. Dimock drive away, I wished I could go with him. Aunt Charlotte stood next to me and silently put her arm around my shoulders.

When I left Aunt Charlotte's house to walk across the street to my house, my mood was as gray as the clouds in the early summer sky. There really wasn't a way out for me. I had to take care of Mama and continue to pray that the Voice would remember me. So I prayed as I walked. I prayed for a new life and courage to face Mama every single day. Believing that the Voice would someday save me was cold comfort, but it was all that I had. I went back to Mama, resigned to be a good girl and keep hoping.

Toward the end of the school year, Denise was busy auditioning for track. She ran like the wind for her coach, and he was so impressed he asked her, "Are there any more like you at home?"

Denise innocently said, "Yes, my cousin."

So at the encouragement of the coach, Denise sought me out. Grabbing me by the arm, she stated, "The coach wants to see you. Hurry up!"

I ran for the coach as fast as I could, but it was no use. I wasn't a runner. I was a reader and writer. I could feel my face burn when he thanked me and turned away. I knew I wasn't good enough. In silence, Denise and I walked home. *That's what happens when a pudge-muffin tries to run*, I thought to myself. I'd put on so much weight since moving back with Zodie that I couldn't even run anymore.

I was in a new school, making new friends, and the last thing I needed was to be known as a loser. If I was going to make my mark with these kids, I realized, I was going to have to use my other skills.

So when the talent show announcement came, I jumped at the chance. Maybe I couldn't run, but I knew I could sing. Even Nana admitted I had talent. I had learned a song at Conservation Camp, "500 Miles," so I decided to sing that song. I practiced every morning as I got ready for school and every night when I did the dishes. The day of the talent show quickly approached, and I was so excited I thought I'd explode. But Mama wasn't interested in going to school to see me perform, so I went all alone.

Walking on stage with all the kids watching me made my stomach do a slow roll toward nausea, but I fought it off and stood alone in front of the microphone. The kids were laughing and jabbing each other, waiting for the chubby new kid to flop. Taking a quick breath and saying a silent prayer, I started to sing as loud and as perfectly as I could. The gym got real quiet, and I finished the whole song without any mistakes. When I finished, there was nothing but silence, so I ran off the stage, mortified. I never even heard the applause.

I was stunned when I was awarded second place and won a big box of Whitman's chocolates. The boy who won first place did a lip sync of Elvis with four of the popular girls as backup. They deserved to win, but I was so proud of my chocolates.

I hurried home to tell Mama what I had done, but she wasn't there. The house was all locked, so I set my chocolates down on the porch and crawled through a back window to get in. Then I hurried around to the front porch to get the box of chocolates before the dogs did. I couldn't wait for Mama to arrive! But she didn't come home for a long time.

I sat in the living room and waited, holding my chocolates in my lap while the room grew dark.

When Mama finally came home, she was too busy dressing for her night out with George to notice me or my chocolates. It was their anniversary. Her hair was styled, and she had glitter in it. She looked glamorous, like she used to look when I was little.

"Mama," I said, finally, "I won a box of chocolates today at school." I held the box up for her to see, so proud of myself. I'd never won anything before, and this wasn't something I won because I was lucky. I won it because I was good at something.

"Oh?" she asked, not looking up. "Why was that?" She spread out her dress and jewelry on the bed and took a step back to admire her ensemble.

"Because I won second place in the talent show!" I blurted out, glowing with pride. "I sang!"

She turned slowly from the bed and looked at me. "That's nice, Mary Zoe, but why didn't you win first place?"

I felt the joy drain out of my body, flowing straight from my heart to the soles of my feet. I wasn't good enough, again. So I took my box of chocolates, went into my room and closed the door. Then I ate the whole box.

CHAPTER 25

Another Move

It wasn't long before George and Zodie had amassed twenty-five dogs, thirteen cats, and one pathetic pigeon and another landlord kicked us out. This time, George decided it was time to own his own home, so he could fence in the animals and not worry about the landlords. Zodie didn't want to move, and I sure didn't want to leave Aunt Charlotte, but the writing was on the wall—we were moving.

George and Zodie found a little house they could afford, and it had the yard and kennel they wanted. It was really small, though, and I couldn't imagine living in such a tiny house with no real escape from George and Zodie and all those animals. What was worse was it was all the way to Lake City, which meant being even further away from anyone I'd ever known. Zodie wasn't too keen on the idea of moving again either, but she tried to rally and just be happy that she finally owned her own home. Once we actually moved in and she started painting the walls, however, her spirits quickly waned and she took to the couch.

"You'll have to finish painting the walls," she said. "I'm just too tired."

"But, Mama," I protested, "I don't know *how* to paint walls."

"Then it's time you learn," she said.

And so I painted all the walls while Zodie sat on the couch drinking and directing and telling me what a sorry job I was doing.

By the time I got to the kitchen, we'd run out of money for paint.

"Just pour the leftover colors together," Zodie said, fixing herself a scotch and water and retreating to watch her soaps.

I dutifully mixed up all the colors and painted the dark-blue kitchen a liver-colored "pink." But at least it was clean—for a while.

I settled into my new school and did my best to endure the tiny house with its menagerie, but it seemed that no matter how hard I tried, I just couldn't get ahead. Changing schools so often had made it hard to keep up and make friends, and the new place was so small and filled with so many animals that coming home was like stepping inside a box of foul-smelling noise. Dogs barked, cats meowed, Zodie yelled, the TV blared, and my stomach growled. Garbage cans overflowed, dishes were piled high in the sink and on the counters, and cat litter boxes steamed with stink. Nothing I could do could get it under control, and nothing I could do could get Zodie under control. I was constantly seeking a moment of peace, but it seemed to constantly elude me.

I was thirteen years old, and the court no longer watched over Zodie and neither did George, leaving her to drink and take pills without limit. At night, she'd wander the house and fall into things, banging her head or splitting a lip. It became a nightly occurrence. George had long since given up trying to pick her up and get her to bed. He just left her where she fell. But I just couldn't leave my mama on the floor, so I tried to help.

It was the vicious swearing that woke me. Zodie had fallen again and was lying in a heap of dirty clothes outside the bathroom. Lifting her to her feet, I walked her toward her bedroom.

"No!" she slapped at me. "I want to go to the couch."

"Okay, Mama." I placed her on the sofa, put a blanket on her, and prayed she'd fall asleep. It was the second time that night she had gotten up and caused trouble.

"Goddammit! Where are my cigarettes?" I handed them to her. "I want coffee too," she added with a nasty snicker.

"But, Mama, that'll keep you awake."

"No, it won't. You do what I tell you, young lady!"

It was 11:00 p.m., and Zodie had kept me waiting on her all evening so I still hadn't gotten my homework done and I had to go to school the next day. But I went into the kitchen and dutifully brewed the coffee while I steamed with anger. My head hurt, and I was *so* tired. How was I ever going to get my homework caught up? I had no idea. Zodie didn't let me have any time for my needs. I had to be at her beck and call constantly. I quietly cried, the big tears rolling down my face while I wiped them away with the sleeve of my nightgown so Zodie wouldn't hear me and start screaming at me for being such a crybaby.

When I finally got my face under control, I brought her a mug of coffee and started to go to my room.

"Don't you leave me!" she demanded. "Stay here and keep me company."

"But, Mama," I said, trying to conceal my anger, "I have to finish my homework."

"You can do that later," she said. "I need you here with me."

So I sat in the dark living room and watched the red tip of Mama's cigarette go bright and dim, dip to the ashtray and then to her mouth, and then the sequence was repeated. Zodie didn't like to be isolated, and ever since we'd moved to Lake City, she'd felt isolated from everyone she knew. She hated the house and George and expected me to compensate for her losses by never leaving her side. I just needed to sleep, but I was bone weary and out of ideas on how to get her to bed. If she'd only sleep, I could get some rest, but instead, she told me to get her another cup of coffee.

"You like this crappy house, don't you?" she said when I returned with her refill. She knocked a couple of cats off her lap and shoved a big dog aside.

"It's okay," I said, knowing that it didn't really matter what I thought about it.

"Well, it's a dump," she said like Bette Davis, so bitter and dramatic. When I didn't reply, she added, "You don't love me anymore, do you?"

"Of course I love you, Mama," I answered automatically.

"No, you don't. You've listened to that Dimock bullshit, and you think you're better than me." She was quiet for a moment and then added, "If you leave me, I'll kill myself. You know I can do it. I have nothing to lose."

While sitting in the dark, memories of fires, of fights, of suicide attempts, of rages, and of being left alone, all flooded into my mind. And now Zodie was adding suicide on top of it all. There would never be an end to the constant fear that life with Zodie brought me. I knew deep in my heart that I would not survive if I stayed with Zodie much longer. I had to escape. I just didn't know how.

As I huddled in the armchair, wrapping my arms around myself to keep warm, I heard the Voice. It spoke quietly.

"Don't worry. She'll fall asleep, and you'll get rest." I startled, jerking my head up, and I looked around the dark room. Mama's cigarette stopped its movement and settled in the ashtray. She had fallen asleep.

"Thank God." I breathed and went to bed.

Zodie was still on the couch when I left for school the next day. I escaped the dank house and faced the new day knowing somehow, some way, I had to do something.

Again the Voice came to me. "Get help!"

It sounded in my head like a man with a megaphone to my ear. I felt it more than I heard it. It stopped me in my tracks, and I just stood and breathed.

Yes, I thought to myself, *I have to get out.* I had to follow the path that Sissy had set. Adjusting my books on my hip, I strode on, straight to Jane Addams Jr. High. The Voice made it clear to me. *When I got there, I had to find someone who could help me.*

I knew the way to get help. When I'd first started at the school, a few months before, the school counselor had said if I ever needed help to come to her. Though I knew she probably said that to every new student, I was now ready to take her up on it. If Gale could get out, so could I.

I entered the counselor's office with the green tile floors, dark desk, and big brown wood chair. I was told to sit down and asked what was on my mind. I dutifully sat down and cried out all the things that had been happening to me. I sat gripping the arms of the chair while occasionally wiping my face with my hands. I cried so hard I gave myself the hiccups, but I got the story out. I had been taking care of Mama, staying up late for fear of fire, for three straight months, and I couldn't take it anymore, I cried. And I told her about Mama and David Walz, about seeing them have sex and not liking it—but I stopped short of telling her about what David Walz had done to me. That wasn't something I wanted to talk about.

When I left the counselor's office, I felt such a lightening of my heart that I didn't even remember I had visited her. The day just felt better, and I felt whole again.

But later that day, I was called out of class and told to go to the counselor's office. When I got there, I saw a police lady. At first, I thought I was in big trouble, but then the counselor smiled at me and wiped her glasses. She had checked out my story and called the authorities.

"Your mother has quite a dossier," the counselor stated. "I wasn't sure your story was true until I read the history of prescription drug abuse and all the family violence."

The police lady turned to me and said, "You don't have to live like this."

I gripped the chair and began to cry in frustration. Suddenly, the reality of what I had done hit me. And it wasn't good.

"You don't understand. If I leave Mama, she'll kill herself! She's tried it before," I cried. "She cuts her wrists!" I hung my head, and the tears fell into my lap.

The police lady knelt by my chair, and brushing the hair out of my face, she asked quietly, "How does your mama cut her wrists?"

I looked into her eyes and saw her concern. "Like this," I said, drawing a line across my own wrist. "I've seen the red meat inside." I shuddered.

The police lady put an arm around my shoulder. "Sweetie, if your mama really wanted to commit suicide, she would slice her wrists lengthwise along the tendons." She pointed to my wrist and ran her finger along the length of my wrist. In that same calm, quiet voice, she continued, "Or she'd cut an artery in her leg."

If she was trying to make me feel better, she wasn't doing a good job. An image of Zodie with her legs slashed opened flew through my mind, but before I could respond, the police lady looked into my eyes and said, "Your Mama isn't trying to kill herself; she's just trying to frighten you to stay." I let that thought settle into my mind when she stood up, smiled, and repeated, "You don't have to live like this."

That was the first time anyone had told me that I didn't need to live the way I was living. The thought that there might be a way out was too shocking to handle. My mind and my heart were spinning as I tried to make sense of it all.

"Come with me," the police lady said. "We'll help you."

I followed her out the door and into the police car.

"Where are we going?" I asked her as the car pulled out of the school parking lot.

"To the youth center," she told me, turning toward me with a smile.

Here we go again, I thought. What had I gotten myself into? I had no idea what was up ahead, but one thing was certain: now Zodie really *was* going to kill me.

CHAPTER 26

The Youth Center

I HAD NO IDEA WHEN the police brought me to the youth center that it would be such a difficult fight. They put me in the primary unit for "protection," though they didn't really explain why I needed to be locked up in order to be protected. I knew Zodie would be furious with me, and I was glad that the bars on the window kept her away. I was terrified of what she'd do to me if she got me alone.

I had heard the court's comforting words before of, "We'll help you," but so far, those assurances were meaningless to me. Although I was thrilled not to have to return to that house, for all the talk of my "protection," I secretly wondered if the court would really protect me any better than they had last time. All I knew was I was in for a battle and I had no guarantee that I would be safe from an angry Zodie, not if they decided to send me home. And they might very well do that if Zodie put on an act again and pretended she was doing her best.

At first, the police lady who brought me to the youth center offered to let me stay with her, but that fell through right away. She took me to a stairway and explained privately to me that she didn't want anything to mess up the case. What if Zodie's lawyer claimed that the police had some special attachment to me and this prejudiced the whole case? They didn't want to take the chance. She apologized to me and told me to adjust to the youth center; it might be a long stay.

The next morning, I was taken to a cold and impersonal room, asked some questions, and informed that I would continue to stay in the primary unit for my own protection. My case was complicated, I was told, and serious, and they wanted to be sure I was safe.

"But why can't I be around the other kids?" I asked. "I hear them and see them going by, but I'm locked away and I haven't even done anything wrong!"

"We know you haven't, Mary Zoe," the director explained, "and I wish we had a better place for you. But those other kids are juvenile delinquents who are being punished for breaking society's rules. They stay in the main unit instead of jail. It wouldn't be fair to you to put you in with them."

So the solution was to lock me in a cell and let the juvenile delinquents walk around. It was during that first meeting that I was introduced to my caseworker, Mrs. Pierce. Mrs. Pierce was a thin woman with a prim smile, and she wore a lot of tweed. The hearing would be later that month, she explained to me, turning back to the adults in the room.

Before I could say much to her, I was excused. On my way back to the primary unit, I was directed to a visitation room. There stood a beefy man who introduced himself as Zodie's lawyer.

When he saw me flinch, he said, "I don't care that your mother hired me, Mary Zoe. I work for you. I want what is best for you. Now tell me the truth. What happened at home?"

I didn't believe that he worked for me, but I told him everything while a lady wrote it all down.

When I was finished, there was absolute quiet, except for the scribbling of pen on paper. The beefy man shifted position in his chair, pulled at his collar, and cleared his throat. During the deposition, I had managed to shred a series of tissues, and the bits were all around my busy fingers. He gently placed his hand on my hands, tissues and all. "You are a very brave little girl. I have a daughter just about your age. I want the best for you, Mary Zoe, just as I do for my own little girl." Before he left, he smiled at me and said, "Don't worry." But I had heard that before. I had reason to worry.

Life in the youth center was rigidly regulated. We lined up for everything. Seniority was what mattered, and I was a newbie, which meant I was the last in line. I received cold looks from the other girls as I took my place at the end of the line. I was wearing the clothes I had worn to school—a skirt and a white blouse; they wore clean but mismatched hand-me-downs.

"Lucky girl!" someone whistled, sarcastically. "Wish we got to wear skirts!"

Then the catcalls began.

I didn't feel lucky as I watched the cooks slap food onto the divided metal trays. As I reached the steam table, I discovered that most of the other girls had gotten the good food, and I got what was left.

I sat alone.

After dinner that first night, the matron took me aside to the wardrobe room and told me to strip for a shower. The wardrobe room smelled sweet. The wood-lined walls were filled with shelves holding assorted pedal pushers and various tops. There was a whole cupboard lined with white panties, undershirts, and socks. It smelled so good to me, it reminded me of the freshly washed clothes and folded socks that Mrs. Dimock would give me.

Abruptly, the matron turned me around and searched my hair. She was looking for bugs, I assumed. Then she stepped away from me with a disgusted look.

"Do you smoke?" she asked.

Alarmed, I answered, "No, ma'am. But both my parents smoke."

She sighed and said that she'd take care of that right away. She took my clothes and stuck in me in a hot shower of needle-sharp spray. She stood watching me as she made me wash my hair twice and scrub myself until I was pink all over. I was handed my towel, my new clothes, and my bed linens, pillow, and blanket.

I spent the next three weeks waiting for my future to be determined, until finally the day of the hearing arrived. I hadn't seen or spoken to Zodie during all that time. Sitting in the witness's seat in the courtroom, I was frozen, afraid to look at Zodie, but there she was, right in front of me at last. Under the fluorescent lights of the juvenile court, her painted mouth looked like a deep red gash. Her face was pointed directly at me, and her eyes were icy cold with rage. A tall sheriff stepped between us, cutting off her blistering stare. He asked me to tell the truth, the whole truth, and he had me swear to it on a Bible. I swore. When he stepped away, Zodie was again in my sight, but she looked away and busied her hands by picking imaginary lint from her wool suit. Then she regained her cool composure.

I answered the lawyers' questions as best as I could, occasionally noticing the barely concealed fury on Zodie's face but doing my best not to look her way. They asked me about food, and fires, and drinking, and pills. And then eventually they asked me about David Walz.

The judge asked me a question, which I didn't hear. I was still frozen in place. Zodie had looked as if she could kill me with her bare hands. Tearing my frightened gaze off of Zodie, I asked, "Could you repeat that, sir?"

The judge then signaled the lawyers to his big desk and after whispered conversation, the lawyers returned to their seats and the judge looked at me through his glasses. His brown eyes were surrounded by caterpillar-white eyebrows, which were drawn in an inverted "V" as he pinned me with his address.

"In order to get a full statement from this minor, it is the court's decision that the remainder of the session will be held in my chambers. Bailiff, please assist the witness to my chambers." Then his eyebrows relaxed, and he smiled at me as the sheriff took me away from the courtroom and Zodie's furious stare. He had brought me there to clarify my testimony away from Zodie's intimidation.

"Tell me, Mary Zoe, how did you know the man in your house was having sexual intercourse with your mother? Do you know what sexual intercourse is?" He paused and fixed me with his stare. I could feel my face flush and my heart pound.

I remembered that night and many others. Pictures flashed behind my eyes—walking in on Zodie and David Walz having raw sex, Grandpa Jerre sliding his hand up Zodie's dresses, Daddy David showing me the clock and the "mouse." I remembered the night he came into my room, the sensation of being suffocated by man stink and my desperation as I looked into his black, soulless eyes. His hand had touched my privates, and my own mother just stood by and watched. She did nothing to protect me. I despised her for that.

I remembered David Walz had said, "You aren't like your mama, you know." Little did he know how true he was. Because of him and men like him, I refused to live her kind of life filled with hate and fear. But I was sufficiently like Zodie to be willing to do whatever it took to achieve my goal.

I wasn't going to tell the judge about Zodie letting David Walz touch me. That was my secret. I knew it was enough that I had seen them having sex. With Zodie's past, that would surely show the court that she couldn't be believed. But I didn't trust the system enough to protect me from her, so I saved the damning information of what David Walz had done to me for an emergency. I'd use it only if I needed it. It was dangerous to cross Zodie, and I wasn't going to take any chances with being tossed back into her care. Zodie wasn't the only one who could plan and use the system.

Like mother, like daughter, I thought. Besides, I was still afraid that she would retaliate for anything I said. It was risky to fight with her.

"Sir," I answered the judge carefully, "I saw them both naked. He was on top of her with his penis between her legs."

There was a pause in his chamber as the judge made a notation. "Yes, well, that clarifies that issue." He cleared his voice. "Thank you very much. You may go back to your primary unit now. You don't have to go back to the courtroom."

I was taken back to the youth center and waited for what seemed like forever until Mrs. Pierce finally came to see me and told me about the judge's decision. I was officially a ward of the court.

"What does that mean?" I asked her.

"It means you'll be placed in permanent foster care," she said without expression. "You'll be living with the Dimock family; I understand you already know them?"

I couldn't believe it! I was going to live with the Dimocks!

"Wh-wh-when? For how long?" I was bubbling over with excitement!

"It will still take some time to get everything finalized," she said, pulling a stray thread from her tweed jacket. Then she looked at me and smiled a thin, abrupt smile. "But until that happens, you'll have weekend visitations with them."

"What did Zodie say?" I was afraid to even think of it.

Mrs. Pierce's smile softened, revealing a trace of actual humor. "She was certainly surprised," she said.

"Surprised?" I asked. "What does that mean? She didn't make a scene, did she?" I had an image of Zodie kicking and screaming and throwing a fit in the courtroom, though I knew in reality she was far too savvy for such antics in public.

"No, she didn't make a scene. But the disbelief was written all over face; that's for sure. I don't think she anticipated it turning out quite like this," Mrs. Pierce concluded.

No, I doubt that she did, I thought. But still, I was worried. Would I be sent back to Zodie's? Would I have to visit her on weekends again? I couldn't bear the thought of going back there ever again. It was bad enough as it was. After I'd said all that in open court, I wasn't just Zodie's daughter; I was Zodie's enemy.

I blurted out my worries to Mrs. Pierce, who assured me that I would not be having any visits with Zodie. She had lost all parental rights. Then Mrs. Pierce gathered her files and stood to leave. "Once everything's taken care of, you'll remain with the Dimocks permanently."

Then she left. Case closed.

I was ecstatic! I had finally proved to the court that Zodie couldn't take care of me. I had proved that she was not a good mother. Without a doubt, Zodie had lost. She had to sign the papers that would relinquish me to the Dimocks for good.

Another one of the girls in protection, Val, met me at the door as I entered the dayroom. Tiptoeing through the maze of bodies playing jacks, I finally collapsed on the beat-up sofa.

"All over?" asked Val.

"Yeah, all over." I sighed.

"How was it? I mean, was she mad when you testified?"

I gave a weak laugh. "You might say that." I closed my eyes, rested my head on the couch, and let the image of the courtroom fill my mind.

Interrupting my thoughts, Val asked, "Do you think you'll have to see your mom again?"

"God, I hope not." I shuddered. "My caseworker and the judge said they would make sure Mama wouldn't see me. I'm glad. You should have seen her face when I--"

The phone rang. My heart stopped, Val paled, and a deadly silence descended on the girls in the primary unit. It always happened that way. Phones ringing in the youth center always meant bad news.

"Mary Zoe Carmichael!" barked the supervisor in her mesh cage. "You're wanted in admissions!" I jerked in reaction. I still wasn't used to my legal name, Carmichael. I had always assumed the name of my current stepfather, which for years had been George Victor. I didn't even realize that Victor wasn't my legal name until I got to the youth center and they told me I had to use my "real" name. My real name was so unreal to me that I had to practice spelling it.

The room tilted at a crazy angle as I stood. My voice sounded weak and far away. All I could hear was the pounding of my own heart. "But I'm not supposed to see anybody," I protested. "My caseworker said I didn't have to see anyone."

"I haven't heard a thing from your caseworker," she snapped. "All I know is you're wanted in Admissions. Get going, Carmichael." She unlocked the door, turned to me, and smiled. "Good luck."

"Yeah, right," I mumbled to her as she locked the door behind me. "I'm so lucky."

The steam and detergent from the lunchroom at the end of the hall burned my throat and stung my eyes as I pushed the button of Admittance. An electric buzz jangled my nerves, and I watched the heavy metal door sway open. The harsh light coldly illuminated the visitation room where I sat. The chairs were cracked with the dirty white stuffing oozing out from the dull plastic. The salmon-pink plaster was chipped away, exposing its raw white underside. The room smelled of dirt, sweat, and cleaning solvents. *So unlike the judge's chambers,* I thought to myself, where the chairs were smooth leather and the walls were warm brown and lined with countless books.

Worrying and speculating ate up the wait. *Maybe the Dimocks had been in the courtroom and wanted to see me. Or maybe the nice policewoman had come back. Or maybe it's Gale! No, not Gale,* I sadly realized. *She has her own life. She left a long time ago. She has her husband to take care of.* I sighed. *Maybe it's Daddy George?* A shiver of dread passed over me, as I wondered if my testimony had made him crazy with rage. I didn't want to face him if he was angry, murderously angry. The thought of what George would do to Zodie if he learned about David Walz was something I hadn't even considered when I testified about it. I almost felt sorry for Zodie. Almost.

The sharp click of the key in the lock shattered the silence of the room as Zodie stalked into the room, her heels making staccato bursts on the tiles. I felt the air get sucked out of the room, as if it had been vacuumed away.

Then Gale rushed in behind her. *Thank goodness,* I thought. *I'll be safe with Gale here.*

Zodie waited until the door was closed before she started her onslaught.

"Now are you satisfied?" she hissed.

I cringed.

"Look at what you've done to me!" Her fury was like a slap in the face. Suddenly, I felt the room close in on me and my racing heartbeat pounded in my head. My frightened gaze turned to Gale, who was hanging back against the door. Silently, I pleaded to Gale for help, but Zodie's enraged voice brought me around and I turned to face her. "This is the way you repay me," she shrieked. "You stupid bitch!" The force of her rage should have blistered the walls.

"I'm not stupid," I cried to myself. "I'm not." But I was too scared to say it out loud.

"You'll be sorry that you did this to me!" Zodie warned. She waited for her threat to sink in. Then she announced, "I won't sign the papers. You'll be stuck here. And you're going to find out that home was a hell of a lot better than this place!"

"You have to sign the papers!" I blurted back. "The court said!"

"The court said you can't come home. But they need me to sign the papers if you want to go live with the Dimocks. And if I don't sign them, well, you can just stay here as far as I'm concerned."

My stomach lurched, and I jumped up, tipping my chair, which fell to the floor with a clatter. Frightened, I blurted, "But I don't want to stay here!"

"Tough," she said. "I hope you rot in this Goddamn place. You deserve it."

No! I thought. *No, no, no!* But my own thoughts were drowned out by Zodie's screams. She had made her triumphant declaration that she was going to let me live in a jail cell, and still, she was screaming at me. *How can I think when she's shouting at me?* I buried my head in my hands, covering my ears so I wouldn't hear her mean words, but still they penetrated my thoughts.

"You can't do this to me!" I heard her saying, her voice climbing to a scream. "I'm your *mother*!"

"Leave her alone!" Gale shouted. "Leave her alone!" Her voice shattered Zodie's screams, and we both looked to her. Then she stepped forward, almost standing between me and Zodie, her face turned toward our mama. "Mary Zoe tried a hell of a lot harder to help you than I ever did. She stayed with you. I didn't."

I stared at her in amazement and thought, *This angry woman is my sister Gale?* She had always tried to protect me, but she never crossed Mama directly. Never in all the years I knew her did she get in Zodie's face, especially when Zodie was in full rant.

Gale focused her flashing hazel eyes at Zodie. "At least she had the courage to tell you to go to hell!" Her voice trembled, and Zodie remained dumbstruck. "You don't deserve children," Gale told her. "Thank God they were all taken from you. You poison people. Just let us be!" Then she burst into tears and dropped her face into her hands as she broke down and cried.

The room fogged as my eyes filled. Gale was very brave. I had no idea she had it in her to stand up to Mama like that. Then the sharp intake of Mama's breath drew my attention, and I looked back at her.

"Go to hell!" She spit viciously. Grabbing her purse, she paused at the door. "Go to hell, both of you!" Flinging the door so that it crashed on the wall, she stormed out of the room. I could hear the crack of her steps fade down the hall. Then Gale faced me. She looked different. There was a sad defiance in her that I had never seen before.

"I'll come and visit you here. And when you're settled in your new home, maybe we can spend time together. Like regular sisters."

Taking a deep breath, I realized how much I loved Gale and how much I owed her. "Thanks, I'd like that," I answered and smiled.

I missed my Sissy. And now that I was free from Zodie, maybe I'd get my sister back.

CHAPTER 27

The Blue Light

THE BLUE LIGHT IN THE ceiling of the isolation ward of the Seattle Youth Center had been my constant and only companion for a month. It cast an eerie light across the room during the night and looked blue and cold during the day. I learned to embrace the light, rather than let it scare me. Like a ghostly but benevolent presence, the blue light calmed me night after night, as I wondered how long I'd be there.

Zodie had held true to her word and refused to sign the relinquishment papers so that I could begin an independent life as a foster child of the Dimock family. For weeks, I lived like a prisoner, unable to see the Dimocks, unable to leave.

Day after day and meal after meal, I got to know the girls who waited in line around me. I learned that when the phone rang, everyone froze. The matron would call out a name, and another girl would disappear from the seniority line, sent back to her home or the foster system, for better or worse. And with each departing girl, there was another new arrival.

I quickly worked my way up the line until I met a pair of sisters who believed they would never leave. Their father had sexually abused them, and their mother didn't believe them. After they told their mother what their father had done, she didn't want them anymore, so the sisters stayed in the youth center. By that time, I had been there so long I was third in seniority, which gave me better jobs, a choice of seating in the dayroom, and better food choices in the mess hall. The girl standing next to me was my friend, Val. We were soon third and fourth in the line and stayed there for a long time.

We got better jobs. I got to run the floor polisher; it was so big and vibrated so strongly that it could bounce me around the walls of our main hallway. But I got good at it and the floor shone brightly when I was done. At least I didn't have to clean the bathrooms; that was miserable work. Val mopped, and I polished the floor; we made a good team. I liked her. She wasn't getting out anytime soon either. We learned to make our beds using the top sheet as the bottom sheet and each Saturday, we were given a fresh sheet and pillowcase. Our dorms were inspected, but my bed always passed muster because I knew how to make a bed, even with hospital corners. Mrs. Dimock had taught me. I rarely got demerits.

School was very lax. It was one room, filled with primary-unit girls in different grades. It seemed to me to be impossible for the teacher to address all the different learning levels, but he did try. He was a kind and gentle young man who pretty much just read to us. I don't remember learning much at all.

One afternoon as we left mess, someone spoke out of turn and the unit was put into a "sit down" in the dayroom with no talking. I sat by a girl, and she pushed me away, whispering that spot was "saved" for someone else. I promptly got up to seek another seat.

"Carmichael!" the matron yelled. "What are you doing? You are to be in sit-down!"

My face flushed. I was one of the "good girls." I didn't get yelled at by the matron.

"But I sat in a seat that was saved for someone else," I told her. "I had to move." The explanation sounded lame even to my ears.

"Sit down, Carmichael. There will be no seat saving in this unit. Is that understood?"

"Yes, ma'am!" We all sang out in chorus.

I found a seat by Val. She patted my hand and whispered, "You can always sit by me." So I did.

Eventually, Mrs. Pierce arranged weekend passes for me to visit with the Dimocks. I got to leave before dinner on Friday, and I had to be back on Sunday before 6:00 p.m. During those precious hours, I was free—free to go to movies with Marti (as Martha by then preferred to be called), go to football games, listen to the radio, go window-shopping, and get my hair curled with rollers. Marti was very good at that. She'd roll my long hair up in her rollers, and when they unrolled, it was like warm honey. I lived for those times.

But by 6:00 p.m., I was back in my cell, as if I were a prisoner on weekend furlough.

One night, I woke up and my throat was on fire. There was a lump in my throat I couldn't swallow away. I climbed out of my cot and yelled through the metal mesh for the matron. "Med call! Dorm 4!"

The matron took me to the infirmary where the doctor looked me over. "No fever," he reported. "Your throat is a little red but not too bad."

I explained that I was to have a weekend pass the next afternoon. He understood. "It doesn't seem too bad," he said. "I think you can keep your weekend pass."

But all day my throat hurt. The matron made me eat the grapefruit pieces in the fruit salad at lunch even though I told her it hurt. "Do you want that pass?" she asked. I did. So I ate the grapefruit. And it hurt. I hung my head to hide the pain in my face since my long hair hid the fact I was crying. I didn't need any demerits to take away my weekend pass.

Finally, Mr. Dimock came to pick me up. I was quiet, so he asked me what was the matter. I told him I had a sore throat.

"Well, Mrs. Dimock can take care of that when we get home," he said, his warm smile warming my heart as he took my weekend bag and escorted me out the doors of the youth center. But by the time I got to their home, I hurt all over and asked if I could take a nap before dinner. I must have slept right through it because Mom came to wake me and discovered I had a fever—a high fever.

They took me across town to Group Health Hospital that night, and I was diagnosed with strep throat and given some medication to take. I felt absolutely miserable, but the best thing was that I got to eat lots of ice cream. The weekend sped along, and by Sunday night, I had to return to the youth center. Regulations wouldn't let me stay with the Dimocks, so when I was brought back and they saw how sick I was, I was taken directly to the infirmary rather than to my regular ward and put in isolation, since I could be contagious.

Back in isolation, I was once again alone with the blue ceiling light. I only saw the nurses when they brought iced apple juice and medications or ice water and soft food. The doctor rarely came.

After my sore throat healed, however, I discovered that they had given away my bed in Dorm 4 because the center was overcrowded. There was no more room for me. I would have to remain in the infirmary, in isolation, even though I was well.

I was so alone. I wasn't even allowed to go to the dayroom anymore, because they said they were at "maximum capacity." It was as if I had to be hidden from view, in case someone came by to count us.

As the days progressed, I watched the patterns on the white walls change position and imagined stories in the shadows on the walls. There wasn't a clear window, just glass blocks that let light in. So I watched the patterns on the walls during the days, listened to the radio, and read magazines, the same magazines over and over, wondering if anyone remembered me, wondering what was going on outside the glass. Days passed, then weeks, and then over a month had passed.

I think I was beginning to experience what prisoners go through in solitary confinement: despair, distortions of time, abandonment. Maybe Zodie was right—even though I was protected from her, this *was* worse than home. There was no one to talk to. My meals were delivered wordlessly or with a few harsh commands not to make a mess. Then I was alone again. As I lay in the white hospital bed, tears rolled down my cheeks and into my ears, wetting the pillowcase. I wanted out. The youth center was keeping Zodie away from me, but it was time to get out. I was tired of being alone.

And then it happened. I heard the Voice again. Very simply, it said, "Get help. Now."

My heart thudded, and I could feel the sting in my throat. I hadn't heard the Voice in so long. I was so relieved, so grateful I was no longer alone. I remembered the last time I had heard the Voice. It had been after a period of isolation and despair, those never-ending nights staying up to watch slack-eyed Zodie with her burning cigarette, too tired to concentrate on school. But I was different now. I refused to be a victim. I could take action. I had done so before, and I could do so again. Even though I didn't know how or when, I knew then and there that I'd get help.

It wasn't long before the opportunity arose. Mrs. Pierce came to visit me. She stood leaning on the other bed, explaining that the medical personnel wouldn't let her visit me when I was sick, and then she became so busy. She was sorry I had been alone so long. She admitted that she was frustrated that it was taking so very long to have the final paperwork completed.

"I don't know what to do," she admitted.

I did.

I would tell my secret. If there was ever a time, this was it. My strategy had to work. So I told Mrs. Pierce all about that horrible night when my mother stood by the bed drinking and swaying back and forth while she let a man fondle me. Mrs. Pierce never interrupted and never said a word. She just kept writing in her book. When I finished, she raised her head, looked at me, and asked, "Was there any penetration?"

I was shocked. My mind reeled. I'd never thought of such a thing, but to hear her say it like that, it dawned on me—it could have been much worse. "No," I answered. "He stopped just short of that."

Then something else hit me—what if it didn't matter that he touched me? What if all that mattered was that he didn't *penetrate* me? I felt sick and so scared and confused. Just talking about it made me feel even sicker.

"But Mama let him do it!" I protested. "She stood there and watched! She never stopped him!" Anger curled my hands into fists as I added, "If my stepfather, George, hears about this, he'll kill her for it!"

Mrs. Pierce closed her book and stepped closer to me. She took my fist in her hands and smoothed it out, as if it were a crumpled piece of paper she was trying to preserve.

"I think we have what we need now to encourage your mother to sign those papers and get you out of here. I will speak to her myself." I looked into the drooping brown eyes of that tidy little lady in her tweed suit and sensible shoes and saw an angel looking back. Her smile told me all I needed to know. She'd heard me. And she believed me.

That night, I gazed at the calming blue light a long time. I knew what I'd done. I'd just blackmailed my own mother so I could have a life. Zodie was afraid of George. He was a violent man, there was no doubt about that, but he had tried to be a good father to me. I knew he felt a father's bond for me and that he had tried to protect me as best as he could. I knew he was an imperfect man who loved me. I also knew he suspected Zodie had continued to see her ex-husband and that grated on his soul. He hated David Walz almost as much as I did.

Over the years, as we got to know each other more, I had come to respect my stepfather. George was a good man with an out-of-control rage bottled up inside him. I never knew what made him so mad, but it did wear on his soul. For all his faults, he had tried to be a good father to me. I loved him for it, and he loved me. Banking on that love, I had just gambled my entire future on his rage level. I was betting short. Between his hatred for Zodie's ex and his loyalty to me, his rage would be unpredictable. The chance of his rage going beyond his own limits was a real possibility. He could kill Zodie. She wouldn't risk it. She would have to let me go.

A day later, I was released from isolation and allowed back in my seniority position in the Primary Unit. Val was still there, as were the sisters who'd been abused. I was there only a few minutes when the matron called, "Carmichael, your caseworker is here to see you."

This time, I wasn't surprised and I wasn't scared. I knew I had finally done something to put me in control of my own life.

I had told the truth in court, but finally, away from the court and the burning gaze of Zodie, I had told the whole truth. And I knew that truth would set me free.

I stepped into the shiny hallway. Mrs. Pierce smiled at me and spread her arms like great eagle wings. "We've done it!" she sang. I rushed into her embrace. "We've done it!" she said again, with a giant squeeze. We held each other for just a moment longer than necessary because saying thank you was so very hard. But finally, Mrs. Pierce gathered her resolve and held me out at arm's length. Smiling broadly, she added, "Zodie signed the papers! You can get out of here!"

I was overwhelmed. I was so grateful to this funny little woman I barely knew—who had believed me. I didn't know if I should hug her again, cry, or kiss her. I stood rooted to the spot, unable to move.

"Go on now," she gently pushed me away. "Get ready to be picked up by your new family."

"Now?" I asked.

"Now," she said and went to inform the matron.

I stepped into to the dayroom; Val had been listening, as well as the sisters. We had a group hug and shared our tears.

"Get outta here!" Val shouted with joy. We started singing, "We Gotta Get Out of This Place!" hopping up and down, yelling at the top of our lungs.

The matron came to me with a brown paper bag, containing all my belongings from the first day. "Good luck, Carmichael!" She smiled. "Don't you dare come back."

"I won't; I promise."

I walked along the main hall with Mrs. Pierce. As the barred doors unlocked, I turned to her, clutching my few belongings. Nothing came to my mind that was adequate to the situation. I paused and looked into her eyes and said, "Thanks for believing in me."

She smiled and waved to someone behind me. I turned and stepped into the sunshine. There were Mr. Dimock and Marti, waiting to take me home.

CHAPTER 28

The Walk Home

THE SUNLIGHT WAS SO BRIGHT it made me blink rapidly to clear my watering eyes. I had to watch the street signs to make sure I was on the correct street on my way home from my first day at school. My new school, my new life. The trees were crystal clear against a background of ice-blue sky. It was a little cold, being November, but where the sun was shining, it was warm. As I walked home, I thought about my day.

That morning, I had sat in the front seat of the car, my hands clutching the piece of paper where Mom had written my new address and phone number. Mr. Dimock was driving me to my new school, James Madison Junior High, and I was going to enroll for my first day of seventh grade. I had resolved to put all the anxiety regarding school in the very same place I banished all thoughts of Zodie—out of my conscious mind and into a very deep, dark hole. Things were going to be so much better for me now that I was free. I was sure of it.

Mr. Dimock was pointing out the streets I would walk past to and from school. I needed to remember them, since I was going to walk home alone after school. As the car was being parked, I had a good look at my new school. It looked serious, old-fashioned, and formidable, not sleek and modern like my last school, Jane Addams. This one was red brick with blank, staring windows.

When we opened the main doors, a wall of noise hit us. In front of me, there appeared to be a mad calliope of tall and short kids circling around the main hall, clumping in groups, running and shouting at other kids in the whirl, forming a chaotic color wheel of life. Suddenly, a loud bell sounded and the calliope began to break up. Kids clutching books headed down the halls, laughing with their friends as they entered the classrooms aligned down the hall.

Mr. Dimock and I stood there for a moment, stunned by the sudden silence; he put his arm around me. "It will be okay. You'll do fine." Then he propelled me toward the principal's office. Once I was inside, a woman I assumed was a secretary assigned me a seat and gave me a clipboard and a pen and told me to fill out the forms in order to sign up for school.

Mr. Dimock smiled at me when he handed me my brown bag lunch. "See you later, Mary. I know you'll be fine." Then he left. I watched as the door swung shut. I was left alone with the efficient woman and the clipboard.

I filled out the papers. I had to remember my new last name, Carmichael. C-a-r-m-i-c-h-a-e-l. I had practiced spelling it in the youth center. I had decided the night that I was finally freed from the youth center that I was going to change my name. My name would never again be Mary Zoe Victor. I had nothing against George, but Victor was Zodie's name, not mine. My new name would be Mary Z. Carmichael, the name I was born with. I would have a new name, my true name, for a new—and true—life of my own.

So as I filled out the paperwork, I had to keep referring to the note Mom had given me that had my new name, my new address, and my new phone number. By the time I finished the clipboard paperwork, the note in my hand was a sweaty wad. But I must have done it right because the efficient woman smiled at me. As she took the papers back to her desk, she tossed over her shoulder, "Someone will be along in a moment to take you to homeroom and help you find your locker. And I'll give you a list of your classes."

I waited. It seemed like a long wait, but after months at the youth center, I had grown accustomed to waiting. Finally, an older woman paused before me, checking her paperwork. "Mary Carmichael?"

I nodded.

"Come with me, dear." She sailed by me, pushing open the door to the main hall. I trailed in her wake clutching my lunch bag, but I was so excited I could have danced! I had just laid claim to my new life, a life free and clear of Zodie and her name.

The details of that morning were a fog to me: getting my locker and its combination, getting my class list and books, and finally being led to my homeroom. As the door opened, I felt heat rush to my face. I was the new kid in class. Again. I felt my newfound confidence crumble as a wave of fright rose from my stomach. It had happened to me so many times before. I should have been used to being the new kid. By the time I'd finished sixth grade, I'd already gone to nine or more schools. But no matter how many times I started at a new school, I could never get used to it.

I felt my throat tighten as all the faces turned to the door. The woman who'd escorted me introduced me to my homeroom teacher, and I did my best to be polite. But all I could see were the faces of the kids in the class staring back at me in various poses. Some open-mouthed, some in the process of passing notes, and some with cold calculation in their eyes, but it was always the same. They were sizing me up, looking me up and down to decide how I would be treated. My clothes were secondhand, but they didn't know that, so I lifted my chin a little higher. Walking to my seat, I tried to smile, but my mouth was completely dry. As I passed one of the kids, he looked vaguely familiar, but I thought nothing of it. Sitting down between two girls, I nodded a shy hello. Another one looked familiar, the girl sitting to my right, but I knew I didn't know her.

A bell rang, and everyone leaped to their feet and rushed to the door, clutching books and yelling greetings to other kids in the hall. I was jostled in the crowd, trying to read my schedule of classes. I had no idea where my next class was and only had five minutes to find it; I knew I was going to be late. My stomach was in knots, and I started chewing my lip until I tasted blood. I couldn't bear the thought of entering class late, all eyes on me again.

Despite my nerves and a chewed lip, however, I somehow found all my classes. I even managed to open my locker, all the while feeling sweat trickling down my back.

I was so nervous, so out of place. I longed for the familiar youth center school. I leaned into my locker and laughed aloud. I found it very funny that I would look back fondly at the youth center, after I had tried so hard to get out! But the morning had been tough and the day had been anything but lax. The only restful moment in the chaotic day was lunch. I sat down to a table and opened my brown paper bag. Inside, right next to my sandwich and apple, was a note from Mom. "We know you can do this, Mary. Be brave." She'd remembered! She'd remembered how special her notes had been to me. Her note gave me courage, but it was secret courage. I was still so embarrassed to be the new girl that I ate the remainder of my lunch with my head bent down so my hair hid my face from the staring kids.

As I walked home after that first day of school, I thought about the kids in my classes who looked familiar to me. There was the girl who said, "Hi," as I passed in the hall; I didn't know her at all, but she, too, had a familiar face. There was the boy in math class who snickered with his pals, glancing up at me as if he knew me. Looking back at him, I felt as if I knew him, too, but I didn't.

Still, I couldn't escape the nagging thought that I had seen them before. Puzzling it over, the shock came as a cosmic slap in the face. They were kids I knew at Alki Elementary School when I first came to live with the Dimock family. *They knew me!* They were the kids who'd ignored me or bullied me, who picked on me for dressing in shabby clothes, for being too skinny, for being too shy—for being held back.

My heart sank. I wasn't going to have a completely free new life after all. As I walked along in the bright sunshine, I remembered how it had been for me at Alki Elementary with those kids. They'd bullied me then, and they would bully me now.

What in the world had I gotten myself into?

Kicking some red and gold leaves along Hinds Street, heading for home, I remembered the games I had orchestrated with Martha before I was sent back a grade. The first summer I lived with them, I created a game named, "EE and AA." I would set up tables and chairs like a classroom and give Martha her instructions to pretend she was a kid in the class who made fun of me, calling me "EE," the failure. The taunting would continue, until I gave her the sign to become my fairy godmother. Then Martha would don a gauzy purple sari around her and magically turn me into "AA" who was smart. "AA" could understand all the classwork and even teach other kids in the class. Martha's role was to act impressed with my newfound intelligence, and that gave me more confidence as I transformed from EE to AA. We played that game over and over all summer, and by the time the new school year came around, I no longer felt like EE; I felt like AA all the way.

My musings vanished from my mind like smoke when I walked to the crest of Hinds Street and Belvidere. As I reached the corner, my breath caught in my throat. In front of me in crystalline detail was Seattle's Harbor Island. Harbor Island is a container port where all the ships unload their cargo to be shipped off by rail or road. Looking across the Puget Sound, I could see every crane, boat, and car on Harbor Island. The trees on either side of the road were outlined against the bright blue sky with remarkable clarity.

It had been a very long time since I had been outside to look at the sky; the bars of the youth center and the white infirmary walls had defined my world for months.

Now as I gazed at the brilliant colors of the neighborhood, the trees began to blur as my eyes grew wet with tears and a wave of gratitude filled me. I was out of the youth center, and I had another chance at life. I could see beyond my own small world if I only opened my eyes. I stood there staring at Harbor Island, imagining all the many worlds that crossed paths on that one small island, all the comings and goings of a million different lives as ships from every nation on earth sailed into its harbor.

In my little life's carousel, I thought I had just grabbed the brass ring. This was my chance. I could be better than Zodie ever thought I could be. I could be anything, go anywhere, and meet anyone. All I had to do was work hard. And that was what I would do.

Determinedly, I entered the front door of my new home, greeting Mr. Dimock and Marti, who had just got in from high school. Mom was running errands, but she'd cleaned the house and prepared some snacks for us. There'd be no more coming home to hunger and filth. This was my home now, my real, permanent home.

After putting my things away, I chatted briefly about my first day, but still, something was gnawing at the back of my mind. Yes, the day had gone smoothly; no, there hadn't been any problems. But I couldn't shake the realization that some of those kids were the kids who'd teased me for being held back. But I shook those thoughts out of my head and resolved with all my heart that no one was going to call me stupid ever again—not the bullies, not Zodie, not anyone. Smiling at Dad and Marti, I headed straight back to my room to begin my homework. I had my chance, and I was going to grab it with both hands.

But little did I realize that along with my battered brown paper bag full of my old clothes, I had brought with me an invisible suitcase crammed with the demons left in me by Nana, Grandfather Jerre, Zodie, and David Walz. I had done a "geographic" as they say in AA. Just like Zodie would do when she moved from house to house in hopes of escaping herself, I had changed the externals of my life, thinking it would automatically change my inner landscape. I had a different kind of homework ahead, I realized, if I was going to do more than just survive. I didn't want to just survive; now that I was free of Zodie, I was going to thrive.

The only problem was, I had no idea where to begin.

CHAPTER 29
Sisters

AS I SETTLED INTO MY new life with the Dimocks, Marti turned from a friend into a sister. I was delighted to have a big sister again, and she was delighted to have something other than brothers. Though there were times she didn't want to be seen with her "little sister," we mostly got along well. We grew even closer as we shared clothes, TV shows, popcorn, swimming, making cookies, sewing, dieting, hairstyling, and astonishing memories.

But it was the time we spent curled up in our pajamas talking that built our sisterhood. Marti would come in from a date while I was still awake in bed, and we would talk about everything. I peppered her with questions late into the night, and she shared her deepest secrets with me. We were fast becoming sisters in every sense of the word.

People even used to stop us and remark that we must be sisters when they saw us. We would snicker in secret knowledge. I was Snow White, and she was Rose Red. I was fair, and she dark. How could they think we were related? Yet these strangers saw into us; we were sisters of the soul, if not of the blood.

It was my relationship with my biological sister, Sissy, however, that gnawed away at my heart. Our paths had diverged instead of converged. We had been split up and farmed out to friends and relatives so many times that throughout our lives we'd had precious little time together. We only really lived together for about two years when I was six to eight years old. The rest of the time either she was living somewhere else or I was.

In that first year when I had returned to live with the Dimocks, I was fourteen and Gale was twenty-three, married and with a baby girl. It was a Sunday afternoon, and Gale had come by to visit; we were chatting in Dad's study as the pattering rain on the window grew louder and louder. I got up to adjust the gold drapes. They were heavy and kept the draft at a minimum and lent a warm glow to the room, which kissed Gale's face. *She was always the pretty one,* I thought as I looked at her. She had pixie good looks. I so envied her.

Returning to my seat, I glanced at the side table and realized I had shredded another tissue. I couldn't ever seem to visit Gale without having a hankie to shred. I was up to several tissues. The litter was in very neat piles, and that was a bad sign. It was a signal to me that I was upset. My nervous habit of tearing paper napkins had gotten so bad that at dinnertime, Mom used to give me at least five, so I could finish my meal. But standing there, next to Gale and staring down at the confetti I'd created, I knew I had to deal with it. The words were out of my mouth before I even knew them myself.

"Why don't you love me?" I blurted out, surprising myself and wishing I could stuff the words back into my mouth. But it was too late. The only thing to do was follow through. I had to know if I had done something to make my Sissy mad, since it was the only reason I could think of to explain her years of aloofness and why she had stayed away from me for so long. "Did I do something wrong?"

I watched the impact of my words smash into my sister as her cheerful face fell apart. In its place, I saw sorrow. Our life with Zodie was such a palpable wound that acknowledging it even obliquely was like poking at a bruise. Being together again brought it all back to us. When apart, we could conveniently forget what it was like living with our mother. But when we were together, we remembered it all with a flash. It was like roller-skating through a swamp: no matter how fast the skater, some of the slime sticks. Although we did our best to push the past out of our minds, our bodies remembered the pain, so inevitably our visits were punctuated with migraines and colds. One or both of us was always sick whenever we were together.

It had become harder and harder for me to find the old Gale. This beautiful woman with the sad eyes and the perky brittle exterior I was talking to was not the Sissy I knew before. She was a grown woman, a woman who'd learned to hold herself back from love and from those who knew her secret pain.

She sighed. Her eyes remained squeezed shut. The silence hung there between us. "I loved you so much when I left," she whispered. "It killed me that the court wouldn't remove you from Zodie. It killed me." I watched a tear gather on her lower lashes. "You were like my first child."

I sat mute. Astonished. All this time, I'd assumed she'd felt nothing when the truth was, she was in such anguish. I could tell by the pain in her face and body that this was the true Gale I was seeing, not the polite china-doll face she wore in public. At that moment, I saw my Sissy completely, through both her pain and her strength. It was so hard to watch, but I couldn't break my eyes away.

A little voice inside me whispered gratefully, *See, it wasn't your fault!* Surprised, a surge of relief filled me. My Sissy did love me! Then as her tears fell, I realized that Gale didn't know how I felt about *her*. Gale had showed me the way out by leaving when Zodie's world became too crazy. It was her greatest gift to me, besides faith (well, to be honest, I never got so far as to let dinner get cold reading Scripture!). Even though I had always thought that Gale was a beacon of light, it had taken a year after my escape from Zodie to really appreciate my sister's courage in leaving when she did. She was my inspiration in leaving, and yet she didn't even know it.

"Don't ever feel bad, Gale," I told her. "I owe you my life for showing me how to escape."

"But how can you forgive me?" she asked, her hazel eyes wet.

"No forgiveness is needed. I love you." Impulsively, I hugged her because she looked so confused and sorrowful. Awkwardly, she hugged me back.

As she prepared to leave, the equilibrium of our relationship settled and the banter of our chitchat resumed. She seemed content with my answer, but I wasn't sure she believed me, not totally. Although the anguish between us had lessened, we would never be free of it.

About a week later, Gale showed up with her little girl and a package. She winked at me and said she had a surprise. Leaving the toddler to inspect Dad in the big green chair in the living room, we walked into my bedroom and sat on my bed. She poked into a paper bag, brought out her pink toe shoes, and laid them gently in my hands. "Sweetie, I don't have any gift to give you to make up for the time we lost as sisters. All I can offer is this token, to represent my love for you even with all those years apart. Please accept them and remember I always loved you."

Inwardly, I gasped. They were her beautiful faded toe shoes, Gale's precious ballerina shoes. Ballet was such a heavenly beauty to Gale. It was something clean and pure in a life so dirty and damaged. The toe shoes were what Gale had aspired to in life. It was the best part of her life and the joy it gave her was infectious. She was giving me her artistic best. She had no need for it now. She was on a different track. By giving me the treasured toe shoes, Gale was passing the hope onto me. As a token of love, it couldn't be beat. We both understood.

And from that moment on, we worked to become sisters again.

I finally had a life that normal people had. I had two sisters, and it was amazing to get to know them both. It was such a gift. It was intoxicating to be loved by the people I loved.

CHAPTER 30

Boys and Men

THE DOCTOR LEFT THE EXAM room, and I was alone on the exam table. I had just finished my eighth-grade year, and I was exhausted. There was nothing he could do for my sore throat, he told me. I had another virus. I had to wait it out. Irritated, I ran my hand across my runny nose because I had forgotten my handkerchief, again. If there was nothing he could do for me, why did I need to sit there? Where had he gone? I shifted my position on the table. The exam room was bare except for the skeleton picture on the wall, which I studied with forced interest.

I hoped that the doctor would come back pretty soon, because my new hip-hugger jeans were very uncomfortable. They were the fashion, but they cut into my thighs and tummy when I sat for long periods. I was just about ready to stand up to get some comfort when the door opened and in came the doctor, clutching my chart and other papers.

"I'm sorry it took me so long," he said. "But I couldn't find what I was looking for." He smiled at me, sat on the rolling stool, and scooted closer. "Mary Zoe, do you know how much you weigh?" His eyes were fixed on my face.

Uncomfortable, I looked away. I knew I was plump. I'd started putting on the weight when I moved back to Zodie's, but she said it was no big deal. She said it was just "baby fat" and I would grow out of it, but I hadn't. My new family never mentioned my excessive weight, but I knew it wasn't baby fat. It had been my secret shame, until now.

Clearing my throat, I answered, "Yes."

There was a pause as he shifted some papers, and handing me a couple of sheets, he continued. "You weigh over 140 pounds. That's way too much for a young lady. You need to lose this weight. Have you ever considered a diet?"

No, I had never considered a diet. I didn't even know what one was, and I told him so.

"Just show this food plan to your foster mother and try it." He smiled. "You're such a pretty girl; you don't need to be this heavy. It's not good for you."

Standing in front of the elevator, clutching my paperwork, I tried to explain to Dad what happened, but I couldn't. I was ashamed because I had eaten my way into repulsiveness. I frequently ate to soothe the pain in my stomach, but I had never considered myself a glutton. Humiliation made my throat tighten, and my stomach turned nauseatingly. Nana was right all along. I wasn't good enough. I was *fat*. The doctor even said so. And it wouldn't go away, unless I did something. My hands fisted. I refused to let Nana win. I had to change. I'd become someone different. I'd become pretty if only to spite Nana.

That night after dinner, Mom came in to discuss the food plan. Settling herself on the foot of my bed, she smiled at me.

"I think we can do this together, Mary Zoe." She briskly explained what was expected of me. In order for this to work, she said, I had to change my whole thinking about food. No longer would it be my sole comfort, it would become what it was food. If I needed support and comfort, she said, I could get it from both of them, Mom and Dad.

"You're already pretty, Mary Zoe," Mom assured me. "It's not because you don't look good. It's because it's not healthy to be so heavy. And if you continue to comfort yourself with food throughout your life, you'll only get heavier. And that's not healthy."

Being healthy was something I needed to do, I realized, but I wouldn't be alone. Everybody would help.

That began the family project. Everyone participated, even Marti. The summer between my eighth and ninth grade years was a time of reconstruction. Dad put little signs in my room, the bathroom, and the kitchen, "Remember: Think, Thin!" Mom planned the meals for me, and I made diet Jell-O by the truckloads to help me with the before-dinner jitters. Marti and I swam at Lincoln Park, and I walked to the big junction for the exercise. I learned. I adjusted. And I lost thirty pounds that summer.

Looking at my reflection in the store mirror, I couldn't believe what I saw. A pretty girl! I had recently cut my long blond hair, and my perky short haircut suited my new look.

"What do you think, Marti?" I asked my new sister, holding up a pretty dress. "Do you think it's worth the money?" We were in downtown Seattle, and I felt so grown up, picking out my own clothes. It was fun. I needed all new clothes because I had "shrunk out" of everything I owned. School was only a few weeks away, and I had to get ready.

"It is if it fits!" she said. "Go on, Mary Zoe. Try it on!"

We went into the dressing room, and I put it on, twirling around in front of the mirror to show it off. The green wool dress fell gently from my rounded chest and gracefully over my slim hips. I loved the dress, but it cost me a whole month's allowance, twenty dollars!

"Well, what do you think?" I looked at Marti.

She smiled at me. Her bright-white smile and sparkling brown eyes set off her new short haircut.

"I think you look great!" she said as she hugged me. The mirror reflected our faces, one blond and one brunette, our hair wreathing our smiles. Yes, I thought to myself, the dress was perfect and I was a new girl with a new chance.

So I bought it, a month's allowance be damned!

The first day of ninth grade was as exciting as a birthday for me. I wore my new dress and fluffed my tousled short hair. I was ready. Entering the loud halls of James Madison, I found a group of my friends walking the halls. I ran up to them and said an excited, "Hi." I watched their faces turn from irritation (being interrupted in mid-gossip) to confusion (who is this girl?) to incredulous surprise.

"Zoe!" They shouted and threw their arms around me. "You cut your hair! You look cool!" They thought it was the haircut, but I knew it was a summer's worth of effort that had made the difference. And so it went for the whole day. I was the new/old friend whom no one recognized until I smiled. I was so thrilled.

I even had a job at James Madison. Good students were recruited to work with adults in the office and other responsible positions. I'd studied and worked so hard in the past year that I'd become an honor student. That got me a job working in the attendance office, helping with the absentee lists and delivering them to the classrooms. It made me feel important to help.

One day in early fall, I was delivering the attendance sheets, as I did every day, and as I turned away from handing the teacher the absentee sheets and smiling a "Good morning," I heard a wolf whistle. I had never been whistled at before! Someone had noticed me. A boy had noticed me. I smiled to myself. I was pretty! It was nice to be noticed, especially when I wanted to be noticed. I still hadn't had a real boyfriend, and I thought it could be nice to have one. But I had to be careful. I liked the boys I hung around with in my church group and the friends I made in the school choir. It was exciting to know that I could flirt and there were lots of boys who wanted to flirt with me. It was great. Flirting became a balm to the soul of the undernourished, unwanted child I had been. I had overeaten to comfort my soul, but now, when I finally became accustomed to regular, modest meals, I discovered that I could fill my soul with friends and the security of my family.

Walking the halls, I thought back to the very start of school, to a day when a neighborhood boy started walking me home from school. He was an eighth-grader, but he seemed nice. We walked together on his paper route. It wasn't really a date; we were just hanging out together. That was when I received my first kiss. It wasn't at all like I had imagined and definitely not like in the movies. His lips were soft and warm, but he had a scratchy upper lip! It tickled. I couldn't help it, but I smiled and he hit my teeth. Laughing, we continued our walk. *Kissing is highly overrated,* I thought to myself. He continued walking with me, but I really wasn't serious about him. It was okay to hang out, but I wasn't all that interested in letting a younger guy from school pursue me. I had my standards.

One day during our walk home from school, he punched my arm hard because I wouldn't go out with him.

"Don't you ever hit me!" I shouted at him. "No one hits me! Go home. I don't want to see you again!"

"But I was just kidding around," he protested.

"No one hits me. Ever!" I faced him in full fury. "Go away!" I stormed across the street and all but ran to my house. I never walked home with him again.

A few years later, I heard that the same boy had gotten in serious trouble for beating his girlfriend and leaving her to cry on the sidewalk. I was relieved it wasn't me. I was grateful that my radar worked so well. I may have had a hard childhood, but it taught me one thing: I knew what I *didn't* want. No one would handle me the way my mother had been handled or the way she'd handled me.

I'd find another way.

Making friends with boys was getting easier in my church group and at camp, as I found out that next summer. I could control who became my friends or not. I was careful. I was not a victim. I had power. I began talking to Dad about how I had found my new strength. He was a kind listener, and he was a man I could trust. And if there was one man I could trust, I reasoned, there could be others. I didn't have to be afraid. I could choose.

From Dad, I learned that treating men and boys as unique individuals was the way out of my fear. My radar for knowing a bad man had been well honed. Trusting began with my Dad, but sometimes my developing trust hit snags. When that happened, I would revert to my old way of thinking and lash out at him. Usually, he understood my outbursts, but once, I really hurt him.

I knew I was in trouble the day I walked home from school and saw his face. He was in pain. His whole countenance radiated sorrow. Putting my books on the kitchen counter, I asked, "Is something the matter?"

"Yes," he answered.

"What?" I was baffled.

"You." Dad explained to me that I had hurt his feelings with my last outburst and that we needed to talk. He explained that a crack I'd made that he was repulsive had really hurt him. Then I remembered. The night before, I had sat on his lap to rest my head on his shoulder for a special time of comfort and trust. But instead of just relishing the wonder of a loving father, I simply saw a man with flaws. I told him that he was really rather repulsive. His head and ears were too big, I had said. He seemed to take it in stride at the time, and I had no idea the hurt I had inflicted on him in that one careless moment.

But I had. Facing Dad in the kitchen that next day, I was ashamed. I ran to my room.

"How could I have been so mean to hurt him?" I asked myself. But I didn't do anything to make him feel better; instead, I stayed in my room, crying for my own pain. I didn't have the nerve to confront him until the next day, when I knew I had to make amends for my rude behavior. Just because he was a man didn't mean he deserved to be my emotional punching bag, so I apologized. His response was insightful.

"Your experience with your mother's men was really very unique. It was full of violence, abuse, dirty words, and offensive sexual contact. There was no love in that tough world. But not all men are like that. When I say I love you, I'm telling you that I will do everything in my power to help your healing. I will do whatever it takes to help you step into a world where people treat people as people and not as objects."

I was speechless.

He continued, "Why don't we let go of anger and be friends from here on?"

It became clear to me at that moment that I had to change how I wanted to relate to men. I needed to treat men and boys as I wanted to be treated, with care and respect. Dad helped me to listen to my instincts but also to trust by treating people as unique individuals, worthy of my trust.

Later, in the summer of 1969, I got my first chance to try out my new attitude. I was returning from church camp and the campers were all riding the ferry. I had learned to play guitar and was singing. A man who must have been at least in his early twenties sat down across from me. He had a red beard, red hair, fair skin, and twinkling eyes. He was polite but very inquisitive. What type of guitar did I play? What was my name? Where was I going? Would I like to go out with him?

I parried the questions as best I could. But I was only seventeen and out of my depth. I was drawn to him but also terrified. He told me his name was Gordon and persuaded me to give him my phone number.

When the ferry docked, I thought that was the end of it. But I didn't count on Gordon's tenacity. He contacted me at home, and it was arranged that we would go out to lunch.

He was intelligent, kind, and absolutely frightening to me. After having a very nice afternoon with Gordon, I went inside and felt thoroughly sick. I had tried to treat Gordon as I would want to be treated, but he was too much of a threat. I knew he liked me. I knew he wanted to be a boyfriend, and that scared me. I simply couldn't do it.

Dad understood my dilemma. When Gordon called again, I just handed the phone to my dad. They met, and Dad explained how it was for me. He explained to Gordon that I had just found the ability to trust and that I needed to be approached with patience and care. Gordon understood. He was indeed a good man.

After discussing my situation with Dad, Gordon called me and said, "Why don't we just be friends and have fun together?"

I agreed, and it was the start of a profound friendship that has lasted for over thirty years.

Through experiences with my church group buddies, my friend Gordon, and my growing trust in Dad, I became more self-assured and less prone to panic attacks. Coed social gatherings were still rough on me through my teen years, but I continued to work on my growth and trust.

Mid-September, 1969, was hot, and my upstairs room was stifling, so I sat on the front porch to enjoy the view of Harbor Island when a car drove up and out poured seven guys from my church group. They all were my friends, and though I knew some wanted to be more than my friend, I also knew they respected my boundaries. Try as they might, they never got far—it was delightful to pit my wits and humor against their persuasive skills. I was better at it than they were, and they liked me all the more for it.

Running into the kitchen, I breathlessly explained to Mom that I needed eight glasses of iced tea, ASAP, because I had a porch full of guys out front! I laughed as Mom and I filled the glasses. Turning to the door and my guests, my eyes caught Dad's face. His eyes twinkled. I smiled, and my heart filled with joy.

I was loved, liked, and admired. At long last.

CHAPTER 31

Two Forces

I HAD CONVERSATIONS WITH ZODIE in my head every day. Most of the time, I had to double-check my thinking and ask myself if I was seeing an issue from Zodie's point of view or from my new family's point of view. There seemed to always be two forces taking up my mind. One kept saying I couldn't do anything right, while the other kept cheering on my progress. The battle raged constantly inside my head with Zodie telling me how disappointed she was that I didn't win first place and the Dimocks telling me how proud they were of every new skill that I set out to master. I was worn out by the tug-of-war. It made everything I did even more difficult.

But I learned to shove Zodie's voice aside. I learned how to push those thoughts out of my head until it became an automatic reflex. Every time I fought that battle between Zodie's discouraging put-downs and the Dimocks' encouraging praise, I grew better at silencing Zodie. And the more her voice was silenced in my mind, the faster I progressed.

I studied hard and watched my grades improve until before I knew it, I was no longer in fear of being held back; instead, I made the honor roll. I started practicing my singing and guitar. By setting my sights on working hard and pushing the past away, I was rapidly transforming. Before I knew it, I had loads of friends. The kids I feared would bully me looked up to me instead. By the end of junior high, I wasn't anything like the dumb girl from the foster home whom no one wanted to play with. I was the smart girl who sang beautifully and everyone flocked around.

But it would be a lie to say that Zodie simply disappeared from my mind. She was always there, tucked in a dark corner of my memories or hiding beneath a thin veneer of confidence. Her voice had seared itself in my ears, and its echo lingered, a barely perceptible chant telling me that I deserved to be locked away, that I deserved to be punished.

And the day I decided to try to get onto the West Seattle High School stage, Zodie's voice took over.

"Who would come to see you?"

"What makes you think you have any talent?"

"That's stupid; anyone can be in a high school play."

"You should be doing something useful."

I couldn't get the thoughts out of my head, no matter how hard I tried. What had I gotten myself into?

I had seen a flyer in the hallway of my high school announcing an audition for the show *1984* (which at the time, seemed so very futuristic), and since I had read the book, I was interested. So I thought I'd try for some supporting role just to see what it was like.

I walked into the auditorium at the appointed time for auditions. It was the grandest hall I had ever seen, except perhaps for the Admiral Theater. Sweeping walkways opened up to a sea of shiny blond wooden seats. It even had a balcony, just like the Admiral. I loved how the lights in the ceiling made the stage curtain look so enchanting. It drew me like a moth to a flame. I stared at the swarm of milling students. A crowd of upperclassmen who all seemed to know each other shouted greetings back and forth and cavorted among the seats, which somehow made me feel both invisible and conspicuous. The lights were dim in the hall, so I found a seat somewhat far back from the crowd and waited for something to happen.

When the lights came up, they illuminated the red velvet curtain, and a stylish thin woman wearing a bright-red smile slipped through the curtains and stood in the light. Noise stopped. She was the director, Mrs. Linehan, and she was organizing the crowd up front to begin the audition. I was terribly nervous, but I knew it was something I could do, so I just breathed deeply and let the encouraging words of the Dimocks knock the badgering voice of Zodie right out of my head.

"You can do this. We know you can," I heard them say.

"You can't get on stage," I heard Zodie say. "Who do you think you are, Nana at Carnegie Hall?"

"Oh, go pour yourself a bottle and leave me alone," I heard myself say right back at her.

When my turn came, I had to walk down the aisle to the stage. It seemed to take a very long time. I turned to face Mrs. Linehan and was suddenly blinded by the bank of lights in the ceiling and floor of the stage. The only thing I could see was the back of my eyes! It was nothing like I had experienced before. But instead of being frightened by it, I was exhilarated. Energy came into me and pulsed through my feet straight through to the stage floor. I had entered a New World, and I loved it.

I don't remember the audition. The only thing I knew was that before the night was over, I had won the role of Julia—the female lead. I also remember after receiving the news that I had whooped and said to Mrs. Linehan, "Man, my mama will never believe this. She doesn't think I can do anything!"

I watched as the red smile on Mrs. Linehan's face faded. "Why in the world would she think that?" she asked.

That was when I realized that she thought my mom was Mrs. Dimock, whom she'd met several times before. "Oh, I don't mean my foster mom," I said. "I mean my biological mom. Thank you, Mrs. Linehan. I'm so honored."

Mrs. Linehan's smile returned to her face, albeit a bit crooked, as if she wasn't sure how to get it back on straight. But as I walked out of the darkness and into the hall, I realized that I had just won first prize! I got the lead! I had redeemed myself from my second-place finish. Zodie couldn't hurt me that way anymore, because I *was* good enough. Mrs. Linehan believed in me and had awarded me the lead! I wouldn't have to be second best to anyone anymore. Feeling suddenly lighter, as if I had shed an old coat that I had outgrown, I ran out into the sunlight to tell the Dimocks what I had done.

Naturally, they were thrilled, but I was the only one who was surprised.

Opening night was a new experience. I was terrified. I was sure I was going to forget all the hard-won lines I had memorized. But once I began, it felt so right, so easy; I was at home on the stage. I enjoyed it, and I had a good memory. I never forgot my lines. At the final curtain, Mrs. Linehan and Mom and Dad came over to congratulate me. I turned to talk to Mom, when over her shoulder, I spotted Zodie, leaning heavily on George's arm.

I forgot to breathe. It was as if all the sound had stopped. All I saw was Zodie staring at me in her mustard-colored coat with its prized mink collar. Zodie still knew how to make a major appearance, because all conversation instantly died. Everyone heard her as she announced, "Good job, kid; I cried all the way through the show. It's what I'd have done if I'd had the chance."

I couldn't articulate a response. Words strangled in my throat. Satisfied that she had made her point, she turned and left, snubbing the Dimocks and Mrs. Linehan by not even acknowledging their existence.

But her exit was flawed. As she turned her back on us in defiance, the dirty tracks on the back of her treasured yellow coat came into view, looking as if she had been dragged through the mud by a caveman towing her by the hair.

It had been three years since I had left her, and it was clear that Zodie had really let herself go. This was no high-styling woman draped in an expensive mink coat; this was a shabby woman in a shabby cloth coat. It had once looked so fabulous on her, but now I was embarrassed for her. Obviously, she had no idea how bad she looked. To see her like that brought back the shame of my early life, and I knew that I had not yet truly cut the cords that bonded me to Zodie. The pain to see her so looking so pathetic was even worse than the shame. As much as I hated all she'd done to me, I knew Mama wanted to be someone. I knew she took pride in her appearance. But the tracks on her coat said it all—she'd been so beaten down by life, that she could barely dress herself.

My breathing was shallow and fast. I felt my heart pound, and the beat of it was all that I heard. When the sound returned to me, my face burned. Everyone had seen my real mother and knew where I had really come from and who I really was. I was no longer filled with pride; in just a mere two minutes of Zodie's presence, I was publicly humiliated and privately heartbroken.

I felt a hand on my shoulder. It was Mrs. Linehan, her smile still bright for me. "Yes, Mary Zoe, you did a great job!"

Her words were so kind and welcomed that I felt as if she had put her arms around me. She accepted me! I *was* good enough! Zodie didn't matter. Breathing deeply, I followed Mrs. Linehan to join the celebrating cast members. Everyone had a smile for me.

That show led to many others. It was the beginning of an amazing new part of my life. Roles came easily to me. I could make the words mine. A senior girl told me she had no idea how I managed to look so natural on stage. The girl didn't know about all the actresses in my life, teaching me from a very early age how to perform for an audience. She didn't know Zodie or Nana or what was *not* natural to me.

When I was on stage, I could make murder, madness, or treachery appear completely natural. Those were emotions I'd learned well. But I sure had difficulty being sexual. In one love scene between the hero and the female lead, which was me, I had to ask Mrs. Linehan's permission to hug the boy. Her answer was a loud bark from the darkness, "Of course you can hug him; you're supposed to be lovers!" It made me feel pretty stupid. But I had to get the blessing of an authority figure in order to be sexual!

After that, I used theater for the freedom it gave me—freedom to find pieces of myself in each role and make it real, make it live. When that senior said I was a natural on stage, it was great praise. I cherished it. I held that compliment close to my heart all the way through each production.

But my junior and senior years turned into the time without laughter. Kids who used to include me in their group began to avoid me. I was accused of being the director's pet because I won too many good roles. Friends turned against me and wrote cruel things in my yearbooks. They made sure I knew I wasn't wanted. I wasn't one of them anymore. They sucked the life juice out of the whole experience, something that became especially painful during one emotionally powerful role.

As much as the role of Julia was a great achievement, the greatest role I had in high school was to play Eliza Doolittle in *My Fair Lady*. When I learned I'd gotten the part, I was struck dumb. I just stood there, trembling. My girlfriend, Jill, put a concerned hand on my shoulder, thinking that my silence was due to disappointment. I looked at her worried face and whispered, "I'm Eliza!" I should have been very happy. But I wasn't. I was afraid. I knew that the role would be the toughest of my experience.

But I'd been through tough times before, so I knew I could conquer it. I worked very hard on that role. I worked with a voice coach to master the Cockney dialect and the rigors of the vocal performance. I even sewed some of my costumes. The part of Eliza was the story of my life writ large—an unwanted girl aspires to have a better life, faking it till she was making it. It was perfect for me. Holding that cast list in my hand, reading my name as Eliza, rooted me in place. I knew what it felt like to change from one life to another; I could be Eliza Doolittle on stage because I was an Eliza Doolittle in my life.

I just wasn't prepared for the pain that came with it. My leading man disliked me. He told people he thought I was a bitch and spread rumors that I slept around, which would have been funny if it wasn't so hurtful. I was so afraid of men that I struggled daily just to interact with them. I had some boyfriends who helped me appreciate the finer points of kissing, but I was still wary of anything more. So I suffered alone when it came to boys, and once the rumors that I was loose started going around, I suffered alone among the cast. They didn't want me.

The destruction of my morale was completed when I was purposely humiliated during the photo shoot for the show. The cast's costumes were all completed, except for mine. The girl in charge of that costume scene made sure that I knew everyone else was lovely before my gown was even started. So I stood on stage, pinned into my dress and looking like a bag of rags while the cast behind me looked stunning. I kept a smile on my face, but right beneath that smile, I was so deeply hurt and angry.

But all that emotional turmoil played right into the role. At the climax of the show, I was to stand alone and cry. It was very easy for me to cry. Drama had given me many wonderful experiences, but it took from me so much more. I cried for the loss of friends. I cried for the cruel things they did and said. I cried because drama made me feel all alone. I felt I was once again that unwanted little girl, singing "Jesus Loves Me" and trying so hard to be good enough to be loved. To be hurt profoundly again after all that I had worked to achieve just enraged me. I was being treated as less valued than everyone else.

And I wasn't going to stand for it anymore.

As I stood on that stage with the spotlight in my eyes, I found the inner strength to use all of my emotions. In that moment, I was no longer Mary Zoe, Zodie's stupid servant child. I was Eliza, a neglected girl transformed into an attentive, knowing woman. But I knew Eliza's transformation wasn't all there was to her story. I knew, deep inside, that her growth had come at a great personal cost. And so knowing, I made her pain universal. Everyone feels a little bit like Eliza sometimes, being reminded they can be even more than they are, while at the same time knowing who they really are isn't good enough for some. I wanted to convey that pain and that confusion and that determination to belong. And I wanted to perform my own life's confusing transformation from wounded child to compassionate survivor.

The audience roared with applause, rising up from their seats to give me a standing ovation, but I didn't hear it at all. Instead, what I heard was Zodie and Nana telling me I could have done better.

But something inside me knew otherwise. Something deep inside me knew, without even hearing the applause, that I had made a real connection with the audience. And that gave me the comfort I so needed.

And the looks on the faces of my cast mates gave me another small, but perverse, comfort. It hurt me that I wasn't good enough for them, but it thrilled me that I knew the reason why. They didn't look down on me, as they had in the past. Now they envied me.

CHAPTER 32

Independence

IN 1970, I TURNED EIGHTEEN. Although I was still only a junior in high school, my life was instantly and profoundly changed. I was no longer a ward of the court and no longer a foster child. Legally, I was alone—emancipated, independent, an adult.

The thought terrified me. I wasn't ready to be on my own. I couldn't. So I asked my parents to adopt me.

The Dimocks seemed as excited as I was at the prospect of finalizing our relationship and truly making me Marti's little sister. When Marti heard our decision, she was delighted. She told me she even prayed for one long ago. And now her wish was to come true.

We initiated the legal proceedings, and I couldn't have been more excited. But as I prepared to sign the document finalizing my adoption, I suddenly felt that I was being asked to give up the life that came before—my whole childhood, my own name, and most especially, my own mother, Zodie. I felt dizzy and had to close my eyes and take a deep breath. What did it mean to renounce my own past, my own identity?

A flood of emotion washed through me, drowning out any sights or sounds. All I saw was my entire life, and all I heard was Zodie's refrain, "Blood is thicker than water."

My life was no longer Zodie's. It was now my own life to choose.

"No one forced you into this? It is your decision to be adopted as an adult?"

I opened my eyes and saw that the judge was waiting for me to answer his question. He stood beside his big desk wearing his black robe and holding a Bible, waiting for my answer.

"Do you swear?"

I swore. Blood may be thicker than water. But water is far more clear.

When it came time for me to sign, the judge instructed me to read the document. Looking at the legal jargon was difficult, but what came across clearly was that in exchange for security, I legally and forever renounced the parents who had given me life. The document listed Margaret and Herb Dimock as my parents. Zodie and Daddy Johnny were completely erased. It was as if they had never existed. And George, who had provided me safety in times of greatest danger, who had supported me throughout my childhood and been the only father figure I'd ever known before I met Mr. Dimock, wasn't even a footnote in this contract of who I had been and was to become.

A deep pain settled in my heart. I wanted to belong in the Dimock family, but I didn't want to deny my birthright.

As I hesitated, the judge spoke softly to my parents, "This is where most people change their names."

So I changed my last name to Dimock. But I put my biological last name, Carmichael, as my middle name. I wanted to keep some acknowledgment of my birth, however symbolic it might be.

To celebrate the adoption, the Dimocks rented a rustic cabin in the rainforest of the Olympic Peninsula. That afternoon, as I sat with my parents in the kitchen nook, looking out at the rain-washed evergreen trees, they were busily and cheerfully preparing lunch. But all I could do was gaze at the gray sky, watch the rain, and think about all that had changed.

Mom handed me my tea, and I smiled at her.

"Look, Mom," I said, pointing to the mugs, "they're the exact color of magic in the old Disney movies."

She smiled. "Well what do you know?" she said. "They certainly are!"

We drank our tea quietly as I thought about the fact that there would be no magic for me. Cinderella had denounced her wicked mother. I had to face what I had done. I tried to swallow the tea and keep up my end of the conversation. They both seemed so happy, but I felt so empty.

As we prepared to walk in the rainforest, I wished I could be as happy as my mom and dad. But I was just going through the motions. The rain fit my mood exactly. The path through the woods was so narrow that only two people could walk abreast, so I walked in front. I couldn't talk. I hurt too much. I strode alone and soon outpaced my parents. The path got deeper and darker as I walked. The evergreen firs were covered in a clinging moss, and webs of Spanish moss hung from the dripping boughs. Even the ferns seemed to droop under the weight of the fat drops of water. The path was black with slippery mud, and I had to step carefully so I wouldn't fall. But deep inside, I was being driven to go faster and faster. I had to get away.

The sound of the rain soon vanished. All I could hear was the pounding of my heart. Mama's voice came to me, screaming, "How could you do this to me? I'm your mother!" My eyes blurred with tears, and I began to run from the sounds in my head.

I heard my grandmother's snide remarks: "You know they only take care of you because they get paid for it," and "I'll never have contact with you as long as you are with that family," quickly followed by, "Your uncle and his family will never speak to you again." My skin slicked with fright. "You'll just be white trash!" I sprinted ahead to drown out her poisonous barbs.

I splashed in the mud as I ran. The sound of my pounding feet echoed differently on a wooden bridge, but by then, I was running too fast to realize I was losing my balance. I skidded, lost my footing, and fell, landing on my back.

My daypack felt like it was gouging a hole in the middle of my back, and my heart hurt so bad it made my arms ache. Every inch of me hurt.

As I lay alone on my back in the mud, the tormenting whispers in my head became a roaring. I had turned my back on my heritage. I was no longer a part of my own family. As the cold mud soaked into my jeans, I realized that I could no longer lay claim to Mama, the mother who played jacks with me, the mother who taught me to appreciate old movies, loved jewelry, and drew paper dolls so I could color them in. And I no longer had a grandmother who sang with the gusto of a gale-force wind. But worst of all, I could no longer lay claim to my most cherished memory, my Sissy. Suddenly, that reality sank in like a knife in my heart. Legally, Gale was no longer my sister.

I could feel the hot tears running down my face, a brutal contrast to the cooling drops of rain. I don't know how long I lay there in the mud with the tears and rain in my face. But eventually, I began to hear other noises, nature sounds, the wind in the trees, and the patter of the rain on the fat green leaves.

I opened my eyes and watched the branches of the trees sway across the darkening sky. I knew one way or another, I had to get up—both literally and figuratively. I couldn't let the slippery slope of my life's path keep me down any more than I could allow the slippery slope of the rainforest path to keep me flat on my back. It was time to take charge of my next move.

I had chosen adoption. And in keeping my birth name as my first and middle names, I had also chosen to keep my heritage. I would always be me, no matter what the court said. I didn't have to deny my past just because I chose a family that could—and would—care for me. I didn't have to collapse under the weight of adoption laws. I could make my adoption fit me. I would keep my family contacts. I would keep Gale and Uncle Tucker in my life. I would keep Mama in my life as best I could—though I knew she might not keep me. And I knew that there were parts of Mama that I couldn't fit into my life ever again—not her abuse, not her lies, not her madness.

But her laughter, her humor, her life, and her pain would forever be in my life and heart. Zodie was a terrible mother, I knew. But what had been her models? Her own mother had hated her, and her own father had molested her. For all her tough exterior, inside Zodie was broken, too damaged to even take care of herself, much less take care of her three children.

They were all still my family. They made me. They looked like me. They even raised me in different ways. But I could choose when and where I would bring them into my new life. I was the one in control of my life.

The rain cooled my face, and I watched the clouds moving. The screaming in my mind had stopped. I had chosen life, my life on my terms.

Carefully and painfully, I regained my footing, and adjusting my daypack, I turned to face the path ahead of me and waited for my new family to catch up.

Part Four

CHAPTER 33

The Hospital

THERE. I'D SAID IT. ZODIE may have been on her deathbed, but at long last, I had told her the story of my life—as I'd lived it, not as she'd defined it. It was growing dark, and the bedside lamp beside Zodie's bed glowed an eerie shade of green, turning her emaciated flesh a ghastly color. I took some deep breaths and waited for the fallout, as Gale sat quietly in her chair, biting her lip.

"Oh, for Christ's sake, does it always have to be about *you*?" Zodie finally spat out.

"Mama, that's not why Mary Zoe told you her story," Gale said, trying, as always, to be the peacemaker. "She just wanted you to hear her story."

"Like I didn't already know it?" Zodie said, shifting in her bed looking for a comfortable spot. "You think it was easy for me? Let me tell you—" But Gale cut her off.

"Mama, we know it wasn't easy for you. But we were just little girls. We needed to be safe, and we weren't safe with you."

Now I was the one biting my lip. I had no idea what Zodie would do or say, but even though I was grown up and the Dimocks—not Zodie—were my parents, in my heart, I was still that small, scared little girl so desperate to please her unhappy mama. And the story I'd just told her of my life was not something that had pleased her. But I knew I had done the right thing by telling her, even if she didn't want to hear it. I told her for my sake, not for hers. I didn't tell her to punish her; I told her because I still wanted—no *needed*—to know why she'd done it. Why had she put me through such a life? Why hadn't she even *tried* to get sober? Why had she risked my life—and hers—so that she could go to Wenatchee when she was too drunk to even sit up? Why hadn't she protected me from David Walz? Why had she always put her needs above ours? What was *Zodie's* story? I don't mean the story of her life, but the story of her living—why had she lived such a life and forced us to live it as well? The more I thought about it, the angrier I got. Maybe there was a part of me that did want to punish her. But more than anything, I wanted to know the answers. I wanted to know the *why* of all that I had suffered and had to overcome because of her needs and her desires. I wanted to know that she was genuinely sorry. Then, before I even realized the words were flying out of my mouth, there they were, flung through the antiseptic hospital air straight into Zodie's face.

"Did you have *any idea* how dangerous it was to take a child over the mountains when you were shit-faced?" I demanded, as Zodie sputtered something about needing a goddamned cigarette. Gale practically dropped her jaw she was so shocked at how mad I'd become. But mad or not, finally, after telling her my story, I was standing up to Zodie.

"I was not shit-faced!" she spat back. "I was *ill*!" Then her voice softened, and she added, "I needed a vacation for my nerves."

Oh, for crying out loud. Where are smelling salts when you need them? She couldn't have been more dramatic if she'd put the back of her hand to her forehead and fainted right then and there.

"But did you have to take a vacation in the dead of night? Why couldn't you have waited? Why did you make me go along?"

"I wouldn't leave you behind with your stepfather!" she said, as if the very thought of it was appalling. A snort came out of me, and Gale and Zodie both glared, but I said nothing. I was thinking of all the times she didn't think twice about leaving me with my stepfather, David Walz. After all he'd done to me and Gale while she turned the other way, she was suddenly acting like leaving me alone with George was somehow more dangerous than making a twelve-year-old drive through the mountains in the dark.

Zodie calmly added, "And *I* needed it. George was working all the time. I needed to get away. My God, you're such a worrywart. Besides, I got you there, didn't I?" She laughed as if the memory of that drive to Wenatchee was just another good story in Zodie's repertoire of lifetime adventures. "Trying to hide that trip from George was such a panic! God damn, the man! He sure was stupid." Zodie howled in laughter, but she was laughing alone.

"I liked him. And he wasn't stupid," I said.

"Oh yeah, I forgot," she cackled, the disdain in her voice unmistakable. "You liked him. Well, swell. Why don't the whole lot of you live happily ever after when I'm dead and buried? It's not like you ever gave a damn about me." She paused to cough up the mucus from her lungs, the deep, guttural hacking sounding like God himself was strangling her. Gale gave her some water, and she took a few sips, then continued, "It's not like we were driving cross-country, for God's sake!"

I tried to stay calm and keep my emotions under control. But the subject was on the table, and there was no sense in clearing it away until I was certain Zodie had digested it. "I just wanted you to know how it felt to *me*. Every time you drove when you were screwed-up, I was terrified! Your escapades put me in a constant panic. I still have stomach problems, thanks to you. I dreamed of that night for months after that trip."

Gale got up and adjusted Zodie's pillow and blankets, cheerfully nursing her as if there was no fight at all going on, though I knew she was secretly thrilled that I was finally letting Zodie have it.

"So bad, so sad," Zodie said in a tone to imply she was bored by the conversation. "It was just a drive, for God's sake. It's no big thing."

"No big thing? Do you know how hard it has been for me to learn to drive? I'd throw up before I drove to the local grocery store! And forget driving long distances or city driving! I have to rely on others. I just can't do it. You wanted me to be an independent soul, but thanks to you, I'm dependent on others for transportation. I hate being helpless!"

"Oh for Christ sake! You *did* it! And at such an early age! I knew you could." She beamed a bright smile, as if at long last, she was finally a proud parent.

I took a deep breath and knocked one back at her. "This is what you've left me with, Zodie, a full-blown phobia of getting behind the wheel of a car."

"Well, okay, maybe it upset your delicate nature, but the fact is that you *did it*! And against all odds! See how *strong* I made you? Hot damn, kid, you're a survivor, just like your mama!"

Gale and I looked at each other, and without speaking, we knew Zodie was beyond our reach. She'd go to her grave unrepentant.

"Well, you can believe that if you want to," I said, "but I know the truth. Most kids learn to drive without trauma. Learning doesn't have to be traumatic. Why was it always the hard way, the sink-or-swim method with you? Couldn't you teach me anything without fear? And what about *your* fear? You forced me to drive that night—we both could have been killed!"

"But we weren't," she said with finality.

But it wasn't going to work this time. This time, Zodie was dying and I was alive. I was going to have my say no matter what she thought of me. Telling my story had calmed me, but in just moments, I discovered that two decades of rage had been stuffed inside me, and now, it was gushing from my mouth faster than I could contain it.

"I hated you for that!" I told her. "And I refuse to be victimized by you anymore!"

"Come on, Zoe," Gale said, trying to calm me. "We need to get going."

Just then, a nurse came in and began checking Zodie's blood pressure and temperature, and Gale and I gathered our things to go.

"There's still another hour before visiting hours are up," Zodie said, her voice shifting to a sing-song tone to impress the doting nurse. "Stick around for a game of cards, girls! It might be the last one; you never know!"

The nurse smiled, finished her ministrations with some teasing remarks, and left. Gale and I agreed to play a game of gin rummy in the day room, but just one. I figured if I was going to have to stick around a bit longer, I'd make the most of it.

"Wait. There's one more thing," I said, realizing this would probably be the last time in my life that I could ask Zodie about our family. "I'm confused about something."

Zodie heaved a heavy sigh. "And what's that?" she asked, disinterested.

I wanted to ask about Nana. I'd learned of Nana's death long after it had happened. No one had told me when she died, and I later learned that she had inexplicably asked that I not be told. Nana had, it seemed, punished me in death as much as she had in life, when she'd had that chance. But she could punish me no more—she could only confuse me. Maybe Zodie couldn't apologize for what she'd done to me, but there was still a chance she could enlighten me about her own abusive mother.

"It's about Nana," I said.

Zodie smiled at that. She loved any opportunity to bad-mouth her own mother, even if she bristled at receiving the same treatment herself.

"Oh, her! What a piece of work that one was." She smiled, again to herself.

"Yeah," I agreed. "What was the deal about dressing me up like Shirley Temple? She was obsessed with making me dress like a little girl. She said that was more 'appropriate,' but I looked ridiculous!"

Zodie howled. "Oh, that! Just another one of Katherine's little jabs. You think you had it bad? You should've seen what she did to me. As soon as I started to develop, Mother would dress me up like an adult and then introduce me as her sister. She didn't want anyone to know she was old enough to have a daughter who could menstruate." Zodie laughed so hard she started hacking again but quickly recovered. "I was inconvenient and a threat to her, not only as a woman, but as a sure end to her cherished opera dreams." Despite the laughter, the bitterness in her voice was palpable.

I began to feel for Zodie, knowing as I did how cold and unloving Nana could be. And I had to admit, even though I always felt safer with Nana, I sure didn't feel more loved. For all her flaws and failings, I knew that Zodie loved me, at least as much as she *could* love. So in a soft voice, I asked her, "How did you feel about that?"

She threw her head back in laughter. "Well, it was challenging, I'll say that much. I sure grew up in a hurry!" She stopped laughing, looked down, and picked at the pieces of red that remained on her fingernails, flipping the bits of cracked polish onto the bedspread where they lay like drops of freshly shed blood.

"But if she dressed you in older clothes," I wondered, "why did she dress me in younger clothes? It just didn't make sense."

Zodie looked up, and I saw the age in her face—the face that had come to nearly mirror Nana's. Her skin dripped from her flesh like melting wax, and her once platinum hair hung like a wilting plant. She really was dying, and I suddenly wanted to throw myself at her, wrap my arms around my mama, and tell her I loved her no matter what.

But before I could budge from my seat, Zodie explained. "Katherine never wanted the challenge to her beauty, don't you understand? You were a budding young woman just when her own beauty was gone; she couldn't have you be attractive. Katherine always had to be the powerful one." Then she looked at me, her face wise and sad. "You never really stood a chance did you? You were *my* daughter, so you were tarnished from the get-go." Zodie shook her head. "Well, hell, where do you think *I* learned to fight? I learned from the toughest teacher there was, and I taught *you* how to fight. You're a fighter, just like her."

I didn't say anything but glanced at Gale. It was time to get going, to have that card game and go home. Zodie would live another night, just to spite me. I stood up and started to gather my things.

"My needs are complex."

Did it never end? I rolled my eyes as Zodie sat back in her bed, a look of defiance growing bolder by the second. Was she nuts? Or was she a masterful actress, I wondered, putting on a kaleidoscope of performances as her final curtain call? It seemed that she'd gone from pissed to mean to sad to triumphant and back to sad again in the time it took to change her bedpan.

My head started to spin as the memories of those drunken moods came back. Her unpredictable and sudden mood swings had haunted every moment of my childhood. I never felt safe to be happy with her, because in a moment, it could turn to rage, just as I never knew if her rage would escalate or turn to loving humor as fast as it had appeared. Now she wasn't drunk, but she was sedated. Though she was only fifty-two, she'd spent most of those fifty-two years drunk or drugged. She didn't know how to sustain a mood any more than she knew how to sustain a job, a husband, or a child. Still, it was a performance. I knew Zodie well enough to know she wouldn't let us be the ones to make the exit, not without being sure she was the one who got the applause.

"How are your needs any more complex than anyone else's?" I asked her.

"Zoe," Gale said, pulling my arm. "Come on; it's time to go. We'll play cards with Mama tomorrow."

"You two don't understand what I've lost," Zodie said, ignoring Gale. "I lost *the one* man I ever loved. I lost a *wonderful* life. Because of *me*, he died." Zodie turned her head and began to cry, the tears rolling down her cheeks as she remembered her first husband, Gale's father, David Grossman, the one who'd been killed in the car wreck. We'd heard this story so many times, so many drunken times. And we were going to hear it again.

"I was the one who *made* him take that vacation. He didn't want to go. We were young, and I had to get away from being a mother." Gale winced, but Zodie didn't notice. She continued to berate herself. "I was young! I wanted to party, gamble, and dance and have a great time!" Her mood began to brighten as she recalled being a young girl in love with the handsome David Grossman. "God, what a pair we made!"

After a moment of nostalgia, she returned to her self-flagellation. "But because of my needs, I got my husband killed. It was my fault." Then she crumpled into a pile of tears.

Timidly, I reached out and stroked Zodie's hair. "Oh, Mama. Don't cry. It wasn't your fault. It was a traffic accident." I sat down on the edge of her bed, and she fell into my arms, crying like a child.

"But he was so broken, so broken..." she cried, her voice giving way to great, anguished wailing. "I must have sat there for hours before helped arrived. I sat there holding his broken head!" She cried some more, hacking and coughing through her tears, and then I felt her stiffen as she sat up.

"Oh, Christ, I don't want to go through this again! I need something to drink. Where's that water?"

I got up, handed her the glass of water, and waited for a comment about it being a waste of good liquid, but she just wordlessly took it from my hand and quaffed it down like a tumbler of vodka and then went back to her story. "Living with the knowledge that I killed my only love just emptied me inside. After David died, I couldn't have the beautiful life I was going to have, and the pain was unbearable. So you see, Zoe, my needs are complex because I don't want to remember what I lost. I did anything I could to *not* remember. That's what led to the men and the parties. But I also had to make a living; I had my little girls. So I did what I needed to do to survive. And thanks to me *we all* survived." Then she quickly added, "So I don't have to answer to you or anybody. But if it's any consolation to you, I did the best I could."

"I know you did," I said. "I did the best I could too. But you gave me nothing but confusion and a rotten view of the world all my life. Thank God I had the Dimocks to set me a good example."

"I don't want to hear any Dimock bullshit from you, thank you. Life is tough. I never lied to you. I taught you the truth. I'm sorry it caused you pain, but you've got to be stronger, Zoe. You've got to 'get your own.'" She laughed at her little joke, then added, "As the song says, "God Bless the Child that's Got His Own."

She was right about that, I figured. I did get my own. I got my own parents.

"Okay, Zodie, I'm going," I said.

"Yeah, Mama," Gale said. "We'll come back tomorrow. Okay?"

"No, it's not okay, goddammit! We were gonna play cards, and I want to play cards! Come on, girls; give your mama one last card game!"

Gale and I looked at each other. How was it that Zodie had managed to turn everything she had done to us into what we and the world were doing to her? I told her my story, and she turned it into *her* story that needed to be told. I wanted an apology but instead ended up comforting her, just as we were now the ones denying our dying mother a game of cards when she'd denied us so much. We both exhaled so loudly that we all laughed, and we assured Zodie we'd stay for a game of cards. We helped her out of bed, and she headed toward the bathroom.

"Okay, just give me a minute, and I'll meet you in the dayroom," she said, the charming, vibrant Zodie coming to life. "And you'd better be ready, because I'm going to beat you girls!" Then the bathroom door snapped shut.

"Okay," I said to the door.

Gale and I waited and waited in the gaudy floral dayroom with its constant TV and assorted patients parked like potted plants in their wheelchairs. We shuffled the cards again and again, but Zodie didn't come through the doors. We finally began a game of Ping-Pong when a nurse walked in.

"Are your Mrs. Victor's daughters?" she asked. I nodded. "Well, I'm afraid you'll have to leave now. Mrs. Victor isn't feeling well enough to receive visitors. You'll need to come back at another time."

"Sure," I said and carefully put the paddle down on the Ping-Pong table. Zodie had been true to her word. She kept us waiting just long enough for us to know she had beat us girls yet again. She showed us who was in control.

"Tell her to get feeling better," Gale said.

We left the antiseptic smell behind and stepped outside.

I never saw Zodie again.

CHAPTER 34

Zodie's Death

I MUMBLED APOLOGIES TO THE nice lady holding my long hair, as I puked in the airsickness bag. I had been vomiting ever since the little plane had taken off into the angry gray clouds over Walla Walla. The clouds blanketed the whole area in a dead white that seemed to stretch forever on the short flight to Seattle. The plane danced around in the rough air as I tried my best to aim for the tiny opening in the paper bag, but it wasn't easy. I begged the lady next to me to forgive me and barfed again.

It was the winter of 1975, and I was flying to Seattle because Zodie had died.

She hadn't died in the hospital like we thought she would; that would have been an intolerable defeat for Zodie, who was defiant to the very end. Shortly after our last visit, she had been released, recovered long enough to go back to drinking and fighting with George, and seemed virtually indestructible. But then, one day, the phone rang. It was Gale.

It had happened so quickly. I hung up the phone and just stood, frozen in place.

Our mother was dead.

My mind screamed that she couldn't be dead; she wasn't old enough. She was only fifty-two and was too mean to die. How could Zodie be dead?

Like batteries that one day just stop working, Zodie's heart one day just stopped beating. George had found her crumpled outside in the front yard, like a dead animal the cats had brought home.

Gale contacted the family members and arranged for the funeral.

But Uncle Tucker wouldn't come. He said Zodie had stolen Nana's topaz ring, and the only way he'd show up at her funeral was if he got his mother's ring back. Nana had worn that smoky, sparkling gem every day, continually boasting of how valuable it was.

She had used threats of leaving it to Uncle Tucker's wife as a way to put Zodie in her place, and Zodie always told her to go ahead and give it to Aunt Licha; she didn't give a damn. But after Nana had died, Zodie somehow got the ring and started wearing it like a souvenir of war. Her greatest enemy had died, and she had plucked the crown jewel from her cold, dead hands.

Now Uncle Tucker wanted it back, because he thought it was worth a fortune.

"Let's just give him the ring," I said to Gale. "It's worthless glass, but Tucker should be at his sister's funeral. Even if he doesn't give a damn, he should be there."

"All right," Gale agreed. "But we're going to need to get it from George."

"Don't worry," I told her. "I'll get it."

Numbly, I called Mom and Dad and gave them the news. They said not to worry; they'd get me on a plane to Seattle. I knew Zodie's death was coming, yet somehow, I didn't really think it ever would. I thought she would live forever.

Everyone seemed so helpful and kind to me, as I got permission to leave campus for the funeral and was instructed by many professors not to worry about class. It had all happened so fast. One moment, everything about my senior year was going smoothly, and then in an instant, the world tilted, my mother was dead, and I was on a plane, barfing my way to Seattle.

After what seemed an eternity of sickness, the plane landed at Boeing Field and we filed off it. Dad was on the tarmac waiting for me. Gathering me into his arms, he hugged me. I told him I had gotten sick on the plane.

"That's pretty obvious," he said, laughing and hugging me again. "You're as green as your wool coat!"

I blushed and gave him another long hug.

"It's so good to see you, Dad," I said. "It's so good to be home." It felt strange, coming home to my parents to bury my mother, but it was such a warm comfort to have a loving family to support me. I had never expected Zodie's death to hit me so hard—I had thought that I'd be relieved. Instead, I felt a deep and throbbing pain.

Dad whisked my luggage and me to the car. I began to shake. I couldn't get warm even with the heater on full blast. My eyes filled with tears. Zodie was dead. Really, really dead. I would never have a chance to be adult friends with her. She would never meet David, the man I loved and was going to marry. Tears slid silently down my cold cheeks.

"I know it's a shock," Dad told me. "But with time, you'll feel better." He reached over, put his hand on my hand, and squeezed it before returning his hand to the wheel.

"But I should be relieved!" I wailed. "After all she'd done to me."

"No," he said gently. "You should feel exactly what you feel. You're in an emotional shock right now. You loved your mother, and she loved you. That will always be true."

I struggled to smile, and my tears began to subside.

"David is driving up from Portland to be with you," he said in a more cheerful tone. "We're going to face this as a family, Zoe. You won't be alone."

I was so grateful for the people in my life. I couldn't have faced it alone. I couldn't have faced the battleground of emotions that were tearing me apart inside.

Later that night, after Mom fixed us a wonderful meal and I got to see my brothers and sister once again, I called George. I wanted to let him know how sorry I was that he lost her. He'd been drinking, I could tell, and he was hurting bad. We chatted a bit about Zodie, and then he told me Gale had made arrangements for us all to view Zodie's body the next day.

Good old Gale, I thought, *still taking care of everything and everybody.* I loved her so much.

"George," I said, mustering up the courage to ask about the ring in the midst of our grief. "Do you know what happened to Nana's topaz ring? Is Zodie being buried with it?"

The question made him explode. Yelling at me over the phone, he made it clear in blunt language that he didn't need to hear from some "jewelry hungry" ghoul.

In the middle of his rant, I'd had enough. "Daddy! How can you say that to me after everything we've been through together with Zodie? God knows we tried."

There was silence on the phone. Then he whispered, "I'm sorry, Mary Zoe; you're right. I shouldn't say those things to you. If you want it, you can have it."

I explained that we needed to return it to Uncle Tucker, or he wouldn't come to the funeral.

After grumbling a bit about Uncle Tucker, George said he'd make sure Gale got the ring, and he looked forward to seeing me. I hung up the phone, put my head on the table, and cried.

The next day found me in Gale's family car. I sat in the back, and David sat next to me, holding my hand gently. We were driving to Orting, Washington, where Zodie was to be buried. It was a small town, very rural. Zodie would have hated it. She was a city girl from way back, but George loved the country, and dead or alive, he wanted Zodie nearby.

George loved the country so much that over the years he and Zodie had moved farther and farther from Seattle until they were living in such a remote, rural part of the state that in her last years, Zodie rarely got to the city. I knew she hated it, and she hated George for dragging her out there, but neither of them would give up their ever-growing menagerie of cats and dogs. As long as they lived in the city, they were constantly being evicted. So they settled for being exiled to the boondocks, where they could drink and curse and fight and make love as long and loud as they wanted and never have to worry about an extra dog or two.

Zodie had always lived a wild life, and in the end, she ended up living with the wildlife. *How poetic,* I thought, as Gale chattered from the front seat, reminiscing about our mother.

Finally, we arrived at the funeral home. George was standing by his pickup truck in the parking lot, waiting for us.

After the initial greetings and introductions, no one said anything as we entered the yellow viewing room with its dim lighting, flowered chairs, and cheap tables adorned with fake flowers and a guest book waiting to be signed. I slowly made my way to the back of the gaudy, quiet room. There in her coffin lay Zodie. It took me only an instant to see that she was dead and the body in the box wasn't my mother. My mother had radiated sexual appeal. My mother had sparkled and sparred. My mother was alive with energy and anger. This was just a tired woman in a rectangular box.

I turned away, ashamed that I could not look at what she had become. I sat in one of the chairs nearest to the door; but Gale stood by the coffin transfixed.

Gazing at Zodie, Gale bent over the coffin as if to make sure she was really dead and not just resting.

"I can't believe how good she looks," Gale said, her gaze sweeping across our mother's lifeless, well-dressed body. "She looks almost better dead than she did when she was alive. They did such a good job, don't you think?" She turned to me for confirmation, and I smiled and nodded my agreement.

I remembered the hospital, how Gale had commented then about how good Zodie looked and how shocked I was at our mother's decline. But this time, I wouldn't argue. Gale needed to believe in the image of Zodie that our mother had so deliberately cultivated in her lifetime. She needed to believe that for all her faults, Zodie was beautiful. Hadn't that always been her defining virtue? Her beauty had attracted the men. Her beauty had propelled her into a world of unrestrained celebration. Her beauty had excused all the neglect, all the abuse, all the damage she inflicted. It was Zodie's beauty that drew sex and violence to her, that had made her needs so much more "complex" than the needs of those around her. Her beauty made her special. That was the myth we had learned to believe.

And my sister needed to believe it. Because the truth—that for all her beauty, Zodie had an ugliness to her she never could, or would, confront—was too painful to think about at that moment.

I shut my eyes, but the tears slipped under my lids and silently down my face. It was all such a waste. She had had such talent, her voice, her art, her wonderful way with animals, and her sense of style were all what made her so mesmerizing and, on her good days, so much fun. She had so much life inside her, but she never did anything with it. She butchered it. Her anger had corroded her life. And my anger arose at the waste of it.

David took my hand in his; I opened my eyes to look into his concerned blue eyes. "I'm okay," I said. "I'm just trying to remember the better part of Zodie."

We sat there in silence while Gale stood over the casket. I don't know how long we waited for Gale, as she stood there motionless. Finally, she straightened her shoulders and without a word walked to the door and stepped outside. I followed.

My eyes could hardly adjust to the bright sunshine. The January day was clear and cold. It made my head hurt and my nose run. We got in the car and followed George to his house, because he wanted to see "if you girls want any of her things."

Bill, Gale's husband, ever the salesman, kept up a cheerful patter of stories as he followed George's truck. David helped him along to keep the conversation going. Gale and I sat mute. As we parked behind George's truck, all conversation died. We were in front of Zodie's house.

The house was dark, due in part to the big fir trees shading it and in part to the mud and soot that marred the gray paint. Patches of mossy green showed through where the paint had blistered off. The window off the living room was covered with muddy paw prints. George let us in.

The smell of the house hit like a fist: urine, dog feces, mud, dust, cigarette smoke, ashes from the wood stove, and old food. George's dogs milled around our feet, and the smell of wet dog permeated our clothes. The rooms were dark, half the curtains drawn. I looked around at the life my mother had lived.

There in the living room stood Zodie's Early American coffee table amid broken sofas and a duct-taped La-Z-Boy. I remembered how Zodie used to polish that table to a golden glow. That table was her pride and joy, a symbol of the life she intended to live—a life of luxury. Now it was scarred and dulled with watermarks and cigarette burns. And on top of it, buried beneath stacks of newspapers and a scattering of empty beer cans, I saw her gold-filigreed lighter. It was so tarnished and dirty that I barely recognized it. I turned away and looked into the kitchen. I wish I hadn't. The white stove was black with burned and spilled food. Long charcoal drips covered the face of the oven, and dirty pans were sprawled across the cooking surface. The garbage sack on the floor was overflowing, and the dogs had gotten into it and spread some garbage around the kitchen floor, leaving behind greasy brown tracks. The room where Zodie fixed her meals looked like a crime scene.

No one said anything as George continued the tour. The bathroom we passed horrified me. The walls were all scratched, and the smell of cat urine was overpowering. George explained that the cats used to stay in the bathroom when the dogs were in the house but that he had gotten rid of the cats because it was such a hassle to lock them up all the time. I wondered how long they'd been gone; from the smell of it, there were probably half a dozen still hiding under the wet towels that were heaped on the floor.

We were finally escorted into Zodie's room. She and George had been sleeping apart. There was nothing on the walls of Zodie's room except cobwebs. A sheet thrown over the window curtain rod served as a window covering. The mattress and box springs sat on the floor, and the only other piece of furniture was an old dresser with a cracked mirror. I pulled out a drawer, and there lay Zodie's jewelry—not the good stuff, that was long gone—but the costume jewelry, her rhinestone bows for her shoes, her rhinestone earrings, and the golden rhinestone necklace that she had loved so much. But now the sparkly necklace was dull and dirty with crystals missing, giving it the look of a tired smile with missing teeth. I put it back in the drawer and turned away. There was nothing there I wanted. Gale agreed. George seemed relieved to leave Zodie's possessions just as they lay. He didn't want to change anything.

The sad truth was that for all his cruelty to her and her cruelty to him, George had loved Zodie all those years.

As we hurried to exit the house, we agreed to meet George after the funeral the next day for a get-together at a local bar, to celebrate Zodie's life. Even Zodie deserved a wake, I thought to myself as we silently drove away.

The flowers on the coffin moved with the wind and rain. Carnations and chrysanthemums bumped heads with the few red roses, while the ferns slapped wetly against the coffin lid. In the white-on-white arrangement, the roses stood out like splashes of blood. It seemed appropriate, given how her life had been so spattered with violence.

Gale and I sat on a little bench just beside the coffin, while Bill, David, and Uncle Tucker stood behind us. I knew that Uncle Tucker had only come because he wanted Nana's ring back, but having him stand behind us was a comfort to me. My tiny bit of birth family was present.

The January wind blew cold against our legs, making the rain sting our skin. We were shivering and crying so hard that the bench shook. I had no idea where Mom and Dad were, although they had followed us up to the cemetery.

The Pentecostal pastor had been speaking for some time, but I didn't hear a word of his sermon. All I heard was my name, Mary Zoe, as he said that she was the one being buried today. It sent a cold chill down my back to hear my name, as if I was seeing a preview of my own funeral. Everyone knew her as Zodie, but her legal name was Mary Zoe; she had named me after herself. Perhaps it was fitting, as a part of me *was* being buried.

I cried for all the losses she suffered and the talents that were ground to dust by bad choices. I cried for all the lost singing, art, and laughter that would be no more. I don't know what Gale cried for, but she cried with an abandonment of a heart being torn right out of its own body. I hadn't seen much of her over the years, but I knew that she had tried in the last couple of years to help Zodie, while trying to make a better life for herself. But it hadn't been easy. Gale was into her third marriage and already worried about her daughter from her first marriage. Her crowded life had made it difficult for her to take care of our mother, just as our mother's crazy life had made it difficult for anyone to help her. It would have been a full-time job for Gale. I had left Zodie a long time ago, and I was determined to live better than she had. But Gale had never been able to forgive herself for leaving us all those years before. She knew she did what she had to do, but she couldn't shake the feeling that she'd let her family down. So once she had a family of her own, she tried her best to make up for running away by going back. It didn't matter that running away had been her only option.

For all the times we'd wished our mother dead, once she truly was, our hearts were broken. We sat together and cried for all that was lost and never had the chance to be.

When the service was over, we rose to leave. I wobbled a little as my heels sank into the grass, but David reached out to stabilize me, and I smiled up at him. Then in quiet voices, we arranged who would ride with whom to go to the local bar for a final toast to Zodie.

Mom and Dad, who'd finally arrived, gave their farewells to Uncle Tucker and George, as they did not drink so would not be joining us at the bar. But they understood that a bar was the most fitting place to celebrate the life and death of Zodie, however sad that fact was.

The tavern was completely unremarkable, dark and smoky, just what you'd expect of a small-town drinking hole, but it had a large room in the back for parties. When Gale, Bill, Uncle Tucker, David, and I entered the room, it was already bustling with people. The mourners may have been a small group, but they were a loud one. Barmaids with tired faces filled the tables with drinks for eager hands. I recognized very few people. It seemed that George, or "Vic" as everyone called him, had lots of friends in town. He was already seated at a table holding his drink with both hands, as if to keep warm.

Making our way past the tables, I noticed a few faces I knew. Aunt Charlotte was there with her daughter, Denise. Charlotte had always played the peacemaker between George and Zodie. I remembered clearly the shadow-puppet-like image through the window of Charlotte begging George to stop while he beat Zodie's head into the floor.

Banishing that memory, I smiled at her and waved to Denise. We moved forward to our table.

Once everyone had a drink, a few people would stand and propose a toast to Zodie. There weren't many. One heavyset lady with improbably black curly hair stood and held her glass up, "To Zodie!" she wheezed. "The best damn poker player I ever met!" There followed laughter and general agreement.

Yes, Zodie was sharp at cards, I thought to myself, *because she knew how to lie and therefore how to spot a liar.*

Once we had absorbed enough cigarette smoke and alcohol, Uncle Tucker was given Nana's ring. George had picked it up at a jewelry repair shop. He held it silently in his big workingman's hands, then passed it carefully to Gale and went back to his drink. Gale took the ring, gazed at it, and handed it to Uncle Tucker. Silence descended around the table as Uncle Tucker fingered the ring and put it in his pocket with the flash of a greedy smile. I knew he thought the ring was very valuable, due to its large size, but it wasn't. I had briefly worked in an antique shop and learned through my sales experience that Topaz didn't come in that smoky color; the stone was quartz. Smoky quartz was popularized in the 1950s as smoky topaz. The ring was fake, like the women who owned it. But to me the ring was a somber remembrance of lost dreams and aspirations, as symbolic as Zodie's coffee table that she'd thought would attract a whole world of gleaming furnishings and class. But all it brought was false illusion.

A little while after the ring exchange, we said our good-byes. Looking through the crowd, I spied George still hunched over his bourbon. Golden liquid spilled from his shot glass as he shakily brought it to his lips. His eyes were red, and he looked lost. Gale and Bill said good-bye to him, as Uncle Tucker had a plane to catch and they were going to take him to the airport. No doubt in a hurry to pawn the ring, I figured.

As they stepped away, George grabbed my hand. "You know that I always loved your mother, even if she couldn't cook," he mumbled, hanging his head.

I put my other arm around his shoulder and whispered in his ear, "Yes, I know you loved her and you did your best. We both know what it was like." I cleared my throat. It was at this moment that my past and future came crashing together. It was a moment that doesn't come often, when clarity dissolves into compassion. "Daddy," I said to George, "I'd like you to walk me down the aisle at my wedding this September."

He looked at me, blinked, and then he looked at David. The French-Canadian twinkle flashed in his eyes, and I saw in that moment flickers of the handsome husband Zodie had brought home so long ago, the man filled with lust for his wife and dedication for his work. "I'd be honored to," he said, his voice betraying his emotion.

Planting a quick kiss on his rough cheek, I told him we'd be in touch because he would have to be fitted for a tux. Groaning loudly, he smiled at me and winked. He would pretend to loathe the tux, but deep inside, I knew he was thrilled.

Stepping out into the cold air was a relief from the stifling heat and cigarette smoke. Turning to Gale, I gave her a crushing hug before she climbed into her truck. She kissed my cheek. I waved broadly as they pulled out of the parking lot. Gale waved back, and Uncle Tucker nodded and turned away. Then they were gone. I stood alone in the gravel parking lot and breathed in the fresh air. David came up behind me and wrapped his arms around me. I leaned on him with a sigh. I was on the road to a life of my own making. I'd found my own.

CHAPTER 35

Wedding

I STOOD IN FRONT OF the bathroom mirror in Plymouth Church. All the bridesmaids had left, and I was finally alone. Sighing, I took assessment of my reflection. It wasn't good. The lovely curls in my long hair that Marti had so lovingly struggled over had melted away in the heat and stress of the wedding preparations. My hair hung completely straight.

"Something old, something new, something borrowed, something blue," I murmured to myself. Something old? The rented wedding dress I found in a trunk in the costume shop where I worked. It fit me and had a five-foot train and even a bustle! I stroked the lovely ivory silk. *Check, old,* I thought. Something new? I had new shoes on. *Check, new.* Something borrowed? Hmm, that was tough. Aha, the veil! The ladies at the shop loaned it to me when I paid the ten dollars for the rental of the dress. *So, check, something borrowed.* Something blue? Now that was a tough one. Struggling to remember, I had a tiny blue ribbon on the center of my white bra. That had to cover it. I turned away from the mirror. Stepping toward the door, I felt the penny in my new shoe. It could give me blisters, but when it came to marriage, I knew I'd need some luck.

I had to laugh. My wedding was the first big production I had completely costumed. My bridesmaids ranged from a pregnant five-foot-tall matron of honor to David's sisters, who were reaching six feet. All David's groomsmen were his height, so that was easy. I put them in black slacks and jackets of bright orange. And then came the bridesmaids.

My mother-in-law was aghast. "You put your bridesmaids in black?"'

"Sure!" I said. I had a vision. All the ladies were in the style of the 1940's and had black velvet chokers around their necks, with fresh roses pinned to each ribbon. Everyone looked great, no matter what size they were. The groomsmen's jackets matched the orange flowers of the girls' dresses, which suited my eye. David and I were dressed in identical shades of old ivory. I thought it was appropriate that we wore a color that was practically white since we started out together as practically virgins.

It all seemed to work together, I thought as I adjusted my skirt. Mom and Dad worked on the ceremony with us. Dad would officiate over the ceremony, and we'd have a priest bless the union to cover the Catholic side of the celebration. David wasn't an active Catholic, but he wasn't ever going to be a Protestant, so we compromised on the service. I felt happy with the solution. Mom was busy acting as the wedding coordinator of the ceremony, the church reception, and the family reception at home. All the church flowers were donated by one of my future father-in-law's customers in Seattle, and they were beautiful. *So far, so good,* I thought to myself.

I stepped out of the bathroom and right into the arms of my sister Gale. She hugged me for all she was worth. I hugged her back, being careful not to bump the baby she was carrying inside. At the same time, I grabbed Marti's hand and we shared a three-way sister hug. I was speechless. I had both my sisters with me on this most important day of my life—Gale, who saved my life by showing me the path to freedom, and Marti, who had taught me how to dance along that new path and enjoy my life. Tears of gratitude welled in my eyes. I owed them both so much. Knowing that this, of all days, was special to me, Marti smiled wryly, and "Merry Christmas" was all she said. We broke into helpless giggles.

It was now showtime! The ladies assumed their positions for the entrance. I could hear music in the large sanctuary. I stepped into the foyer, and there stood George. He looked so handsome in his white dinner jacket and black pants. I was proud to have him represent my biological side of the family. Zodie was gone, and Daddy Johnny was gone, but here stood this strong man who would represent all of those who came before me. He smiled at me and offered me his arm. I smiled at him, thinking this was the man who helped me pick out my first training bra! I laughed and squeezed his arm.

We stood at the doorway to the sanctuary, and the music filled the room. It was our cue. Suddenly, George leaned over and whispered in my ear, "Now is the time to cut and run, if you need to."

Startled, I looked George in the eye. *Cut and run?* I thought. No. Not me. I fought for the life I was about to enter.

A blast of memories came to me like a motion picture: the tiny four-year-old daring to scale a fence to reach freedom, a child dragging a ripped bag of toys down a hill, and the eight-year-old who learned to be alone and survive when her big Sissy had had to leave. And I remembered standing on stage, bowing to applause.

It was at that moment I realized a secret of my survival: I would always pick the path that would most improve the quality of my life. Whether it was biding my time keeping a crazy adult from killing herself or me, or recognizing qualities in my friends and even strangers that I knew would help me make my life better, I had always pursued my own protection. And I had learned that when the Voice in my heart spoke to me and urged me to take action, I would listen.

"Hell, no!" I answered George. "I've come this far, I can go a few steps farther." And with that, my stepfather walked me down the aisle to a life of love and liberation.

Zoe and David Wedding 1975

Epilogue

IT HAS BEEN FORTY YEARS since David and I walked down that aisle, and since that time, our marriage has seen many ups and downs, but through it all, we've been rewarded with a rich and happy life. We've raised a wonderful son, Richard, and seventeen dogs (but not all at once!) and have built a successful horticultural business in Oregon. I never would have thought as a young girl that I could have had such a long and stable family life after the childhood I'd had, but whether it was the example set by the Dimocks or Zodie's example of what *not* to do, somehow, I've beaten the odds and I'm here to tell you, if it's possible for me, it's possible for anyone.

Sadly, however, Gale passed away from cancer in her early sixties. She'd had many failed marriages, and her last one was tumultuous, but not nearly as tumultuous as the marriage between Zodie and George. Unfortunately, her husband kept me from seeing her before she died. But even that wound was healed, somewhat, when after her death, we bridged our differences, united by the love that we both shared for the wonderful woman my Sissy had been.

I lost contact with George but heard that he, too, died many years ago, a much beloved character who worked hard, cared for street dogs, and never gave up on the horse races.

I'm happy to say that David Walz is also dead and buried. Hallelujah! As for "Grandpa Jerre," Zodie told me that he died on his knees begging for forgiveness. Let us hope so.

My parents, Margaret and Herb Dimock, lived into their nineties and both passed away recently. They were an amazing pair, not only devoted to their family and congregation but active in the civil rights movement, the antiwar movement, and other social justice causes. They remained loving and committed parents to me throughout their lives and urged me to write this memoir.

And I remain close to my brothers, Larry and Jon Dimock, and especially my sister, Marti Dimock. We are all of us happy, loved, and growing.

MARGARET AND HERB 50TH ANNIVERSARY

Acknowledgments

THIS BOOK NEVER WOULD HAVE been completed without the support and assistance of the following people: David, my beloved, for supporting and loving me all these years in spite of my being "a bubble short of plumb." Marti, for her editing and for showing me another way of life and not minding sharing it with me. Larry Dimock, my brother, helped by scanning family pictures into the text. Brenda Peterson, for the first comprehensive edit. Janice Harper, for making the manuscript sing! I never would have been able to write this without her level-headed, clear-eyed edits. And finally, Mom and Dad, for always believing in me and supporting me in the writing of this memoir. Although they have both passed away, it was their dream that I bring my story to light, and this memoir is a testament to their love.

Thank you for reading my book. If you enjoyed it, please visit my website: ZoeNiklas.com and leave a comment, or better yet, tell Amazon!